Collins

INTERNATIONAL
PRIMARY
MATHS

Workbook 4

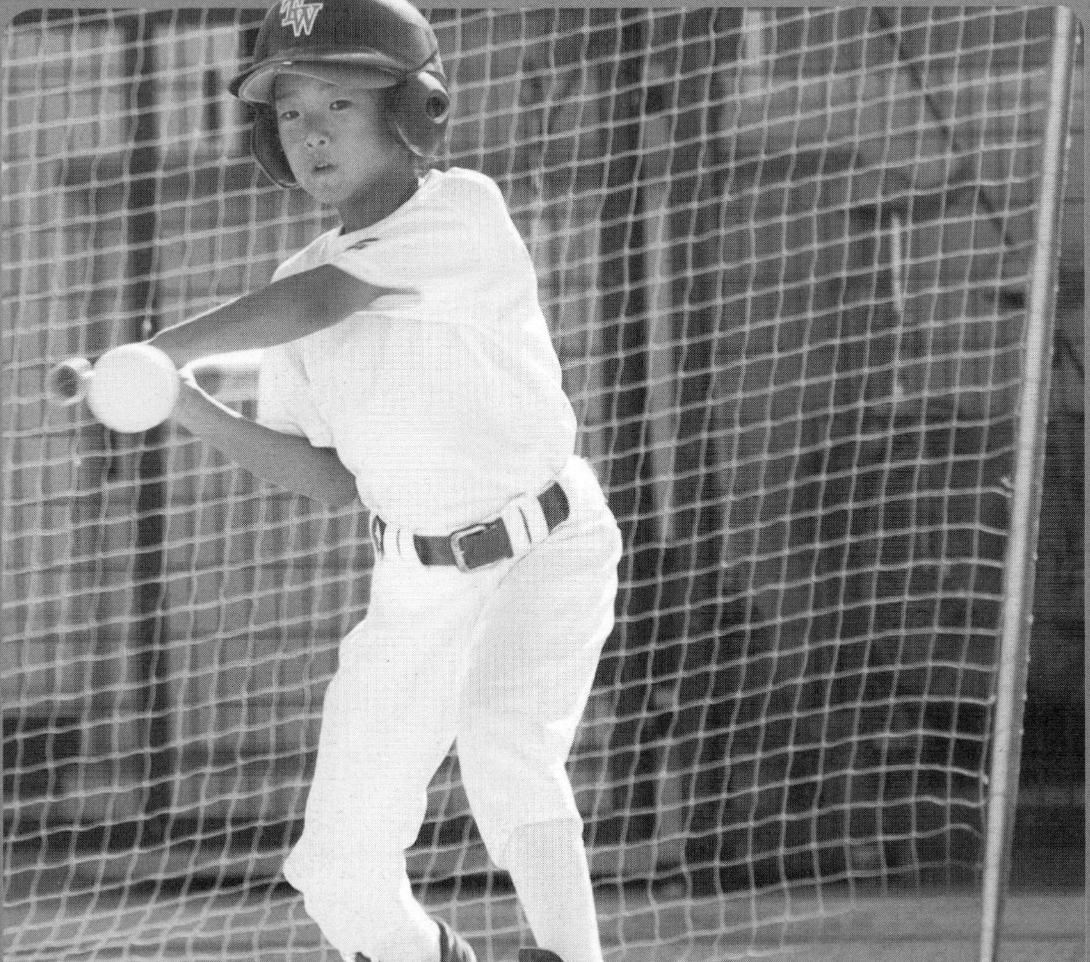

William Collins' dream of knowledge for all began with the publication of his first book in 1819. A self-educated mill worker, he not only enriched millions of lives, but also founded a flourishing publishing house. Today, staying true to this spirit, Collins books are packed with inspiration, innovation and practical expertise. They place you at the centre of a world of possibility and give you exactly what you need to explore it.

Collins. Freedom to teach.

An imprint of HarperCollins*Publishers*
The News Building
1 London Bridge Street
London
SE1 9GF

Browse the complete Collins catalogue at www.collins.co.uk

© HarperCollins*Publishers* Limited 2016

10 9 8 7

ISBN 978-0-00-815995-5

Caroline Clissold and Paul Wrangles assert their moral rights to be identified as the authors of this work.

All rights reserved. No part of this publication may be reproduced, stored in a retrieval system, or transmitted in any form by any means, electronic, mechanical, photocopying, recording or otherwise, without the prior written permission of the Publisher or a licence permitting restricted copying in the United Kingdom issued by the Copyright Licensing Agency Ltd., 90 Tottenham Court Road, London W1T 4LP.

British Library Cataloguing in Publication Data
A catalogue record for this publication is available from the British Library.

Commissioned by Fiona McGlade
Series editor Peter Clarke
Project editor Kate Ellis
Project managed by Emily Hooton
Developed by Karen Williams and Tracy Thomas
Edited by Catherine Dakin
Proofread by Karen Williams
Answer check by Steven Matchett
Cover design by Ink Tank
Cover artwork by KPG_Payless/Shutterstock
Internal design by Ken Vail Graphic Design
Typesetting by Ken Vail Graphic Design
Illustrations by Ken Vail Graphic Design, Advocate Art and QBS
Production by Lauren Crisp

Printed and bound by Grafica Veneta S. P. A.

Contents

Number

Geometry

Measure

Handling data

Lesson 1: **Counting, reading and writing numbers**

- Read and write numbers to 10 000
- Recognise multiples of 5, 10 and 100

1 Write these numbers using numerals.

a one hundred and twenty-five 125

b seven hundred and fifty-one 751

c nine hundred and thirty-three 933

d three hundred and nineteen 319

e two hundred and forty-seven 247

2 Count on in 1s from each of these numbers.

a	7921	7922	7923	7924	7925	7926
b	3567	3568	3569	3570	3571	3572
c	2412	2413	2414	2415	2416	2417
d	1974	1975	1976	1977	1978	1979

1 a Draw a line to match each number in words with the same number written in numerals.

9465 • • six thousand four hundred and fifty-nine

6900 • • nine thousand four hundred and fifty

6459 • • six thousand nine hundred

9450 • • nine thousand four hundred and sixty-five

b Which number in Question **a** is a multiple of 100? 

c Which is not a multiple of 5? 

2 Write each distance in words.

a Tokyo: 4382 km four thousand, three hundred eighty-two

b Dubai: 2690 km two thousand, six hundred ninety

c London: 1462 km one thousand, four hundred sixty-two

d Madrid: 5039 km five thousand, thirty-nine

3 a Fill in each gap as you count forwards and backwards in 1000s.

1597 2597 [3597] [4597] [5597] [6597] 7597

9305 8305 [7305] [6305] [5305] [4305] [3305]

b Fill in each gap as you count forwards and backwards in 100s.

2590 2690 [2790] [2890] [2990] 3090 [3190]

1729 1629 [1529] 1429 [1329] [1229] [1129]

Challenge 3 Use the digit cards to make the numbers. Write each number in numerals and words.

5	0	2	8	0

a A multiple of 100. [52800]

fifty-two thousand, eight hundred

b An odd number. [50028]

five thousand, twenty-eight

c A multiple of 10. [50280]

five thousand, two hundred, eighty

Lesson 2: **Place value**

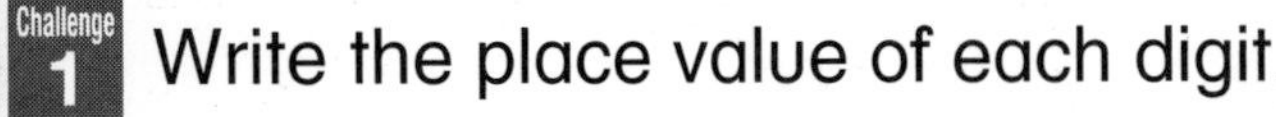

- Know the value of each digit in a 4-digit number

Challenge 1 Write the place value of each digit.

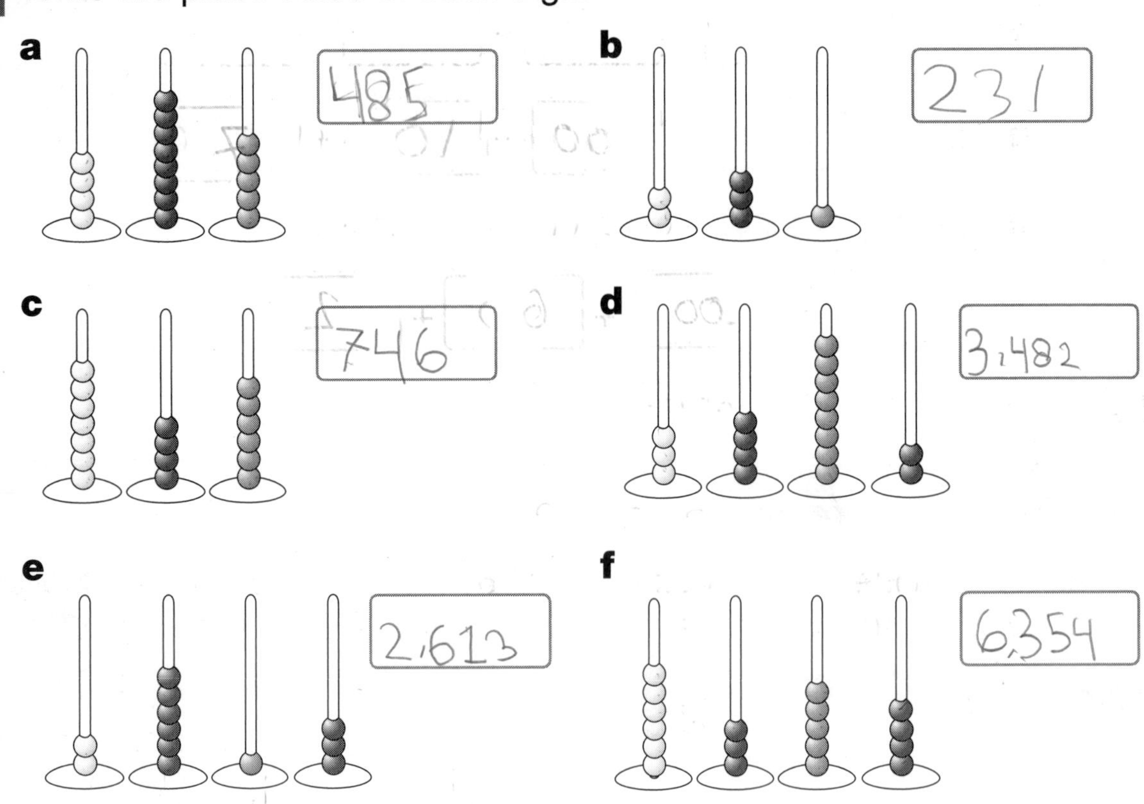

Challenge 2 **1** Each of these forks shows a 4-digit number.

Write the number under each fork and write the letter of the statement that fits.

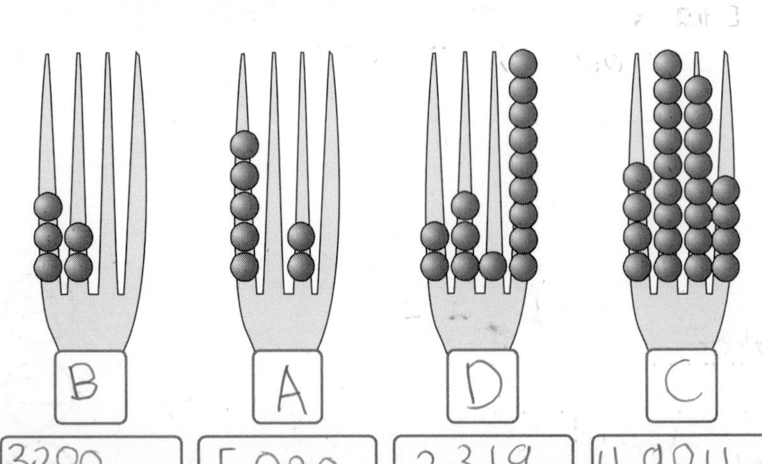

A The largest number.

B A multiple of 100.

C A number where the 4 digit is worth four 1000s.

D A number with an odd number of 10s.

2 Nia makes these 4-digit numbers using corn on a fork. Write down how each number can be partitioned.

Example: 3592 = 3000 + 500 + 90 + 2

a 2634 = 2,000 + 600 + 30 + 4

b 5217 = 5,000 + 200 + 10 + 7

c eight thousand one hundred and sixty-two – 8,162

= 8,000 + 100 + 60 + 2

Challenge 3 You have only eight beads.

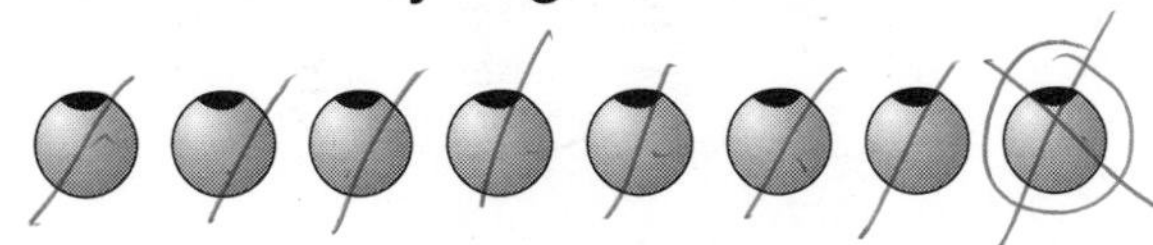

a What is the largest 4-digit number you can make?

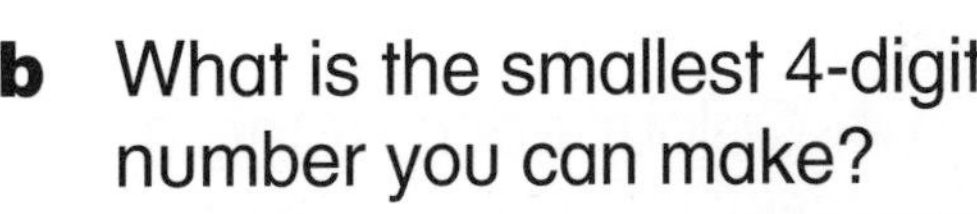

b What is the smallest 4-digit number you can make?

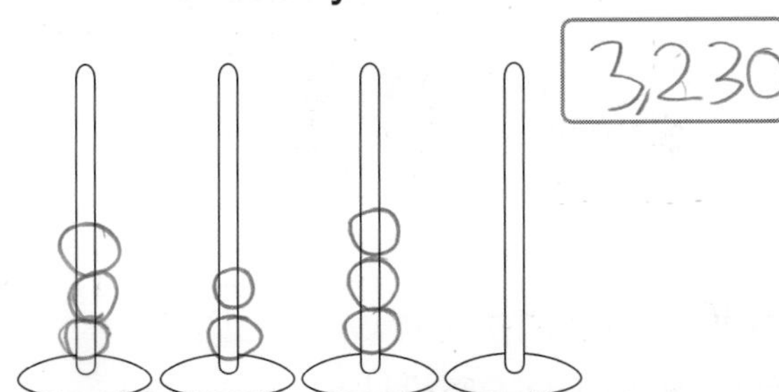

3,230

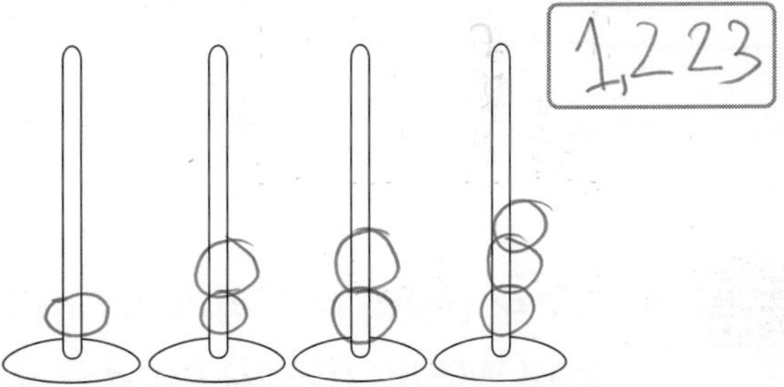

1,223

c Look carefully at this list. Write another eight numbers that only use eight beads and begin with a 5 in the 1000s place.

8000	7100	7010	7001	6200
6020	6002	6110	6101	6011

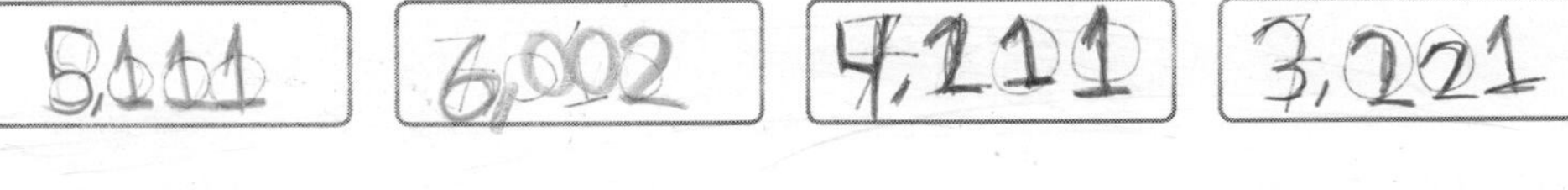

Lesson 3: **Rounding whole numbers**

- Round 3- and 4-digit numbers to the nearest 10 or 100

You will need
- coloured pencils

Challenge 1

1 Colour each of the numbers that rounds to 840.

2 Colour each of the numbers that rounds to 920.

3 Colour each of the numbers that rounds to 300 when rounded to the nearest 100.

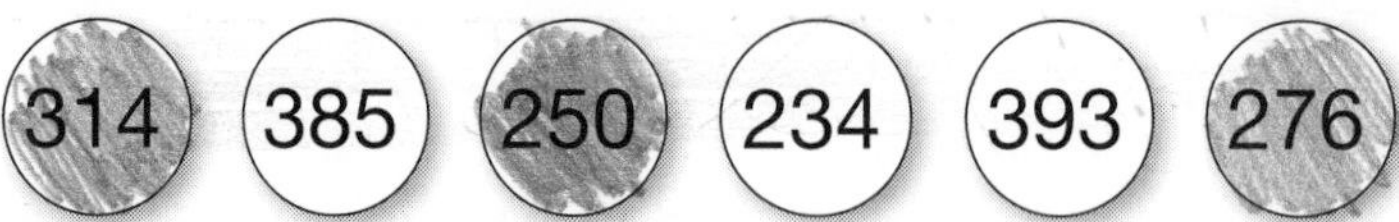

4 Colour each of the numbers that rounds to 600 when rounded to the nearest 100.

Challenge 2

1 Mark each number on the number line and show whether you would round it up or down to the nearest 10.

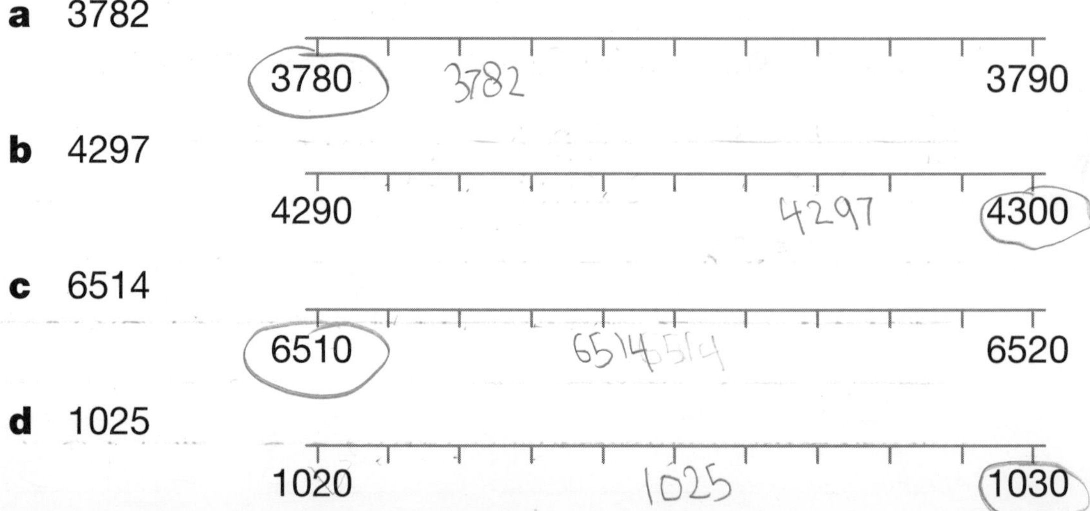

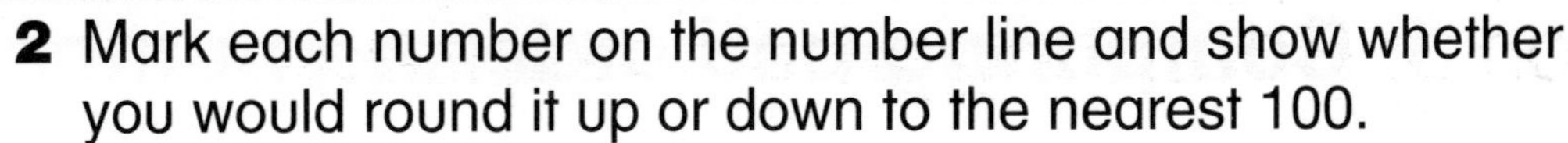

2 Mark each number on the number line and show whether you would round it up or down to the nearest 100.

a 5294 — 5200  … 5294 [5300]

b 1852 — 1800  … 1852 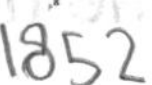 … [1900]

c 4407 — 4400 4407 … 4500

d 2650 — 2600  … 2650  … (2700) 

e 7290 — 7200  … 7290 [7300] 

Challenge 3

If I add the digits of my mystery 4-digit number, they make 25.
If I round my mystery number to the nearest hundred, it rounds to 9000.

Rajesh

What could Rajesh's number be? [9,425]

Invent a similar puzzle of your own for a friend to try.

If I divide my mystery number with 4, they make 800. When multiplied by 4 it 1,280.000

Number

Lesson 4: Comparing and ordering numbers

- Compare 3- and 4-digit numbers using > and < signs
- Order 3- and 4-digit numbers

Challenge 1

1 Write the correct symbol, > or <, in between each pair of numbers.

a 459 < 759 | b 302 < 802

c 644 > 244 | d 592 < 992

e 420 > 120 | f 737 < 837

g 283 < 383 | h 576 > 176

2 Mark the numbers in the correct order on each number line.

a 550 350 750

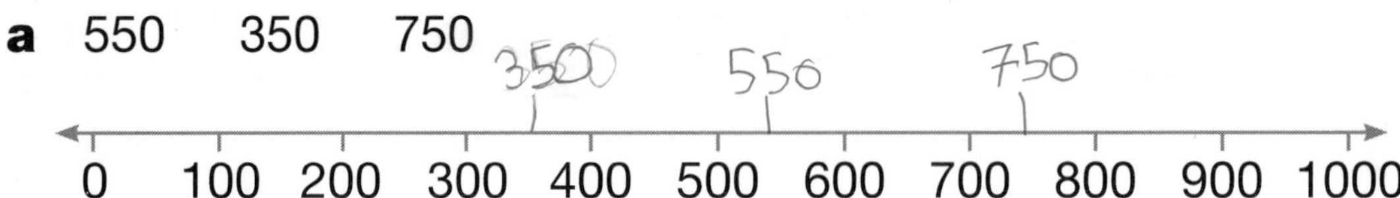

b 620 290 180

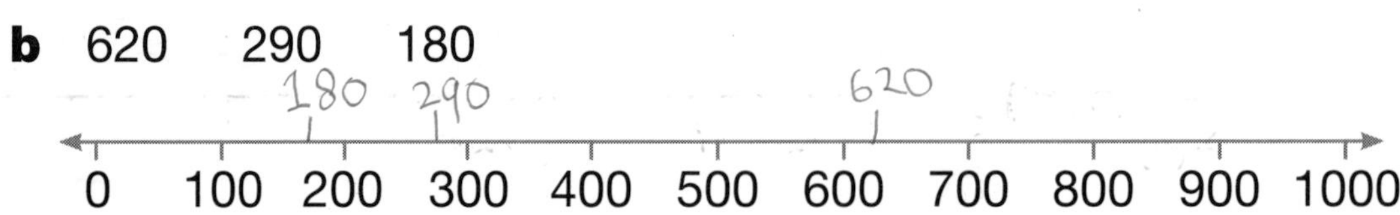

c 940 480 510

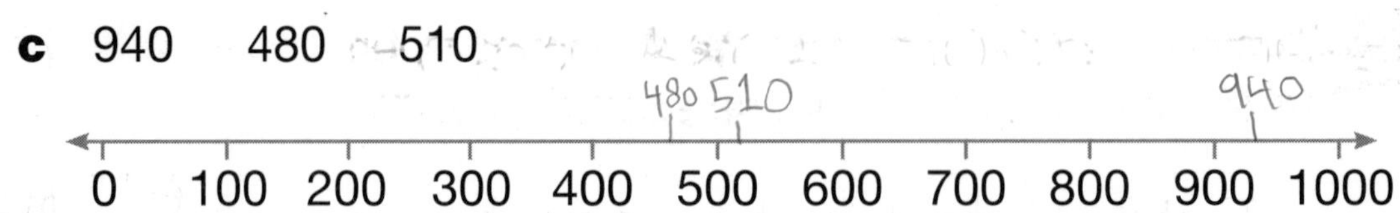

Challenge 2

1 Write the correct symbol, > or <, between each pair of numbers.

a 2580 < 5208 | b 1252 < 5212

c 6933 > 3936 | d 4867 < 8467

e 1569 < 1596 | f 7110 > 7101

2 For each pair of numbers in Question 1, write another 4-digit number that could go between them.

a ☐ **b** ☐ **c** ☐

d ☐ **e** ☐ **f** ☐

3 Mark where you estimate the numbers should lie on each number line.

a 385 358 362 886 680 608

300 1000

b 4219 6380 6308 4921 2977

2000 10 000

c 3053 8071 3503 2789 2987

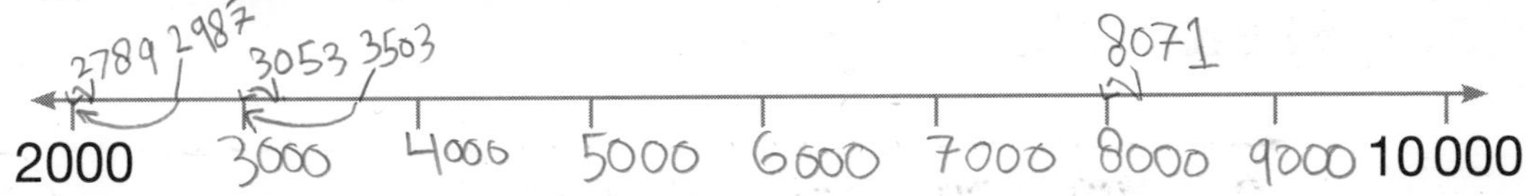

Challenge 3 Complete each list so that the 4-digit numbers are in order from smallest to largest. Only use each digit once.

a 1 8 ☐ ☐ 1 8 2 4 1 8 ☐ ☐ 1 8 ☐ ☐ 1 8 ☐ ☐

b 7 5 ☐ ☐ 7 5 ☐ ☐ 7 5 ☐ ☐ 7 5 7 0 7 5 ☐ ☐

c ☐ ☐ 4 5 ☐ ☐ 9 0 5 1 ☐ ☐ 5 ☐ ☐ ☐

Lesson 1: **Multiples of 10, 100, 1000 more and less (1)**

- Find multiples of 10, 100 and 1000 more and less than a number

1 Write the numbers that are 10 more than these.

a 384 394 **b** 572 582

c 1045 1055 **d** 4928

2 Write the numbers that are 100 more than these.

a 534 634 **b** 278 378

c 9304 10304 **d** 7634 6634

1 Fill in the tables.

a

10 less	7223	943	3010	2257
	7233	**953**	**3020**	**2267**
30 more	7263	983	3050	2297

b

300 less	4163	1283	9005	1368
	4463	**1583**	**9305**	**1468**
400 more	4863	1983	9705	1868

c

2000 less	1045	4279	3510	2152
	3045	**6279**	**5510**	**4152**
3000 more	6045	9279	8510	7152

2 Complete these calculations.

a 2589 + 200 = 2789 **b** 6390 – 50 = 6340

c 5642 + 30 = 5672 **d** 4923 – 400 = 4523

e 7424 + 2000 = 9424 **f** 8203 – 5000 = 3203

Challenge 3

1 Maria thinks of a number. She finds 400 less than it. Her answer is 7283. What was the number she thought of?

7283 + 400 = 7683 7683 7683 – 400 = 7283

2 Maria thinks of another number. This time she finds 500 more than it. Her answer is 4247. What was the number she thought of?

4247 – 500 = 3747 3747 + 500 = 4247 3747

3 Think of your own 3-digit numbers where two digits change when you find 20 or 200 more or less. How many can you find?

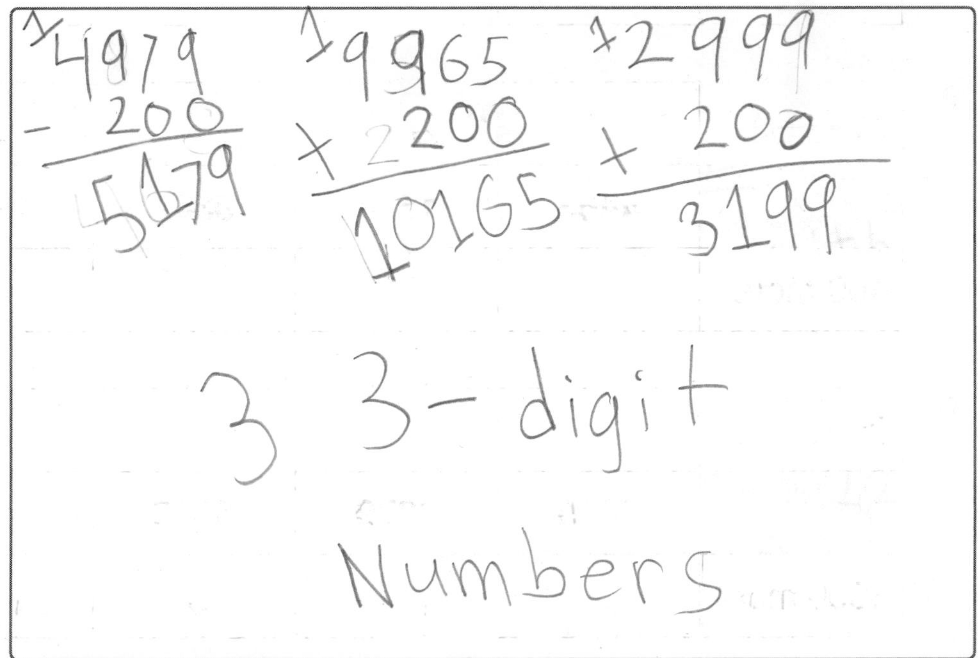

Number

Lesson 2: **Place value and rounding**

- Know the value of each digit in a 4-digit number
- Round 3- and 4-digit numbers to the nearest 10 or 100

You will need
- coloured pencils

1 Circle the number...

a	...where the 2 is worth 2 hundreds.	1320	2031	1203
b	...where the 8 is worth 8 thousands.	8952	9285	2589
c	...where the 0 shows 0 units.	5053	3505	3550
d	...where the 7 is worth 7 tens.	6741	4176	1647

2 Colour each of the numbers that rounds to 50.

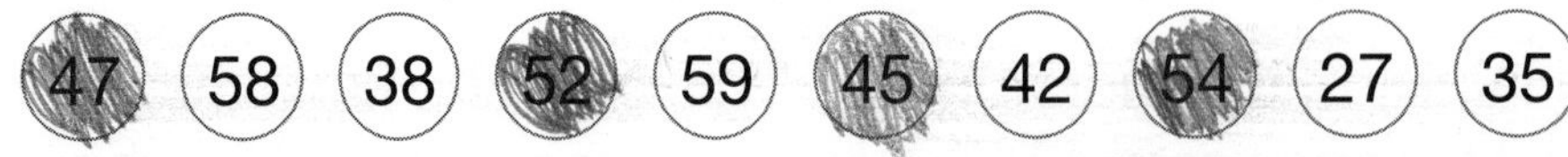

Challenge 2

1 Write the 4-digit numbers that the Base 10 equipment is showing.

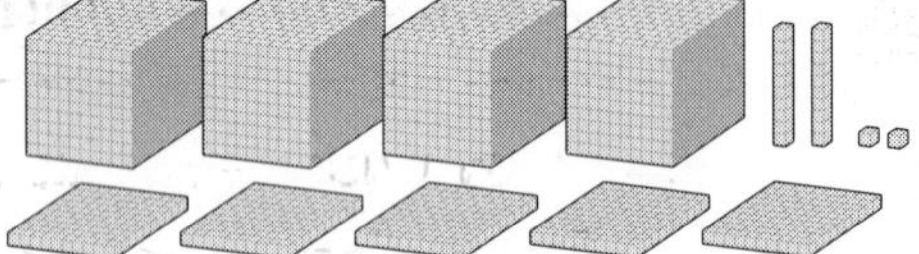

4 thousands, 5 hundreds, 2 tens and 2 units = 4522

a

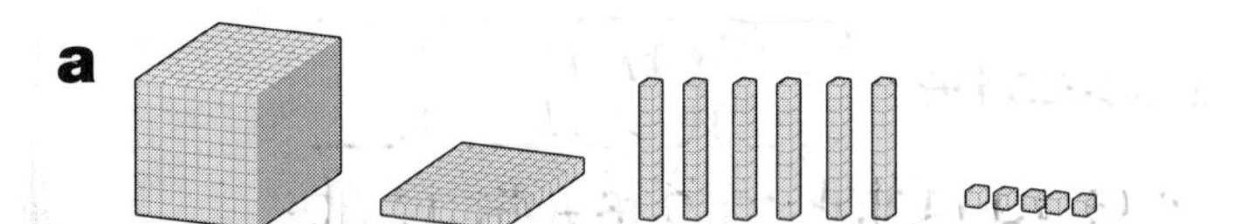

1 thousands, 1 hundreds, 6 tens and 5 units = 1165

b

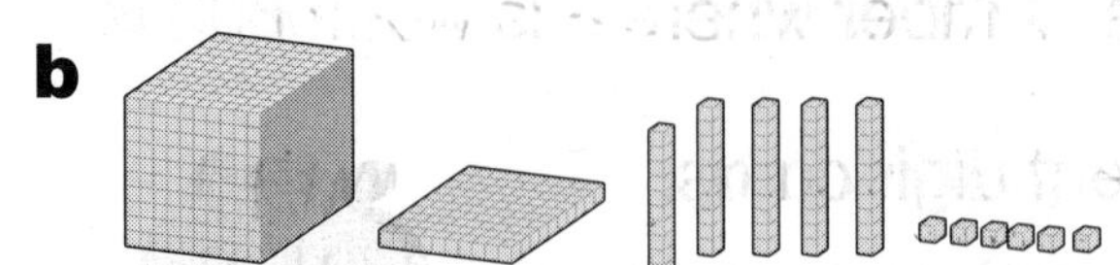

1 thousands, 1 hundreds, 5 tens and 6 units = 1156

c

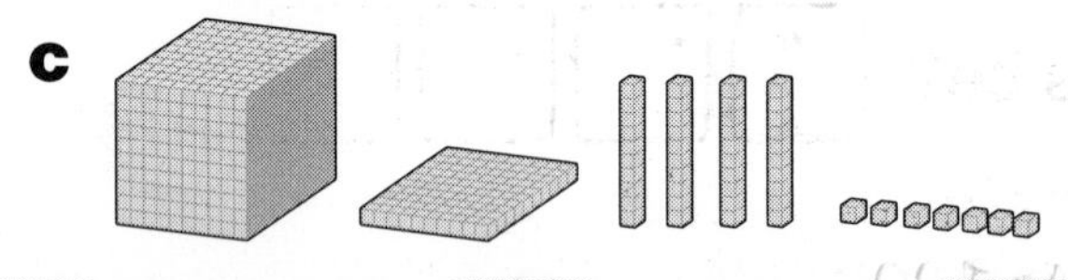

1 thousands, 1 hundreds, 4 tens and 7 units = 1147

2 Class 4 throw balls at a target. This table shows their results.

a Complete the table using the information provided to help.

Name	Thousands	Hundreds	Tens	Units	Total score
Lewis	Three	Zero	Zero	Four	3,004
Aaliyah	five	eight	two	one	5821
Zoe	Nine	Five	Six	Zero	9,560
Jaymie	two	nine	nine	five	2995
Emeka	Three	One	Zero	Two	3,102
Dylan	seven	three	seven	eight	7378

b If you round each of the children's scores to the nearest 10, two scores round to the same number.

Who are the children and what is the number?

Lewis and Jaymie, 300

Challenge 3

1 Hiro picks up four digit cards. He says:

I can make a multiple of 10 with these cards.
I can also make a number that rounds to 5300
and a number where the digit 8 is worth 800.

a What could his cards be? 4 8 3 0

b Write the numbers you think Hiro is talking about.

"The multiple of 10 is 0. The number that rounds to 5300 is ______. The number where 8 is worth 800 is ______."

2 Hiro picks up four different digit cards.

I can't make an even number using these

a What could his cards be?

1 7 9 7

b Use these cards to make a number that rounds to 1800 when it is rounded to the nearest 100.

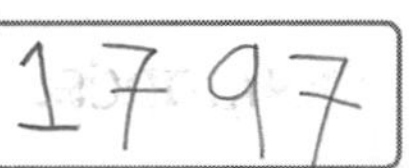

1797

Number

Lesson 3: **Multiplying and dividing by 10 and 100 (1)**

- Multiply and divide numbers by 10 and 100

Challenge 1

Draw a line to match each calculation to its answer.

18 × 10 •	• 140
21 × 10 •	• 230
17 × 10 •	• 210
20 × 10 •	• 200
14 × 10 •	• 250
24 × 10 •	• 180
25 × 10 •	• 240
23 × 10 •	• 170

Challenge 2

1 Complete the table. Circle the direction that the digits move in and write how many places they move.

Operation	Direction the digits move	Number of places the digits move
× 10	left right	
× 100	left right	
÷ 10	left right	
÷ 100	left right	

2 Show how the digits shift when multiplying by 10.

Example: 138 × 10

Th	H	T	U
	1	3	8
1	3	8	0

a 873 × 10

Th	H	T	U

b 558 × 10

Th	H	T	U

c 469 × 10

Th	H	T	U

d 723 × 10

Th	H	T	U

e 104 × 10

Th	H	T	U

3 Show how the digits shift when multiplying by 100.

Example: 84 × 100

Th	H	T	U
		8	4
8	4	0	0

a 71 × 100

Th	H	T	U
		7	1
7	1	0	0

b 33 × 100

Th	H	T	U
		3	3
3	3	0	0

c 47 × 100

Th	H	T	U
		4	7
4	7	0	0

d 85 × 100

Th	H	T	U
		8	5
8	5	0	0

e 20 × 100

Th	H	T	U
		2	0
2	0	0	0

4 Show how the digits shift when dividing by 10.

Example: 620 ÷ 10

Th	H	T	U
	6	2	0
		6	2

a 470 ÷ 10

Th	H	T	U
	4	7	0
		4	7

b 850 ÷ 10

Th	H	T	U
	8	5	0
		8	5

c 530 ÷ 10

Th	H	T	U
	5	3	0
		5	3

d 190 ÷ 10

Th	H	T	U
	1	9	0
		1	9

e 310 ÷ 10

Th	H	T	U
	3	1	0
		3	1

Challenge 3 Preeti takes four different digit cards. She makes two different 2-digit numbers with them. She then multiplies her numbers by 100. Her answers are 8900 and 5100.

a What are her digit cards? 

b Write ten more calculations using Preeti's digits (as well as zeroes). You can write ×10, ×100, ÷10 or ÷100 calculations.

50 89,510 890 80
900
9510 8500 510 89500
100

Number

Lesson 4: **Odd and even numbers**

- Recognise odd and even numbers
- Understand what happens to odd and even numbers when they are added or subtracted

You will need

- green and yellow coloured pencils

1 Colour the odd numbers yellow and the even numbers green.

1	2	3	4	5	6	7	8	9	10
11	12	13	14	15	16	17	18	19	20
21	22	23	24	25	26	27	28	29	30
31	32	33	34	35	36	37	38	39	40
41	42	43	44	45	46	47	48	49	50

2 What do you notice?

They go down.

1 a Harry wants to know how to spot odd and even numbers.

What are the rules for identifying odd or even numbers?

A rule identifying odd and even numbers is that even numbers have two numbers that add upp to that number, and odd numbers don't

b Rhian says:

Whether a number is odd or even has got something to do with the 2 times-tables.

Is she right? Explain your answer.

NO, because only even numbers have 2 times-tables

2 Complete each of these calculations and write **E** and **O** underneath each number to show whether it is **E**ven or **O**dd.

Example: 10 + 12 = 22

E + E = E

a 8 + 14 = 22

E + E = E

b 17 + 9 = 26

O + O = E

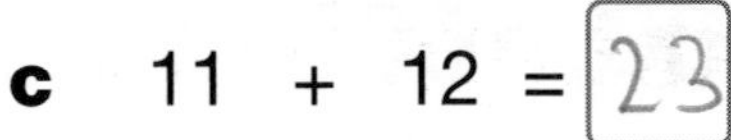

c 11 + 12 = 23

O + E = O

d 18 − 14 = 4

E − E = E

e 13 − 7 = 6

O − 6 = E

f 16 − 11 = 5

E − O = O

3 Tick the statements that you think are true.

a An even number plus an even number equals an odd number.

b Two odd numbers added together equals an even number.

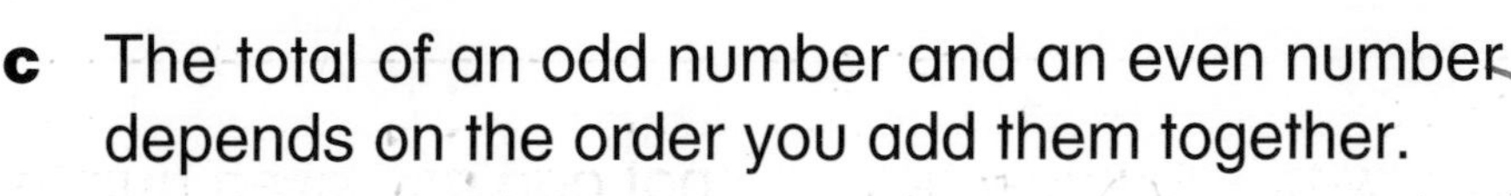

c The total of an odd number and an even number depends on the order you add them together.

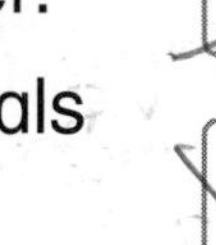

d An even number minus an odd number equals an odd number.

Challenge 3 Carla says:

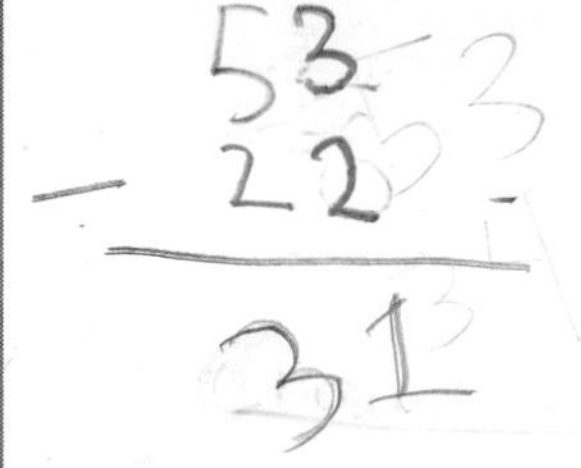

a Use the box below to try out different combinations of odd and even numbers in subtractions.

53 − 22 = 31

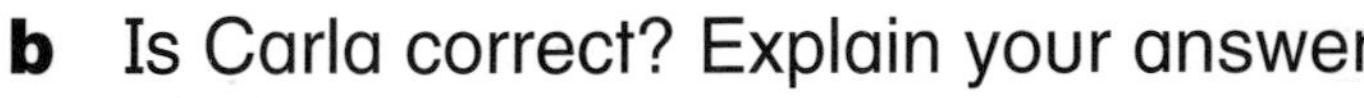

b Is Carla correct? Explain your answer.

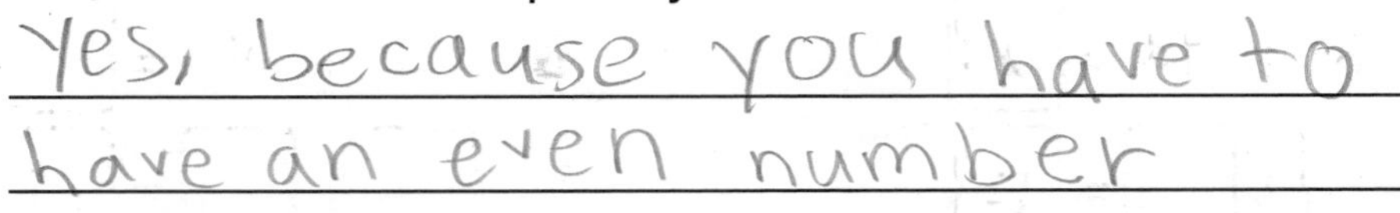

Yes, because you have to have an even number

Number

Lesson 1: **Multiples of 10, 100, 1000 more and less (2)**

- Find multiples of 10, 100 and 1000 more and less than a number

1 Complete the table to show how numbers change when you find 10 less.

Starting number	10 less
629	619
572	562
640	630
4883	4873
1457	1447

2 Complete the table to show how the same numbers change when you find 100 more.

Starting number	100 more
629	729
572	672
640	740
4883	4983
1457	1557

1 Use the blank number lines to help calculate the answers.

Example:

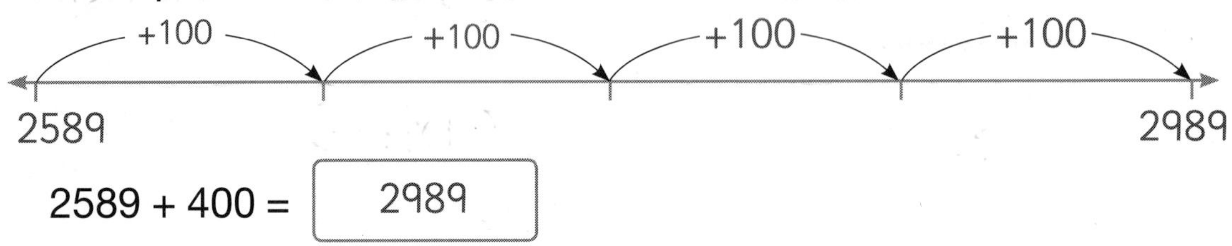

2589 + 400 = 2989

a

4121

4121 + 700 = 4821

b

7202 + 600 = 7802

c

8730 + 400 = 9130

2 In Question **1a** and **b** only the 100s digit changes, but in **c** the 1000s digit changes too. Why is this?

In Question c, 4 + 7 = 11 so you need to change the 8 into a 9

3 Complete these calculations.

a 3680 + 300 =	3980	**b** 6924 – 700 =	6224
c 2555 + 90 =	2645	**d** 1045 – 80 =	965
e 4319 + 5000 =	9319	**f** 7112 – 200 =	6915

4 Start with the number 5766.

You may only add or take away multiples of 10, 100 or 1000.

How many different ways can you find to make a number that has an 8 in the 100s place?

Hint: Start with the lowest number you can add and then write a list in order.

5766, 6766, ~~77~~ 66, 8766, 9766
5766, 5776, 57

1 Max finds 500 less than a number.
He says that the answer is 6328.
What was the number?

2 Bella finds 4000 more than a number.
She says that the answer is 5240.
What was the number?

9240

Number

Lesson 2: **Multiplying and dividing by 10 and 100 (2)**

- Multiply and divide numbers by 10 and 100

You will need

- 0–9 digit cards

Challenge 1

Use digit cards to make each of these 2-digit numbers. Then move them one place to the left to show what happens when you multiply them by 10.

Example: 5 7 × 10 = 5 7 0

a 3 2 × 10 = 3 2 0 **b** 2 5 × 10 = 2 5 0

c 4 6 × 10 = 4 6 0 **d** 5 1 × 10 = 5 1 0

Challenge 2

1 Draw an arrow to show the direction that the digits will move and write down how many places they will move.

Example: 720 ÷ 10 → Move one place.

a 658 × 10 6580 **b** 1300 ÷ 100 13

c 950 ÷ 10 9500 **d** 28 × 100 2800

e 72 × 100 7200 **f** 5500 ÷ 100 55

2 Complete these calculations.

a 670 ÷ 10 = 67 **b** 280 ÷ 10 = 280

c 990 ÷ 10 = 99 **d** 18 × 100 = 1800

e 1400 ÷ 100 = 14 **f** 310 ÷ 10 = 31

g 427 × 10 = 4270 **h** 64 × 100 = 6400

3 529 × 10 = 5290

a

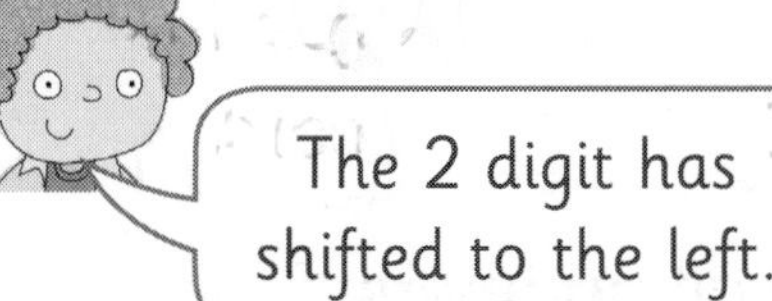

b

The 2 digit has moved because it was worth two 10s. Then it was multiplied by 10 and it is now worth two 100s.

Both of these statements are true. Which one is the best explanation for what happens to the 2 digit?

b

Khalil says:

If I start with a number and multiply it by 100, then I divide the answer by 10 twice, I will get back to the number I started with.

a Use the box below to test whether Khalil's statement is true.

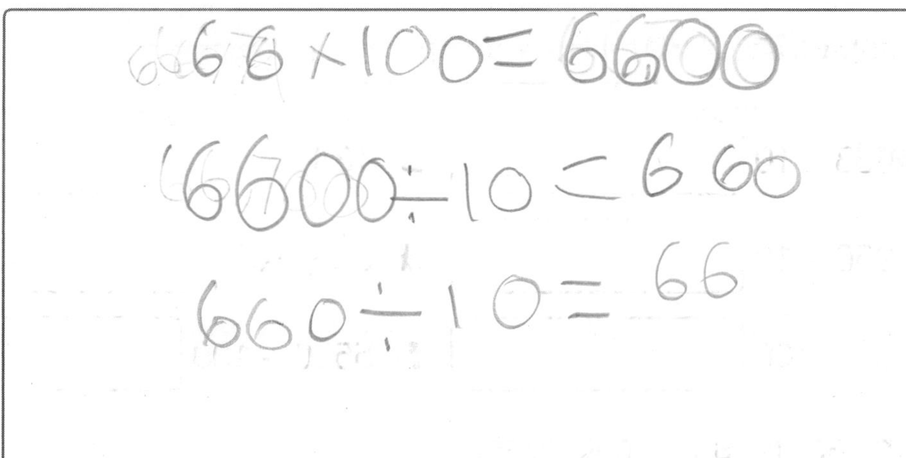

b Is Khalil's statement true? yes

c Explain your reasons for why this does or does not work.

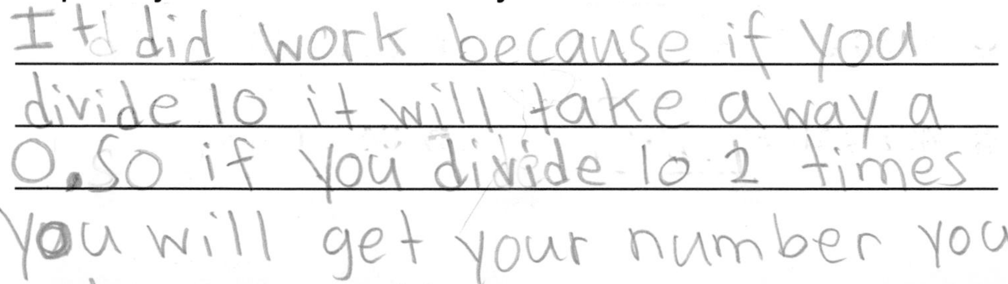

Lesson 3: **Negative numbers**

- Use negative numbers correctly in different situations

Challenge 1 What temperature is shown on each thermometer?

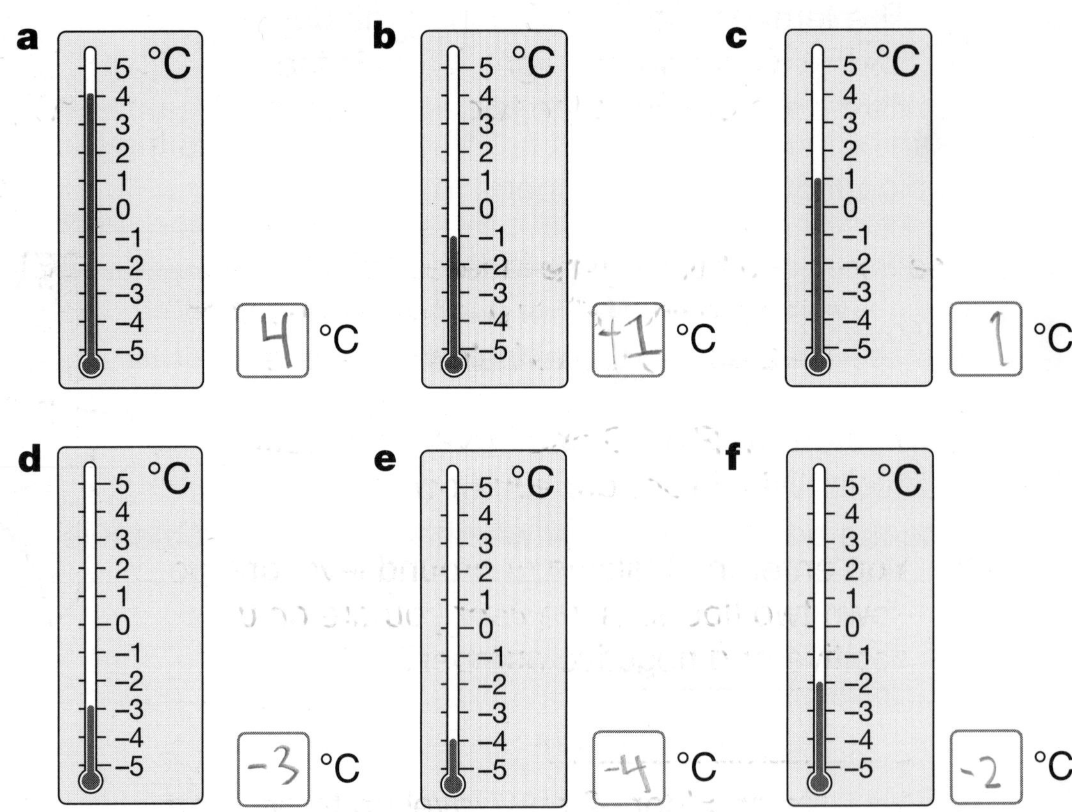

Challenge 2

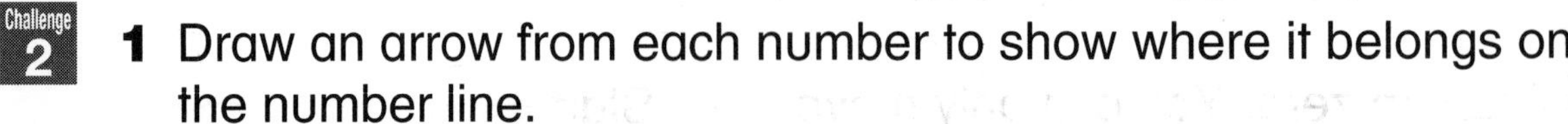

1 Draw an arrow from each number to show where it belongs on the number line.

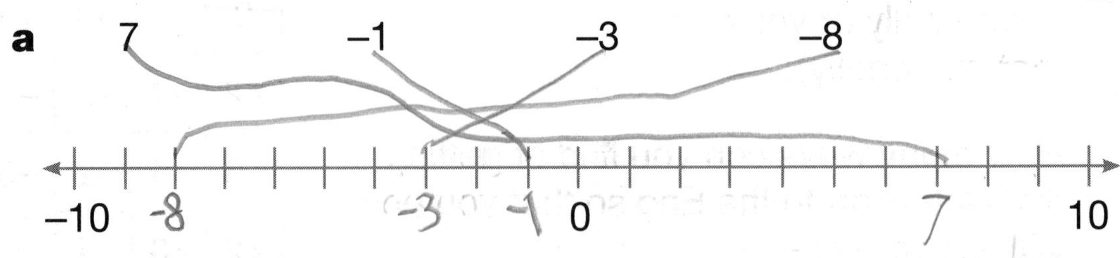

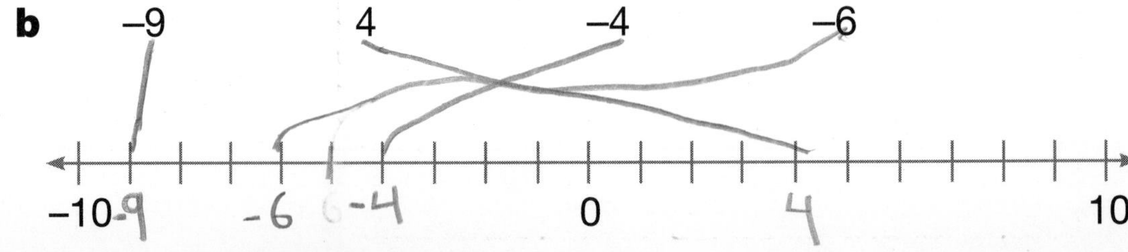

2 a The temperature is 2°C. Overnight it falls by 5 degrees. What temperature is it now? -3 °C

b The temperature is –7°C. It rises by 1 degree. What temperature is it now? -6 °C

c The temperature is 8°C during the day and –1°C during the night. What is the difference between the two temperatures? 7 °C

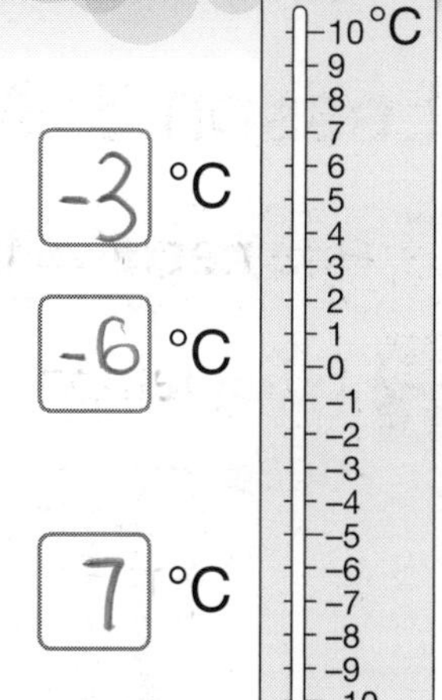

3 The floors of a building are labelled from 5 to –3. Floor 5 is the top floor. Floor 0 is the ground floor. Floors –1, –2 and –3 are all below ground level.

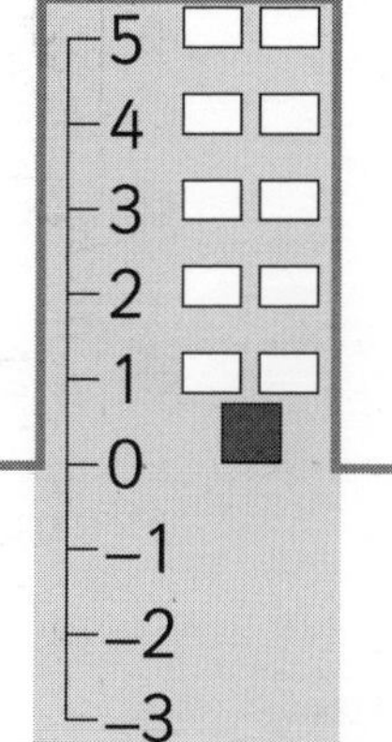

a You are on Floor 3 and travel down four floors. What floor are you now on? -1

b You enter the building at ground level and go down two floors. Is the floor you are on a positive or a negative number?

negative

c You are on Floor –2 and travel up three floors. What floor are you now on?

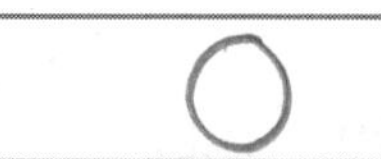

0

Challenge 3 Start on zero. You can only move horizontally or vertically (not diagonally).

How many ways can you find of getting from the Start to the End so that you end with a score of –4?

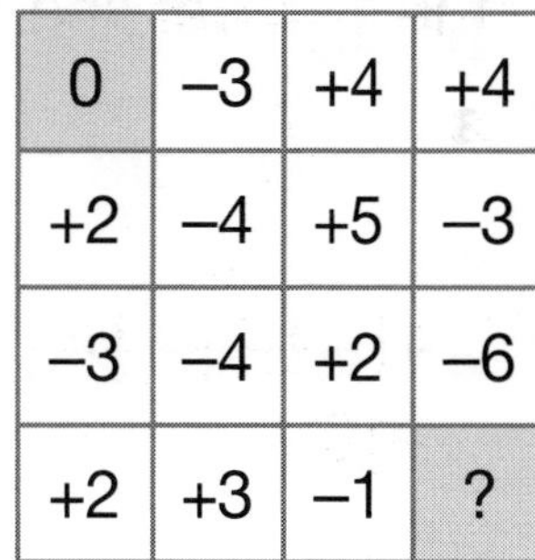

Start

0	–3	+4	+4
+2	–4	+5	–3
–3	–4	+2	–6
+2	+3	–1	?

End

2

Number

Lesson 4: **Number sequences**

- Recognise different number sequences and extend them

Challenge 1

Draw a line to match each number sequence to the rule that describes it.

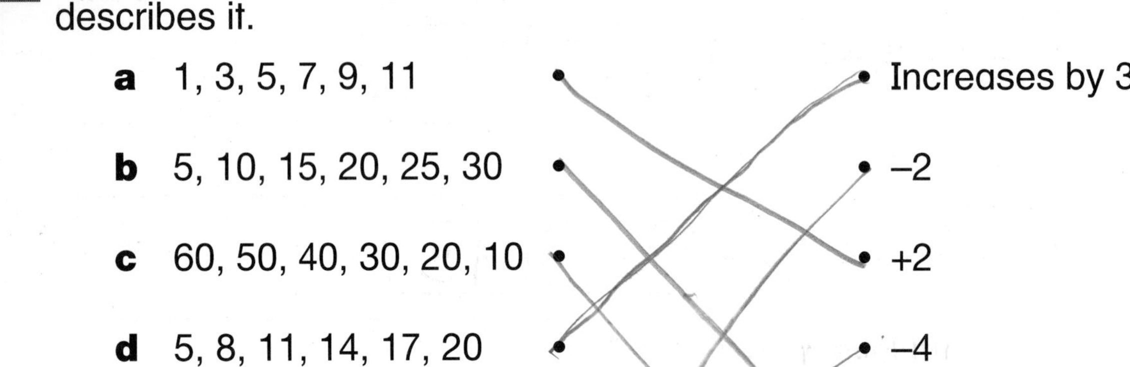

a 1, 3, 5, 7, 9, 11 • • Increases by 3

b 5, 10, 15, 20, 25, 30 • • −2

c 60, 50, 40, 30, 20, 10 • • +2

d 5, 8, 11, 14, 17, 20 • • −4

e 22, 18, 14, 10, 6, 2 • • +5

f 28, 26, 24, 22, 20, 18 • • Decreases by 10

Challenge 2

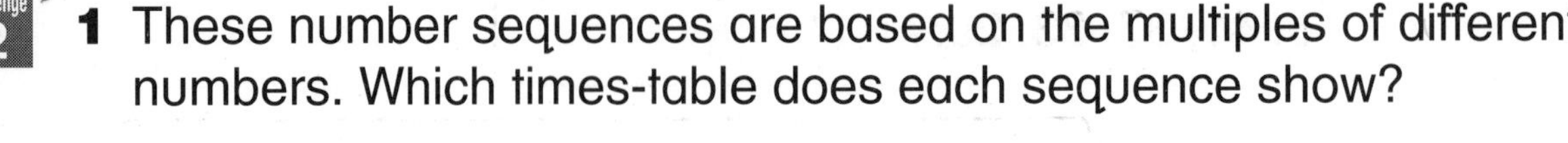

1 These number sequences are based on the multiples of different numbers. Which times-table does each sequence show?

a 6, 12, 18, 24, 30

These are all multiples of [6]. The pattern is [+ 6].

b 40, 36, 32, 28, 24

These are all multiples of [4]. The pattern is [− 4].

c 35, 30, 25, 20, 15

These are all multiples of [5]. The pattern is [− 5].

d 54, 45, 36, 27, 18

These are all multiples of [9]. The pattern is [− 9].

2 Write the next two numbers in each sequence. Then write the rule.

a 25, 20, 15, 10, 5, 0, -5

The rule is -5.

b – 4, – 3, – 2, – 1, 0, 1, 2

The rule is +1.

c 53, 60, 67, 74, 81, 88, 95

The rule is +5.

d 22, 33, 44, 55, 66, 77, 88

The rule is +11.

e 45, 41, 37, 33, 29, 25, 21

The rule is –4.

Challenge **3** Use these boxes to make up five different sequences of your own for a friend to try to work out the rule. Leave the last two boxes empty so that they can write the next two numbers in your sequence.

a	26,	39,	52,	65,	78,	91
b	24,	36,	48,	60,	72,	84
c	28,	42,	56,	70,	84,	98
d	30,	45,	60,	75,	90,	105
e	32,	48,	64,	80,	96,	112

Number

Lesson 1: **Tenths (1)**

- Understand the value of tenths in a number
- Recognise the link between fractions and decimals

You will need
- coloured pencils

1 These strips have been split into tenths.
Colour each fraction and then write it as a decimal.

Example: Colour $\frac{7}{10}$.

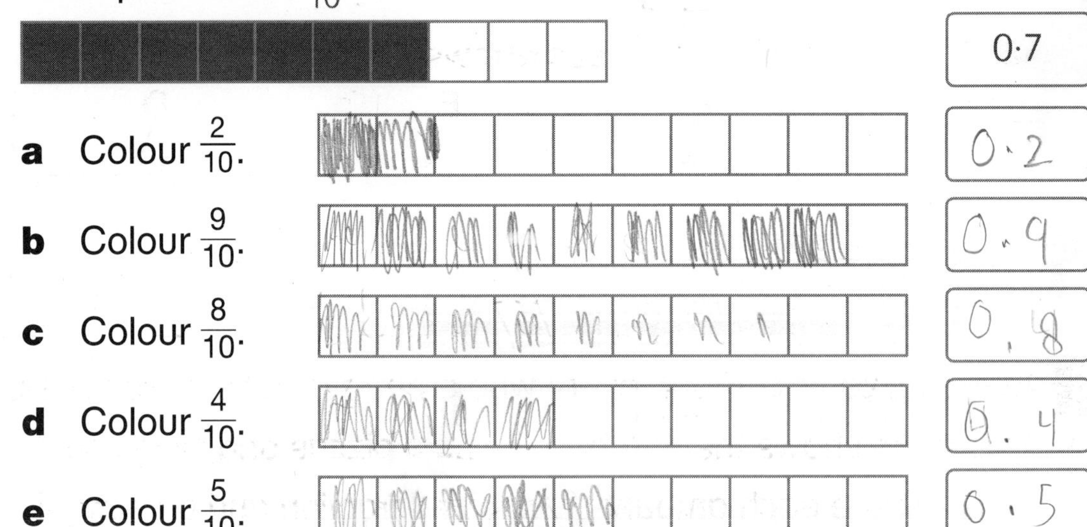

0·7

a Colour $\frac{2}{10}$.

b Colour $\frac{9}{10}$.

c Colour $\frac{8}{10}$.

d Colour $\frac{4}{10}$.

e Colour $\frac{5}{10}$.

2 Use one of your answers in Question **1** to help you circle the correct ending to this sentence.

0·5 is the same as **all** / **half** / **a quarter** of the strip.

1 Label each decimal on the number line.

a 0·6

b 0·3

c 0·5

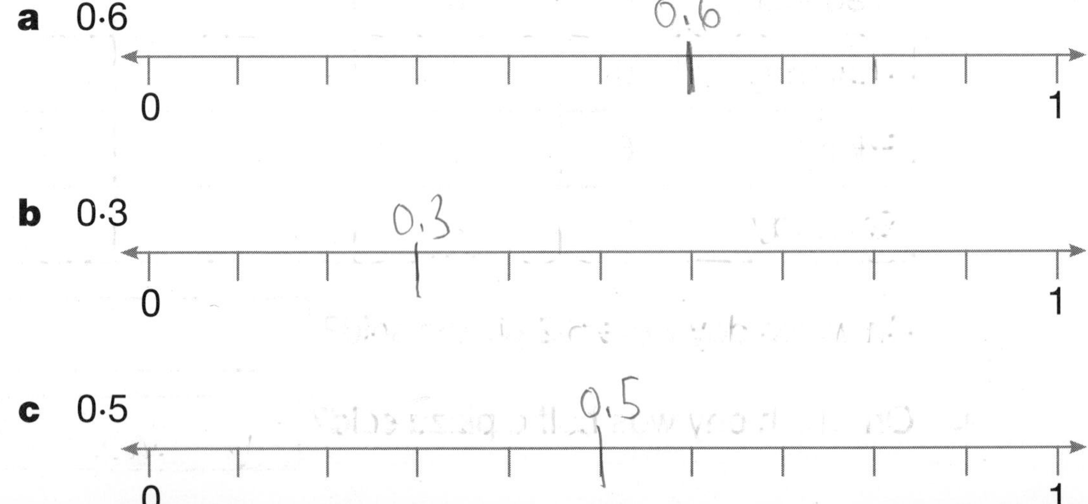

2 Write these decimals as wholes and tenths.

Example: 3·2 pizzas = [3] whole pizzas and [$\frac{2}{10}$] of a pizza.

a 1·3 metres = [1] whole metre and [$\frac{3}{10}$] of a metre.

b 12·5 litres = [12] whole litres and [$\frac{5}{10}$] of a litre.

3 Which decimals are these arrows pointing to?

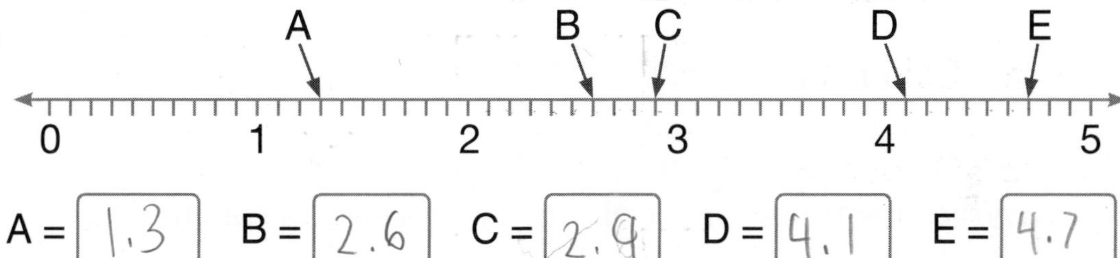

A = [1.3] B = [2.6] C = [2.9] D = [4.1] E = [4.7]

Challenge 3 At the pizza restaurant, every whole pizza is cut into 10 slices. This table shows the number of whole pizzas and slices sold.

a Write each amount as a mixed fraction and a decimal.

Day	Whole pizzas	Pizza slices (tenths)	Total (as a mixed fraction)	Total (as a decimal)
Monday	2	4	$2\frac{4}{10}$	2·4
Tuesday	3	8	$3\frac{8}{10}$	3.8
Wednesday	4	3	$4\frac{3}{10}$	4.3
Thursday	0	5	$\frac{5}{10}$	0.5
Friday	6	2	$6\frac{2}{10}$	6.2
Saturday	5	9	$5\frac{9}{10}$	5.9

b On which day were 6·2 pizzas sold? 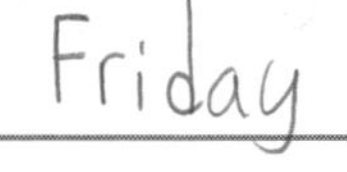

c On which day was half a pizza sold? 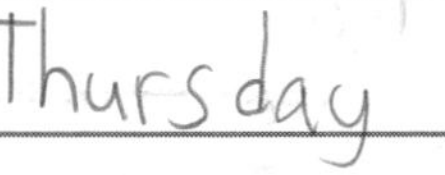

Lesson 2: **Tenths (2)**

Number

- Understand the value of tenths in a number
- Read and write tenths in different situations

Challenge 1 Draw lines to match the same measurements.

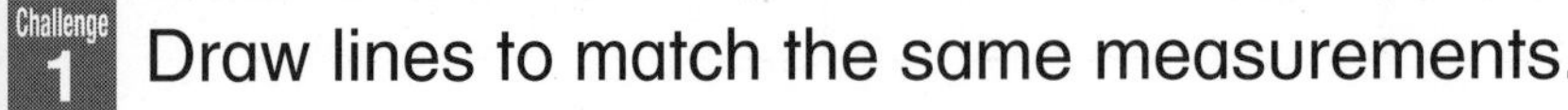

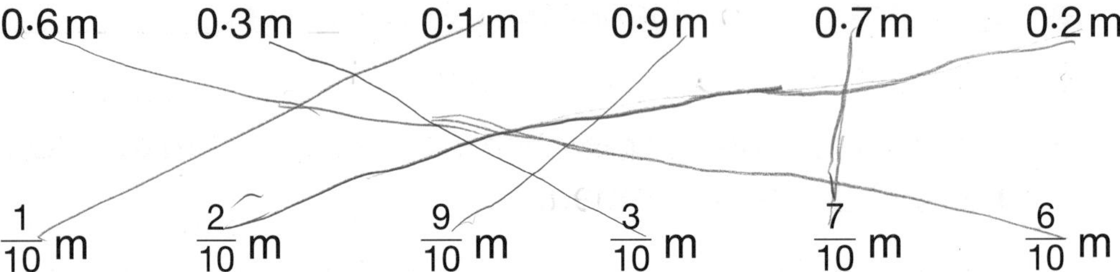

Challenge 2

1 These measuring tapes are 2 metres long.
Write down the different lengths shown as decimals.

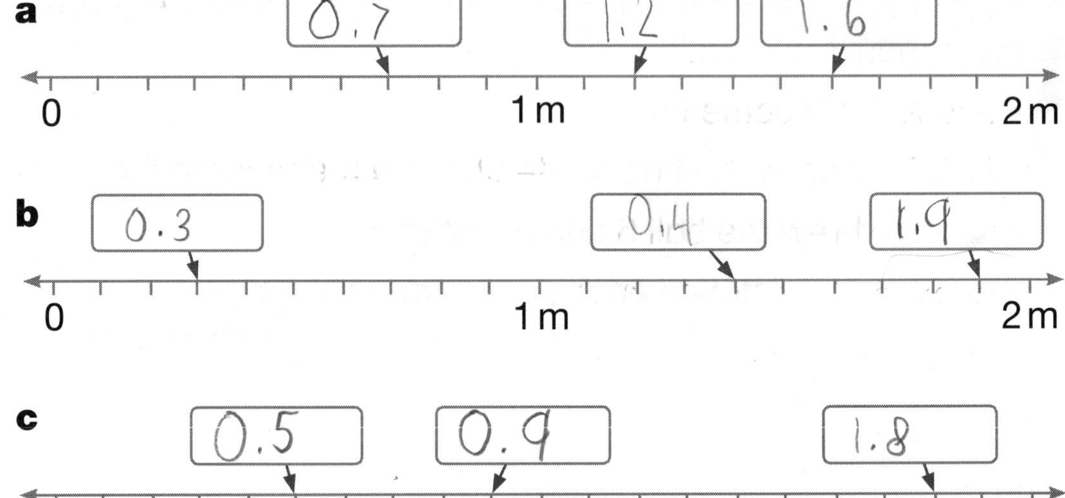

2 Look back at your answers to Question **1**.

a One tenth more than one of your answers is 1·3.

Which answer is it? 0.3

b Which three answers would be written as 2 metres if you rounded them to the nearest metre?

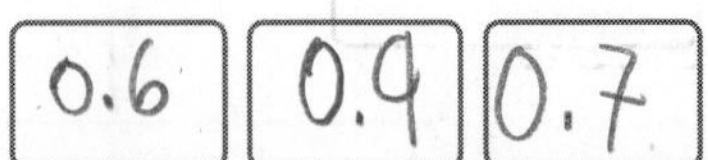

3 Class 4 had a long jump competition. Here are their results:

Class 4 Long jump scores							
Name	Nia	Abdul	Jaymie	Kyle	Zac	Kim	Charlotte
Distance jumped (metres)	1·4	1·3	0·9	1·5	1·6	0·8	1·2

a Who jumped the furthest distance? Zac

b Who jumped the shortest distance? Kim

c Write the names of the children in order, from shortest to longest distance jumped.

Kim, Jaymie, Charlotte, Abdul, Nia, Kyle, Zac

Challenge **3** Class 4 take part in a ball-throwing competition.

- Jaymie: "I threw the ball the furthest. My distance was one tenth more than 7 metres."
- Charlotte: "I came third."
- Abdul: "I threw the ball two tenths of a metre more than Kyle."
- Kyle: "I threw the ball 6 and a half metres."

Work out the distance each person threw the ball.

7.0 + 1 = 7.1   6.5 + 2 = 6.7

Write your answers as decimals.

Jaymie = 7.1 m Charlotte = 6.6 m

Abdul = 6.7 m Kyle = 6.5 m

Number

Lesson 3: **Hundredths (1)**

- Understand the value of hundredths in a number
- Recognise the link between fractions and decimals

Challenge 1

1 These squares have been split into hundredths.

Count the number of hundredths shaded and then write them as a decimal.

Example: 45 hundredths or 0·45

a

82 hundredths or 0.82

b

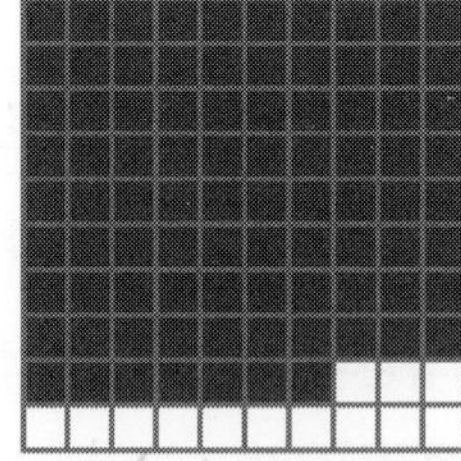

97 hundredths or 0.97

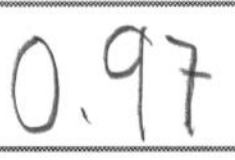

2 Complete the sentence. Circle the correct answer.

50 hundredths (or 0·50) is the same as **all** / **half** / **a quarter** of a whole.

Challenge 2

1 Label each decimal on the number line.

a 0·56

b 0·73

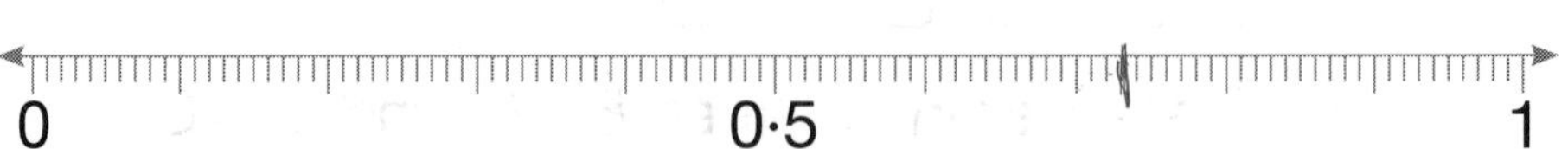

c 0·39

d One of the decimals you have labelled is less than a half.

Which is it? 0.39

2 Which decimals are these arrows pointing to?

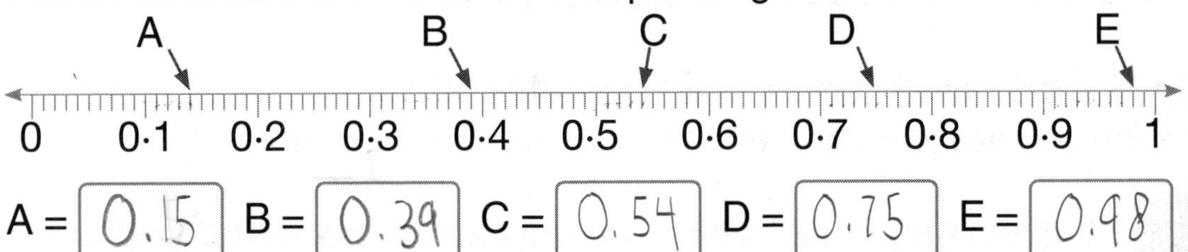

3 Write the decimal number.

Example:

12 whole metres + 5 tenths of a metre + 4 hundredths of a metre

= 12·54 metres

a 4 whole litres + 3 tenths of a litre + 8 hundredths of a litre

= 4.38 litres

b 10 whole seconds + 8 tenths of a second + 9 hundredths of a second

= 10.89 seconds

Challenge 3 Use the digits 4, 8, 2, 1 and 7 to make the following decimals to two decimal places.

a The largest possible decimal.

b The smallest possible decimal.

c A number in between 84·27 and 42·78.

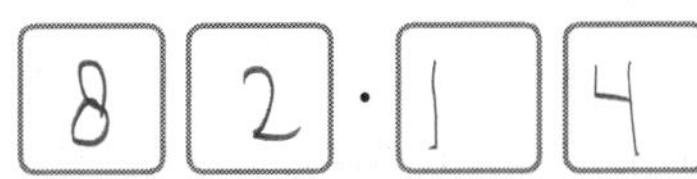

d A number that rounds up to 43.

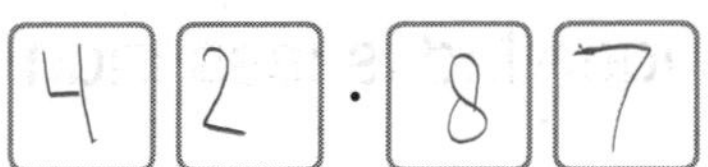

Number

Lesson 4: **Hundredths (2)**

- Understand the value of hundredths in a number
- Read and write hundredths in different situations

Challenge 1 Draw a line to match each amount of money to the fraction of $1.

\$0.04 \$0.03 \$0.05 \$0.08 \$0.09 \$0.07 \$0.06 \$0.01

$\frac{7}{100}$ $\frac{8}{100}$ $\frac{4}{100}$ $\frac{3}{100}$ $\frac{9}{100}$ $\frac{6}{100}$ $\frac{1}{100}$ $\frac{5}{100}$

Challenge 2 **1** Six children have different amounts of money.

a Complete the table.

Name	**Dollars**	**10 cent coins**	**1 cent coins**	**Total**
Ellie	4	8	2	\$4.82
Joe	5	1	5	5.15
Raheem	9	3	4	\$9.34
Nadia	3	4	0	3.40
Georgia	2	9	8	\$2.98
Lily	1	9	5	1.95

b Round each person's total to the nearest whole number.

Example: Ellie's total rounds to \$5.

Joe's total rounds to \$5.

Raheem's total rounds to \$9.

Nadia's total rounds to \$3.

Georgia's total rounds to \$3.

Lily's total rounds to \$2.

2 Write the following in each box.

a A decimal with 25 hundredths. 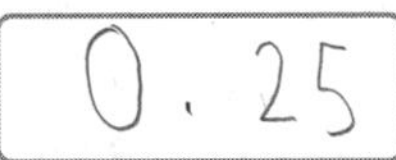

b A decimal with 68 hundredths. 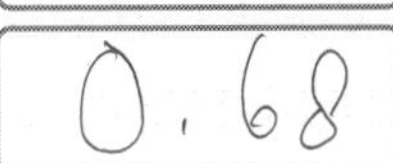

c A decimal with no tenths and 5 hundredths. 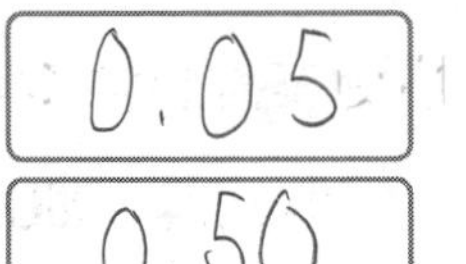

d A decimal with 5 tenths and no hundredths. 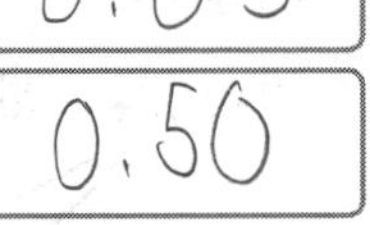

Challenge **3** A shop sells different kinds of clocks. The digits in all the prices add to 10.

a What could the prices of the clocks be?

- The price of the desk clock contains 5 tenths and 0 hundredths.

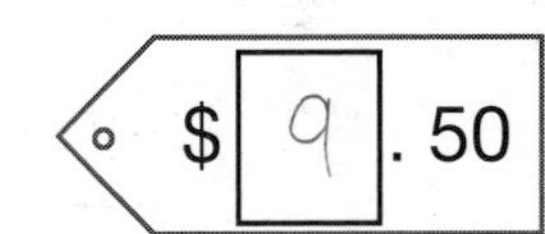

- The price of the wall clock contains 1 more tenth and 3 more hundredths than the desk clock.

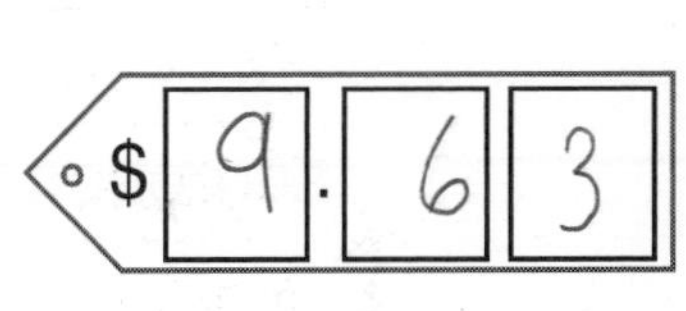

- The price of the alarm clock contains two less hundredths than the wall clock.

b Round each price to the nearest dollar.

Alarm clock = $10.0 Desk clock = $10

Wall clock = $10

Lesson 1: **Tenths (3)**

- Understand the value of tenths in a number
- Label decimal numbers and order them
- Read and write tenths in different situations

Challenge 1

1 a Match each decimal with the correct description.

4·2 •	• 9 units and 3 tenths
6·5 •	• 6 units and 5 tenths
9·3 •	• 1 unit and 5 tenths
5·1 •	• 4 units and 2 tenths
1·5 •	• 5 units and 1 tenth

b Two of the decimals above have the same number of tenths.
Which numbers are they? ☐ and ☐

1 Some children in Class 4 take part in a race.

a Complete the scoreboard.

Name	Whole seconds	Tenths of a second	Finishing time
Ryan	36	5	36·5 sec
Abby	37	8	
Miki	36	1	
Sofia	34	7	
Joe			35·3 sec
David			34·8 sec
Mat			37·2 sec

b Who won? ______________________

c Who came last? ______________________

d Write the names of the runners in order from shortest time to longest time.

____

____

2 a Count on in 0·1s.

2·6	2·7					3·2

b Count on in 0·2s.

0·4	0·6			1·2		

3 Each of these arrows shows a different time in seconds. Write down the decimal each arrow is pointing to.

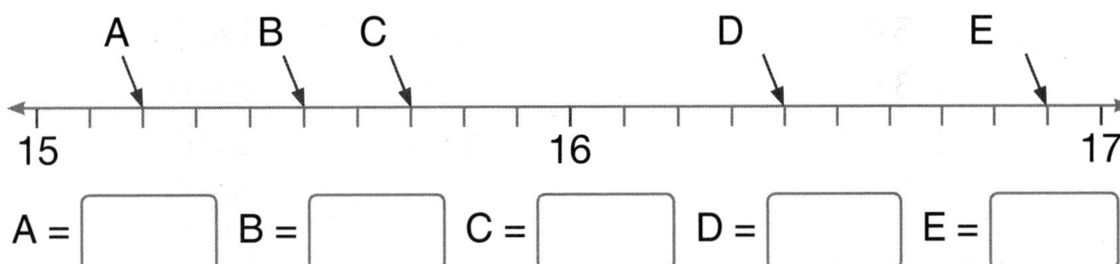

A = ☐ B = ☐ C = ☐ D = ☐ E = ☐

Challenge 3

54·6	55·9	53·1
55·6	54·2	55·2
54·9	53·7	53·9

a Jonathan chooses a number from the grid. He counts on in 0·4s from that number.

He reaches the number 58·0. Which numbers could he have chosen?

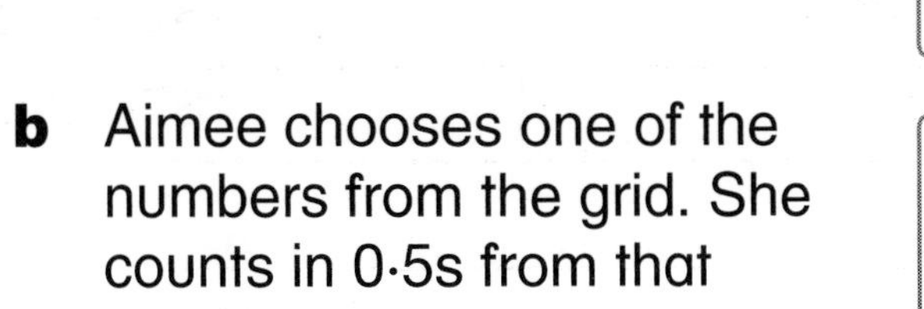

b Aimee chooses one of the numbers from the grid. She counts in 0·5s from that number.

She reaches the number 56·7. Which numbers could she have chosen?

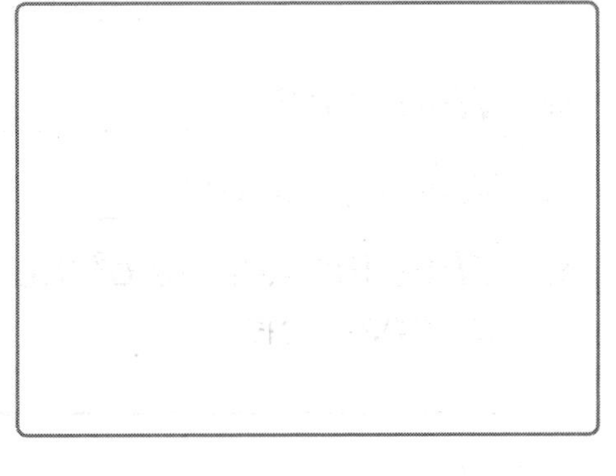

Lesson 2: **Tenths (4)**

- Understand the value of tenths in a number
- Convert whole centimetres into lengths in metres (in tenths)

1 What is the 3 worth in each of these lengths?

a 32·5 m ☐ **b** 84·3 m ☐ **c** 93·2 m ☐

d 70·3 m ☐ **e** 23·0 m ☐ **f** 36·7 m ☐

2 Look carefully at these lengths.

51·8 m 42·3 m 63·2 m 41·5 m 58·7 m 61·3 m

a Which is the shortest length? ☐

b Which two lengths have the same number of tenths?

☐ and ☐.

1 Write each measurement in metres.

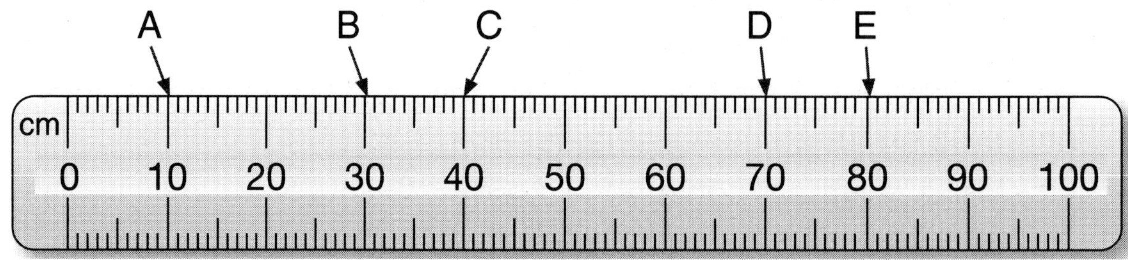

A = 0·1 m B = ☐ C = ☐ D = ☐ E = ☐

2 Divide by 100 to convert these measurements into metres.

a 120 cm = ☐ m **b** 160 cm = ☐ m

c 170 cm = ☐ m **d** 230 cm = ☐ m

3 Class 4 record the distances each child can hit a tennis ball.

Name	Distance (cm)	Distance (m)
Leah	460	4·6
Mo	560	
Nathan	490	
Oscar	640	
Preeti	610	

a Complete the last column by converting each measurements into metres.

b Write the names of the children in order from the furthest to the shortest distance.

____

____

Challenge **3** Four numbers are made using the digits 4, 5, 9 and 0.

4	5	9	0

Each of the numbers has two digits followed by a decimal point and then an amount of tenths, for example, 59·4.

- The first number is a whole number.
- The second number can be rounded up to 55.
- The third number represents something 'and a half'.
- The fourth number is the largest possible number.

What could each number be?

Number 1: ☐ Number 2: ☐

Number 3: ☐ Number 4: ☐

Number

Lesson 3: **Hundredths (3)**

- Read, write, label and order hundredths
- Describe and continue decimal number sequences
- Convert prices written in cents into dollars (and dollars into cents)

Challenge 1 Write down the value of each of these letters.

a

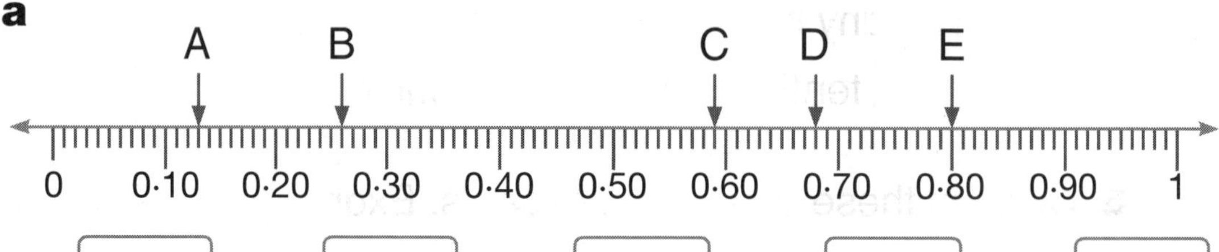

A = 0·13 B = ☐ C = ☐ D = ☐ E = ☐

b

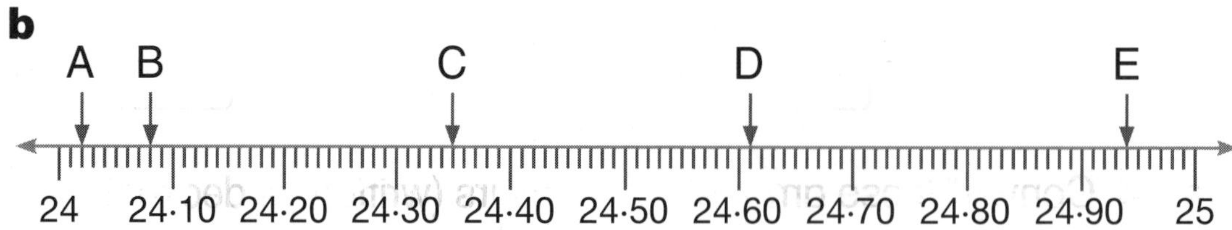

A = 24·02 B = ☐ C = ☐ D = ☐ E = ☐

Challenge 2

1 Look carefully at these sequences and write each rule. Continue each sequence for a further three prices.

a $23.96, $23.97, $23.98, ☐, ☐, ☐

Rule = ______________________

b $5.38, $6.38, $7.38, ☐, ☐, ☐

Rule = ______________________

c $15.97, $15.95, $15.93, ☐, ☐, ☐

Rule = ______________________

2 a Three children bring money to school for a book sale.

William brings \$9.05, Ade brings \$9.55 and Sara brings \$9.50.
Who has brought the most? ______________________

Who has brought the least? ______________________

b A magazine costs \$4.65. How many tenths and how many hundredths is this?

[ ] tenths and [ ] hundredths

3 Convert these amounts into cents. Example: \$2.56 = [256] cents

a \$4.06 = [ ] cents **b** \$8.34 = [ ] cents

c \$3.50 = [ ] cents **d** \$19.52 = [ ] cents

4 Convert these amounts into dollars (written as decimals).

Example: 2513 cents = [\$25.13]

a 582 cents = \$ [ ] **b** 629 cents = \$ [ ]

c 1490 cents = \$ [ ] **d** 2006 cents = \$ [ ]

Challenge 3 This decimal number sequence increases by two hundredths (0·02) each time: 3·45, 3·47, 3·49, 3·51, 3·53, 3·55

Make up three different decimal number sequences of your own. For each sequence, write the rule.

a

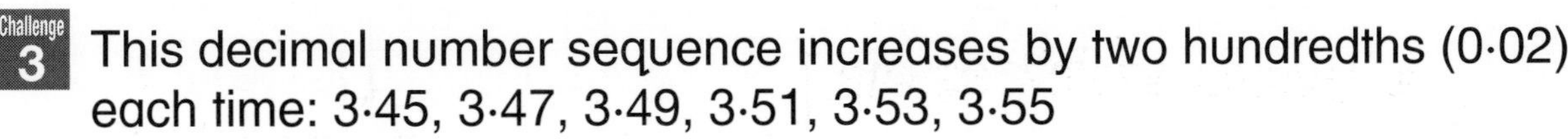

Rule = ______________________

b

Rule = ______________________

Number

Lesson 4: Hundredths (4)

- Read, write, order and round decimals in different situations
- Convert measurements using decimals

You will need
- coloured pencils

Challenge 1

Each small square is worth one hundredth of the whole (or 0·01).

Each row is worth one tenth of the whole (or 0·1).
Colour in the correct number of squares or rows.

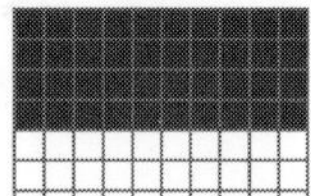

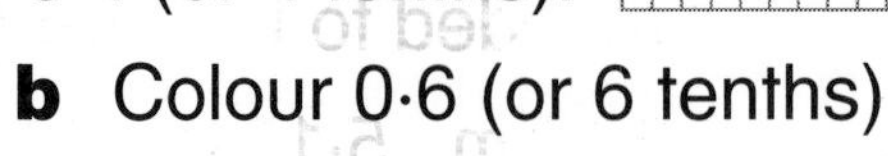
Example: Colour 0·4 (or 4 tenths).

a Colour 0·8 (or 8 tenths).

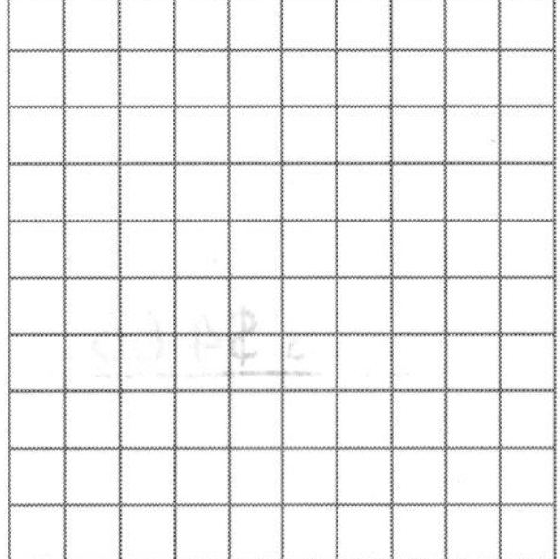

b Colour 0·6 (or 6 tenths).

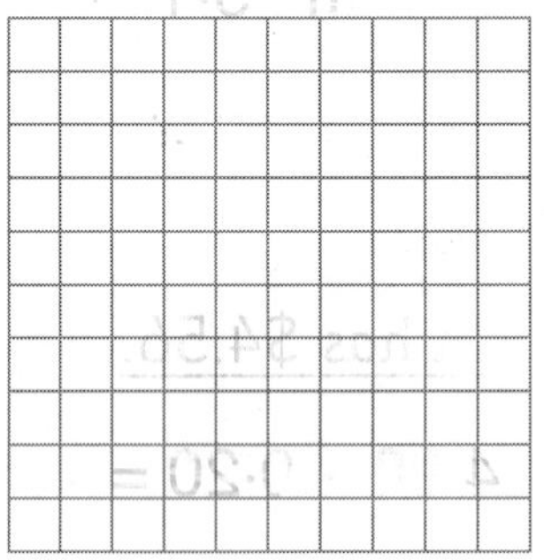

c Colour 0·37 (or 37 hundredths).

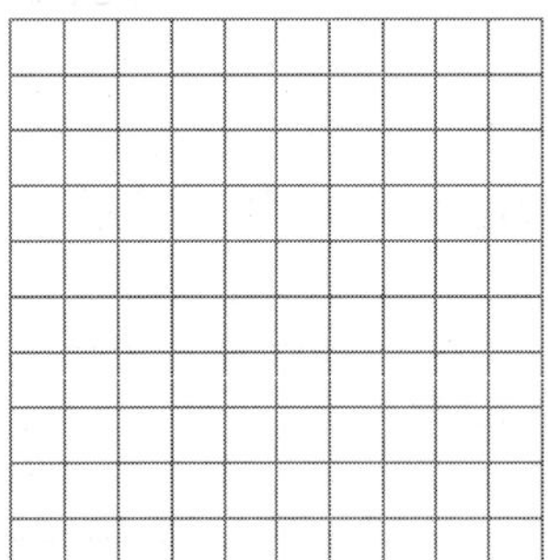

d Colour 0·78 (or 78 hundreths).

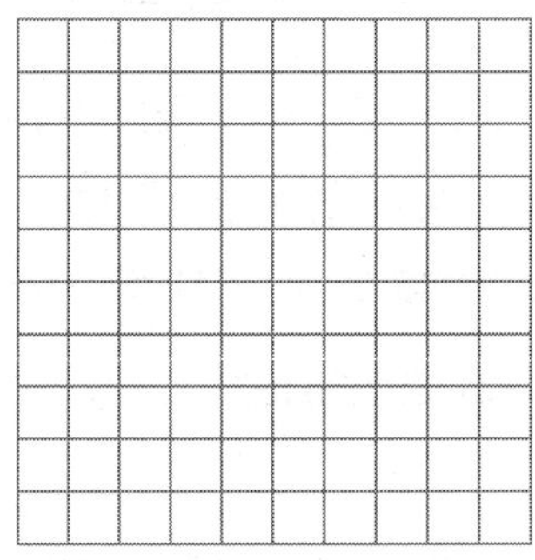

Challenge 2

1 a Write the places in order, starting with the nearest.

____

____

Airport	3·50 km
City Centre	3·21 km
Hospital	3·68 km
University	3·18 km
Bus station	3·02 km

b If you round each distance to the nearest whole kilometre, which distances will round up to 4 km?

____

2 a What is \$3.60 in cents? ☐ cents

b Four containers hold different amounts of water.

Container A = 1·56 litres Container B = 1·65 litres

Container C = 1·55 litres Container D = 1·66 litres

Write the letters in order from the smallest to the largest container.

c Circle the distances that will equal 6 metres when rounded to the nearest metre.

5·87 m 5·19 m 6·52 m 6·50 m 5·50 m 6·23 m 6·09 m

3 Write a number story for the calculation.

Example: 4·56 + 0·10 = 4·66

Liam has \$4.56. He finds 10 cents and now has \$4.66.

a 4·98 – 0·20 = 4·78

____

____

Use these digit cards to make the following decimal numbers. Each number should have both tenths and hundredths.

a A decimal number that rounds up to 4. ☐

b An amount of dollars that equals 135 cents. ☐

c A length in metres that is equal to something and a half. ☐

d The smallest decimal number you can make. ☐

Number

Lesson 1: **Comparing and ordering fractions (1)**

- Compare and order fractions that have the same denominator

You will need
- coloured pencil

Challenge 1 Colour each fraction and then write which is the larger or smaller.

a $\frac{1}{4}$ $\frac{3}{4}$

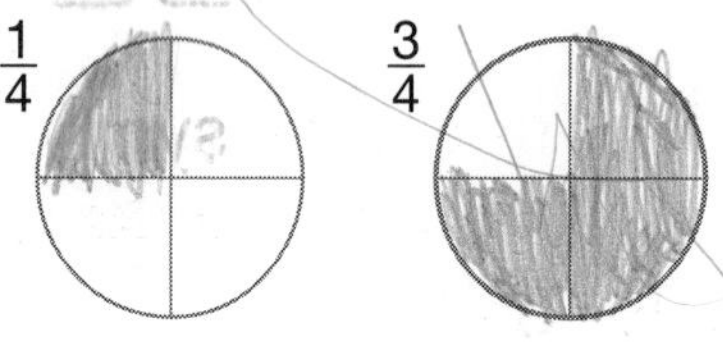

$\frac{1}{4}$ is larger than 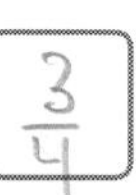 $\frac{3}{4}$.

b $\frac{2}{3}$ $\frac{1}{3}$

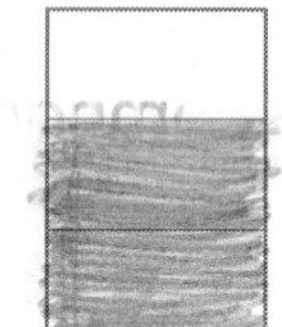

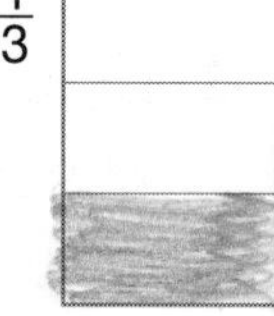

$\frac{2}{3}$ is smaller than 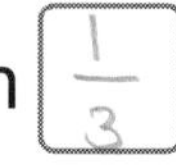 $\frac{1}{3}$.

c $\frac{5}{10}$ $\frac{7}{10}$

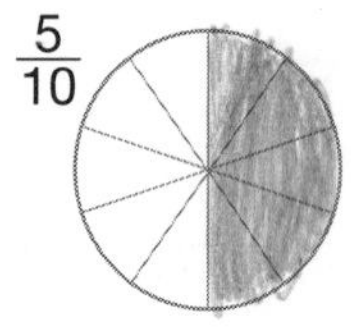

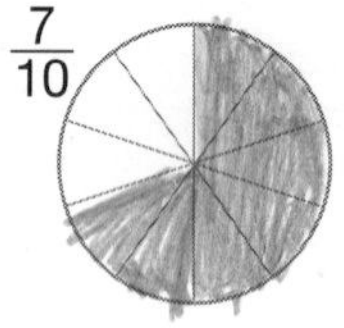

$\frac{7}{10}$ is larger than ☐.

d $\frac{2}{5}$ $\frac{3}{5}$

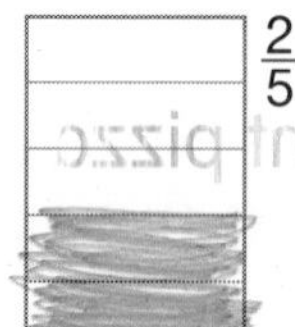

$\frac{3}{5}$ is smaller than  $\frac{2}{5}$.

Challenge 2 **1** Identify each fraction and then use the < or > symbols to show which is smaller or larger.

Example:

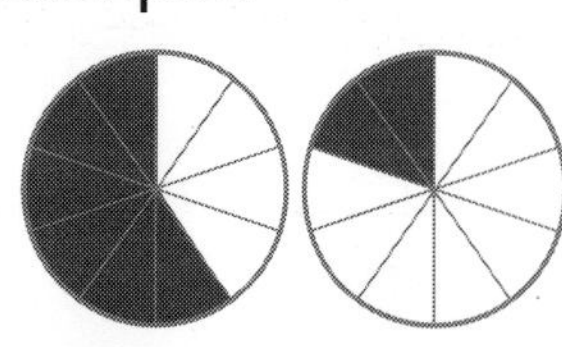

$\frac{6}{10} > \frac{2}{10}$

a 

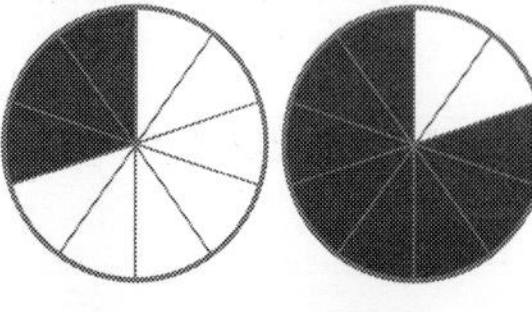

$\frac{3}{10} < \frac{8}{10}$

b 

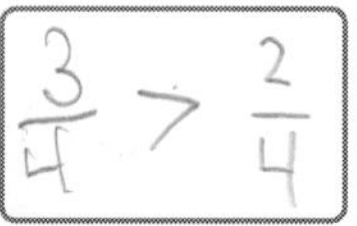

$\frac{3}{4} > \frac{2}{4}$

c 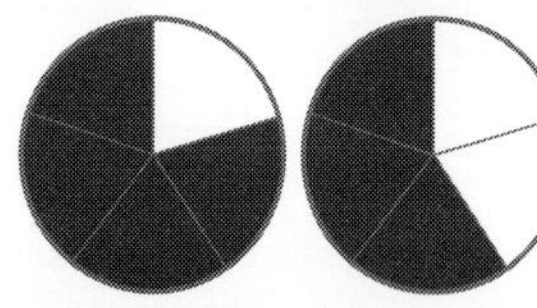

$\frac{4}{5} > \frac{3}{5}$

d 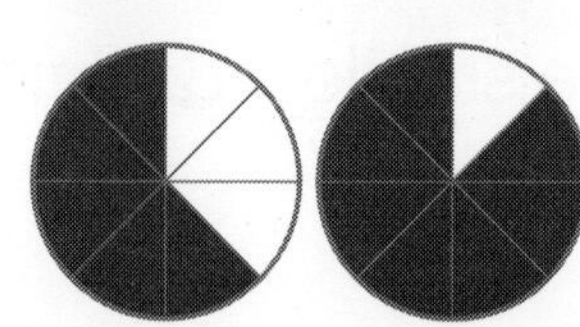

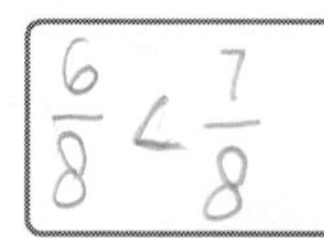

$\frac{6}{8} < \frac{7}{8}$

2 Class 4 make towers containing 5 cubes out of red and white cubes.

Tower 1 = $\frac{4}{5}$ red Tower 2 = $\frac{2}{5}$ red

Tower 3 = $\frac{1}{5}$ red Tower 4 = $\frac{3}{5}$ red

Compare the different fractions and write them in order from smallest to largest.

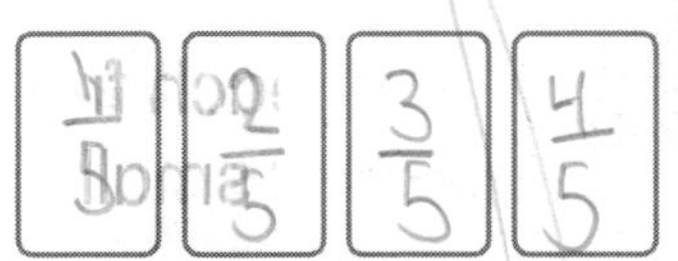

3 Kyle has compared pairs of fractions and used symbols to show which is larger or smaller. Write a tick (✓) or a cross (✗) to show whether each of his comparisons is correct or not.

a $\frac{5}{10} > \frac{7}{10}$ ✗ **b** $\frac{4}{8} < \frac{3}{8}$ ✓ **c** $\frac{3}{4} > \frac{2}{4}$ ✓ **d** $\frac{2}{3} < \frac{1}{3}$ ✗

Challenge 3

Three different pizzas are cut into 5 slices each.

3 slices of the cheese and tomato pizza, 4 slices of the spicy pizza and 2 slices of the vegetable pizza are eaten.

a What fraction of each pizza is **not** eaten?

cheese and tomato = $\frac{2}{5}$ spicy = $\frac{1}{5}$ vegetable = $\frac{3}{5}$

b Explain how you worked out the fractions that were not eaten.

1whole − 3 = $\frac{2}{5}$ 1whole − 4 = $\frac{1}{5}$ 1whole − 2 = $\frac{3}{5}$

c Write the three fractions in order from smallest to largest.

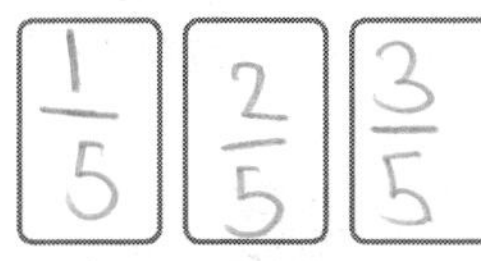

Number

Lesson 2: Equivalent fractions

- Identify fractions that are equal to $\frac{1}{2}$, $\frac{1}{4}$ and $\frac{1}{5}$

You will need

- coloured pencil

Challenge 1 Shade half of each shape.

a

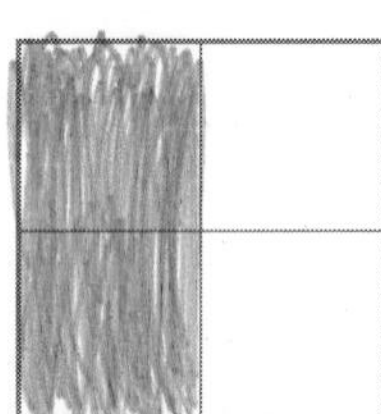

How many quarters have you shaded?

b

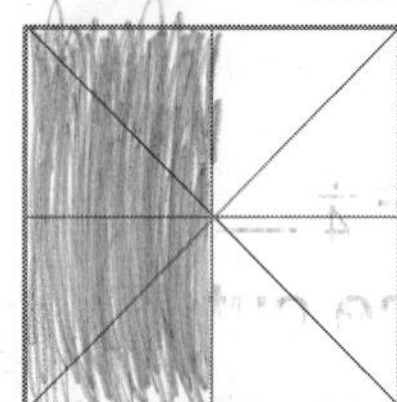

How many eighths have you shaded?

c

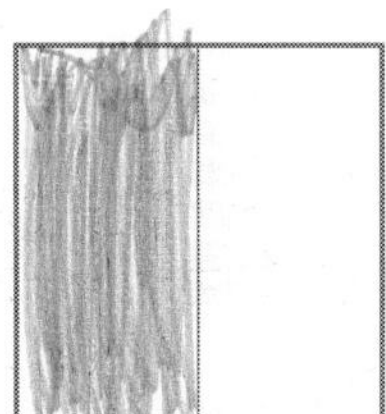

How many halves have you shaded?

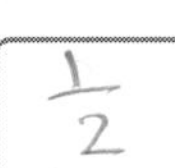

d

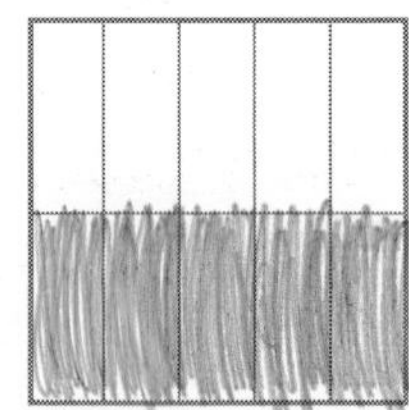

How many tenths have you shaded?

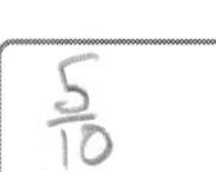

Challenge 2

1 These shapes show equivalent fractions. What are they?

a

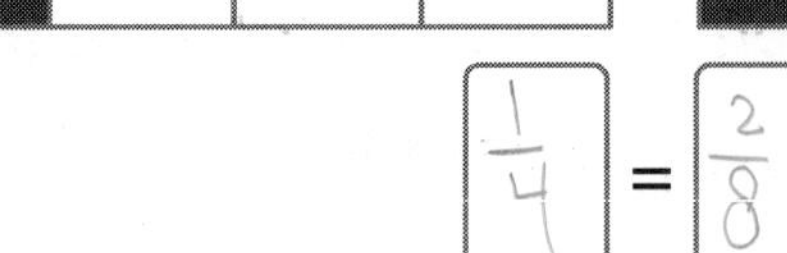

b

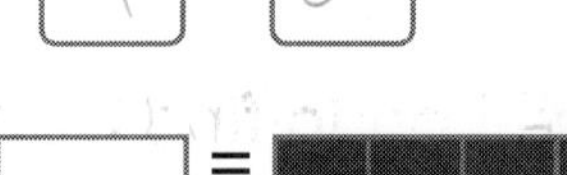

c

d

$\frac{1}{5} = \frac{2}{10}$

2 Write 'True' or 'False' for each of these statements.

a Two quarters are equivalent to one half. true

b $\frac{4}{8} = \frac{1}{4}$ False

c One out of five is the same as five out of 10. False

d $\frac{1}{2} = \frac{5}{10}$ True

e Four eighths are equivalent to one quarter. False

f $\frac{2}{4} = \frac{2}{8}$ False

Challenge 3 A multiplication table can help find equivalent fractions. These two rows from a multiplication table show multiples of 1 and multiples of 2.

		1	2	3	4	5	6	7	8	9	10
Multiples of 1	1	1	2	3	4	5	6	7	8	9	10
Multiples of 2	2	2	4	6	8	10	12	14	16	18	20

a Can you see the fraction $\frac{1}{2}$ anywhere? Circle it.

b Now look for $\frac{2}{4}$ which is equivalent to a half. Circle it using a different colour.

c Use the same method to find as many fractions equivalent to $\frac{1}{2}$ as you can. Write your fractions in a list, in the order they appear in the rows.

$\frac{1}{2}, \frac{2}{4}, \frac{4}{8}, \frac{5}{10}, \frac{6}{12}, \frac{7}{14}, \frac{8}{16}, \frac{9}{18}, \frac{10}{20}, \frac{11}{22}, \frac{12}{24}, \frac{13}{26}, \frac{14}{28}, \frac{15}{30}, \frac{16}{32}, \frac{17}{34}$

Number

Lesson 3: **Comparing and ordering fractions (2)**

- Compare and order fractions that have different denominators

You will need
- coloured pencil

Challenge 1

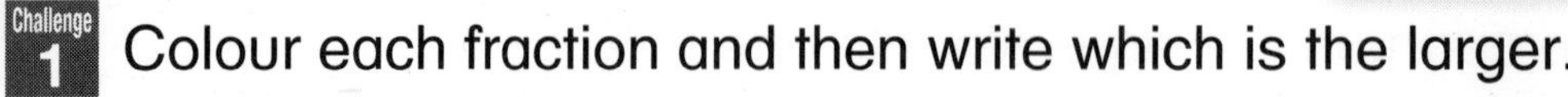

a 
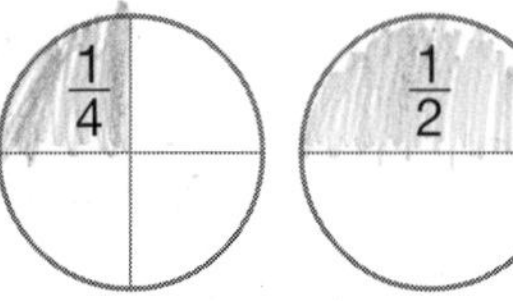

b
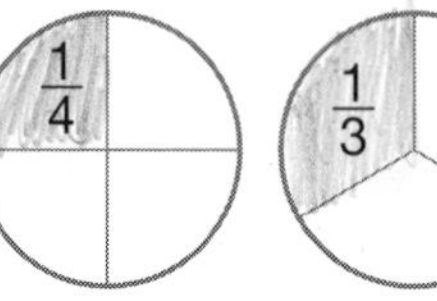

c
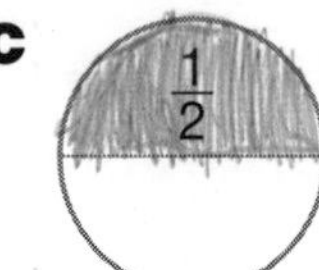

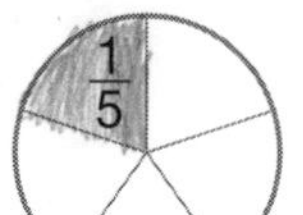

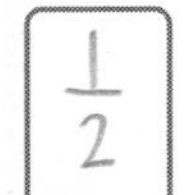

is larger than

1/3 is larger than

1/2 is larger than

1 Use the < or > symbols to show which fraction is smaller or larger.
Example:

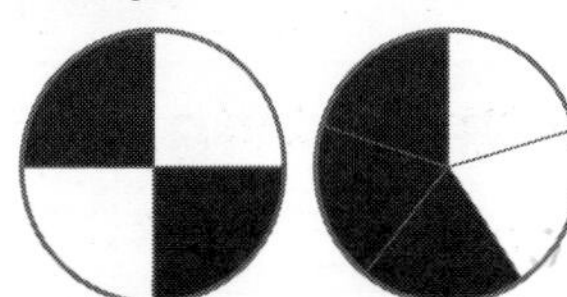
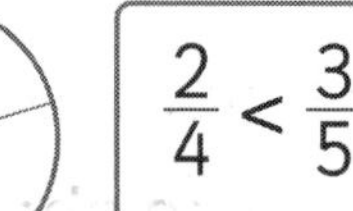
$\frac{2}{4} < \frac{3}{5}$

a 
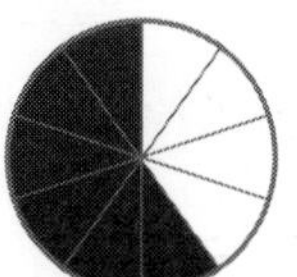
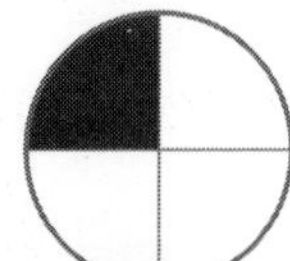
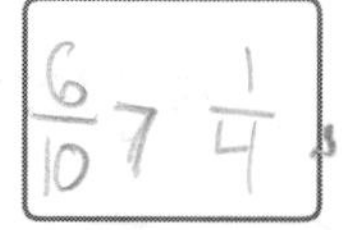

b
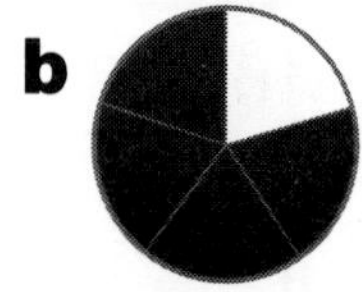
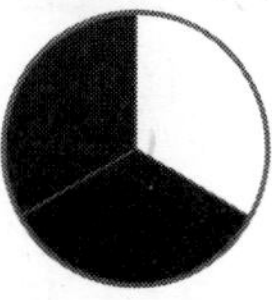
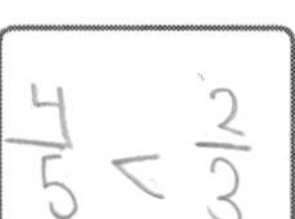

c 
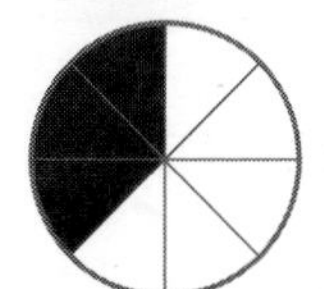

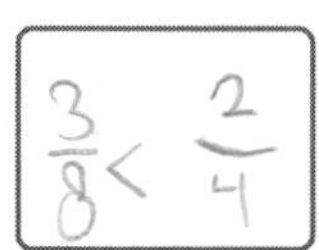

2 Order each group of fractions from smallest to largest.
One fraction is worth less than a half, one fraction is worth a half and one fraction is worth more than a half.

a $\frac{1}{4}$, $\frac{7}{10}$, $\frac{4}{8}$

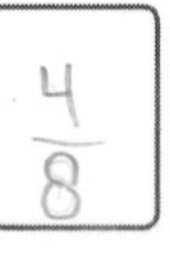

b $\frac{1}{10}$, $\frac{4}{5}$, $\frac{1}{2}$

c $\frac{5}{8}$, $\frac{5}{10}$, $\frac{1}{3}$

5/10

d $\frac{1}{5}$, $\frac{8}{10}$, $\frac{4}{8}$
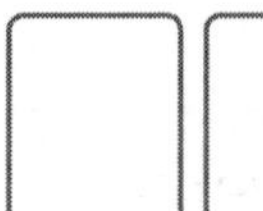
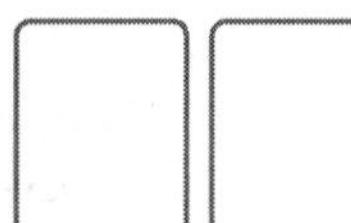

3 Order each group of fractions from smallest to largest. Use this fraction wall to help compare the fractions.

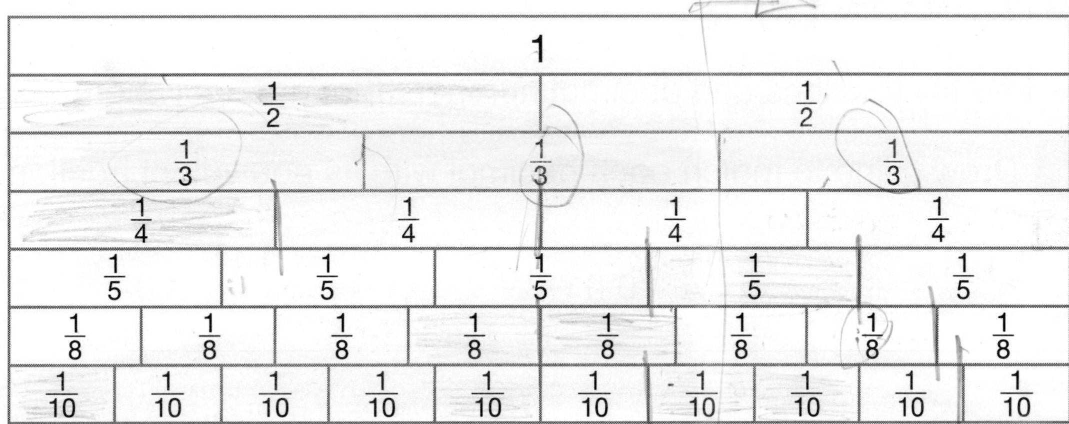

a $\frac{2}{3}, \frac{2}{4}, \frac{1}{2}, \frac{4}{10}$ [$\frac{4}{10}$] [$\frac{1}{2}$] [$\frac{2}{4}$] [$\frac{2}{3}$]

b $\frac{9}{10}, \frac{3}{5}, \frac{7}{8}, \frac{2}{4}$ [$\frac{2}{4}$] [$\frac{3}{5}$] [$\frac{7}{8}$] [$\frac{9}{10}$]

c $\frac{2}{8}, \frac{2}{5}, \frac{1}{10}, \frac{2}{3}$ [$\frac{1}{10}$] [$\frac{2}{8}$] [$\frac{2}{5}$] [$\frac{2}{3}$]

d $\frac{4}{8}, \frac{6}{10}, \frac{4}{5}, \frac{1}{4}$ [$\frac{1}{4}$] [$\frac{4}{8}$] [$\frac{6}{10}$] [$\frac{4}{5}$]

4 Read each question carefully before answering it.

a Ibrahim likes sweets. Should he choose $\frac{1}{5}$ of a bag of sweets or $\frac{1}{3}$ of a bag of sweets?

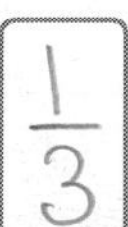

b Alicia does not like apples. Should she choose to eat $\frac{1}{4}$ of an apple or $\frac{1}{10}$ of an apple?

Challenge 3 Write your own fraction comparison questions below. Use the fraction wall above to help you.

a ________________________

____

b ________________________

____

Answers

a	
b	

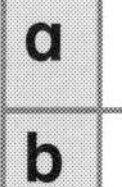

Number

Lesson 4: **Equivalent fractions and decimals (1)**

- Identify fractions and decimal numbers that are equivalent

Challenge 1 Draw a line to match each decimal with its equivalent fraction.

Challenge 2

1 Write each of the shaded areas as a fraction and as a decimal.

Example:

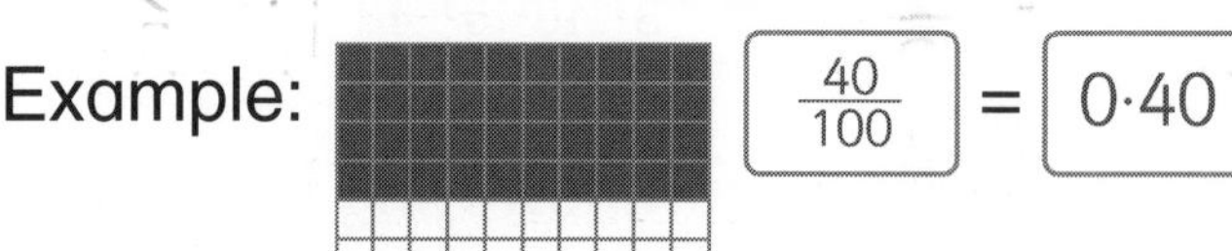

a   =   **b**   =

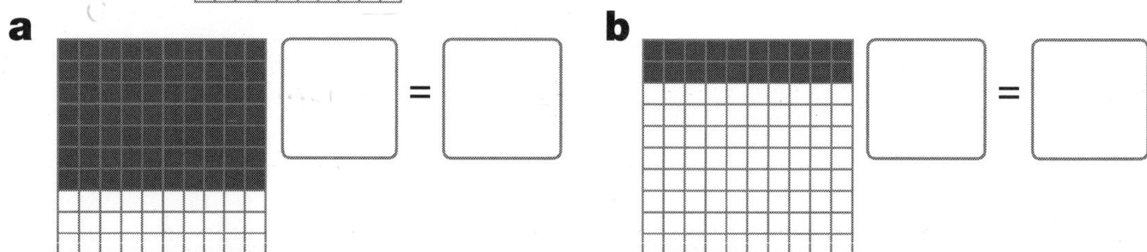

c   =   **d**   =

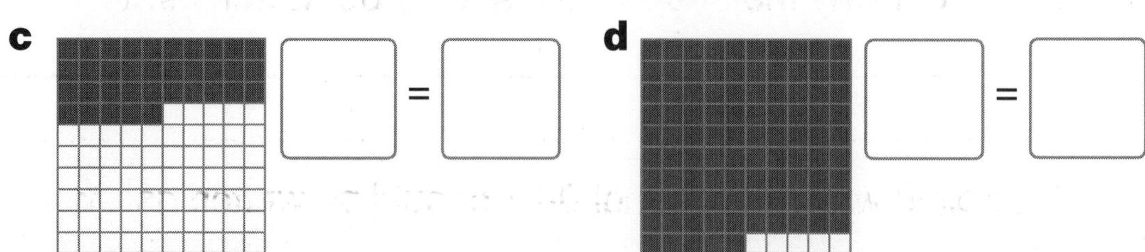

e   =   **f**   =

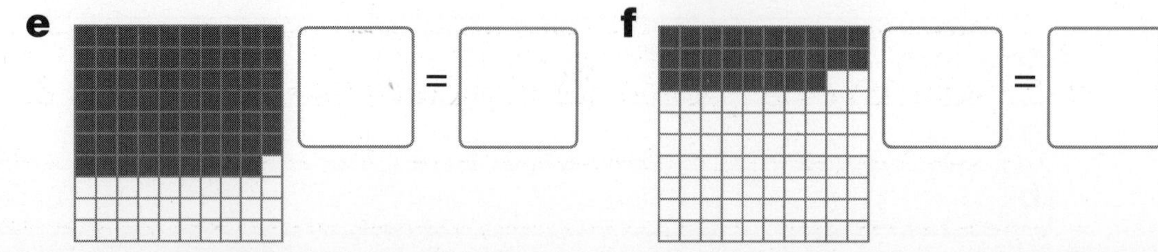

2 This machine converts fractions into equivalent decimals. Write the missing fraction or decimal.

Fractions			Decimals	
$\frac{30}{100}$	←		→	0·30
$\frac{5}{100}$	←		→	
$\frac{90}{100}$	←		→	
$\frac{50}{100}$	←		→	
	←		→	0·70
$\frac{63}{100}$	←		→	
	←		→	0·01
	←		→	0·12
$\frac{81}{100}$	←		→	
	←		→	0·69
	←		→	0·10

Challenge 3

1 Explain why the fraction $\frac{2}{100}$ should be written as 0·02.

____

____

2 Explain why the decimal 0·4 should be written as $\frac{4}{10}$.

____

____

3 Explain why the decimal 0·21 should be written as $\frac{21}{100}$.

____

____

4 Explain why the fraction $\frac{60}{100}$ can be written as 0·60 or 0·6.

____

____

Lesson 5: **Equivalent fractions and decimals (2)**

- Identify fractions and decimal numbers that are equivalent

You will need
- coloured pencil

Challenge 1

Write these amounts as fractions and as decimals.

Example: 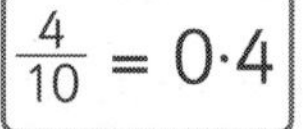 $\frac{4}{10} = 0{\cdot}4$

a  **b** 

c **d** 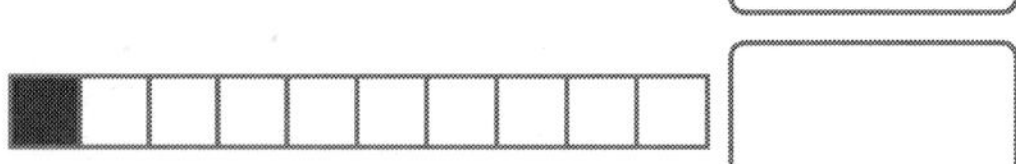

e **f**

Challenge 2

1 Convert these fractions into decimals.

Example: $\frac{9}{100}$ = 0·09

a $\frac{1}{100}$ = **b** $\frac{20}{100}$ = **c** $\frac{7}{10}$ =

d $\frac{14}{100}$ = **e** $\frac{5}{10}$ = **f** $\frac{5}{100}$ =

g $\frac{59}{100}$ = **h** $\frac{15}{100}$ = **i** $\frac{65}{100}$ =

2 Convert these decimals into fractions.

Example: 0·35 = $\frac{35}{100}$

a 0·08 = **b** 0·40 = **c** 0·02 =

d 0·55 = **e** 0·7 = **f** 0·13 =

3 a Colour half of this square.

Count the small squares you have shaded and use this to help you write $\frac{1}{2}$ as a fraction and also a decimal.

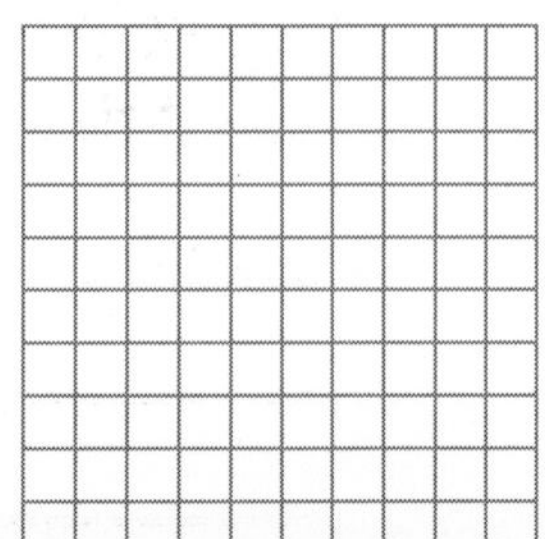

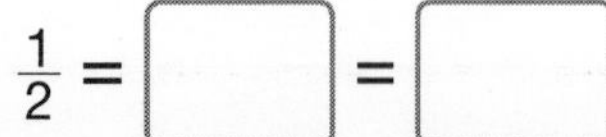

$\frac{1}{2}$ = ☐ = ☐

b Colour one quarter of this square.

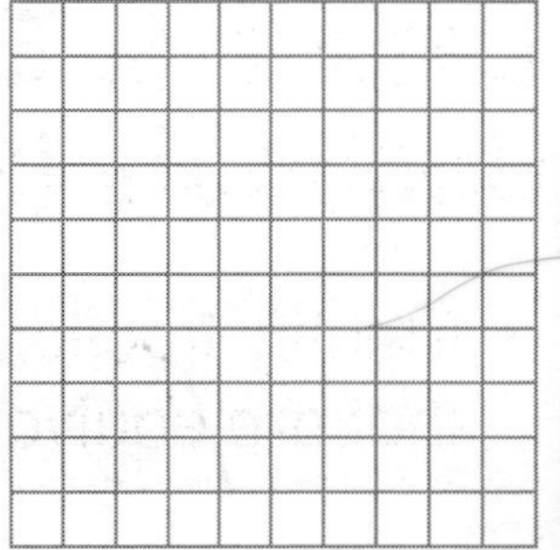

Count the small squares you have shaded and use this to help you write $\frac{1}{4}$ as a fraction and also a decimal.

$\frac{1}{4}$ = ☐ = ☐

c Colour three quarters of this square.

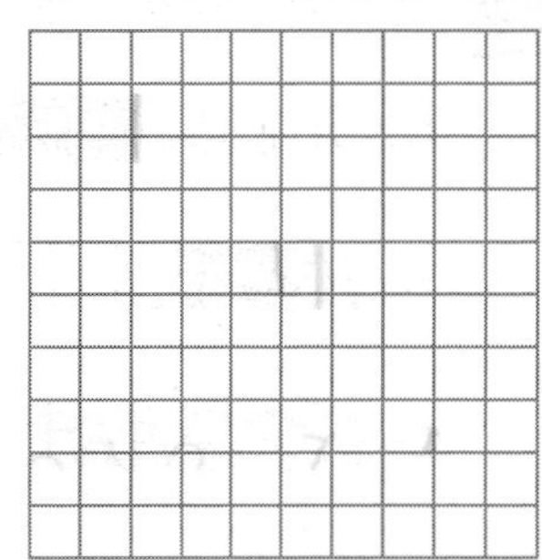

Count the small squares you have shaded and use this to help you write $\frac{3}{4}$ as a fraction and also a decimal.

$\frac{3}{4}$ = ☐ = ☐

Challenge 3

1 This strip shows $\frac{1}{5}$.

Leah says, "If I can change this into tenths, I can write it as a decimal."

Explain how Leah could show the fraction as tenths and write down what the decimal will be.

____

____

____

2 This strip shows $\frac{2}{8}$.

Leah says, "I can write this as a decimal because I know a different fraction that it is equal to."

Explain what fraction Leah is thinking of and write down what the decimal will be.

____

____

____

Lesson 6: **Mixed numbers**

- Recognise mixed numbers
- Put mixed numbers in the correct order on a number line

You will need

- coloured pencils

Challenge 1 Show each mixed number.

a Colour $1\frac{1}{2}$.

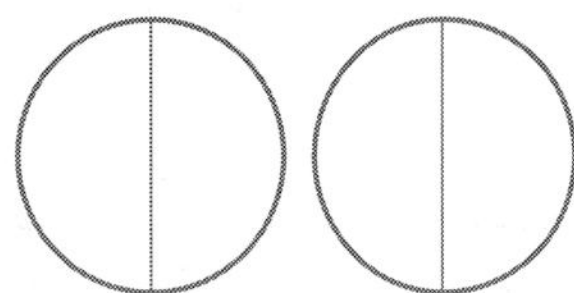

b Colour $1\frac{2}{3}$.

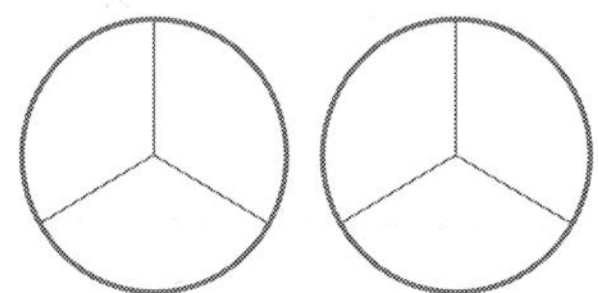

c Colour $1\frac{4}{5}$.

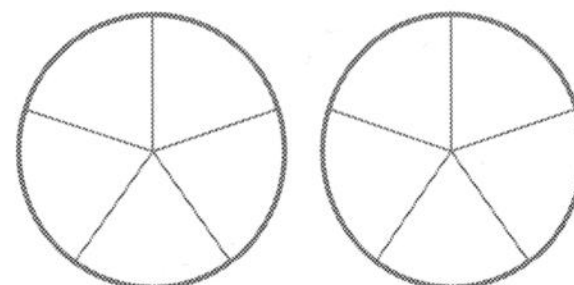

d Colour $1\frac{7}{10}$.

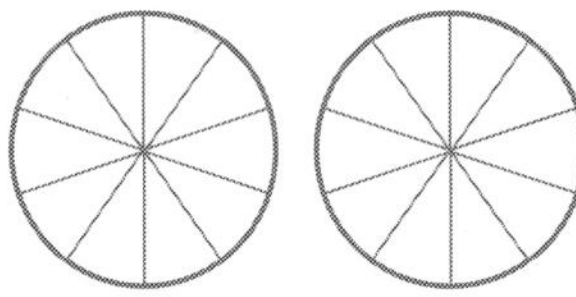

Challenge 2

1 Write each of these mixed numbers.

a

b

c

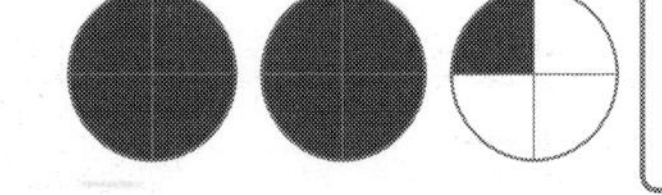

d

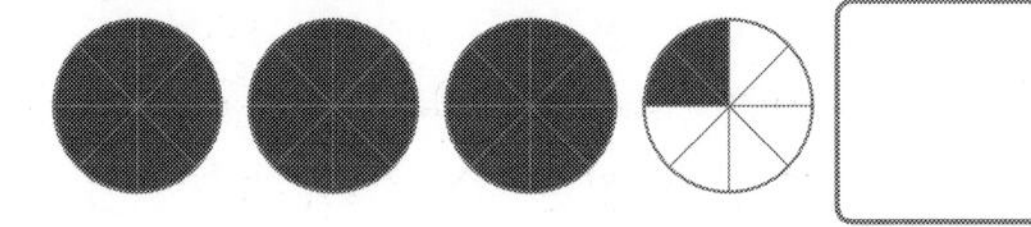

e Look at your answers for **a–d** and order them correctly on this number line.

2 3 4

2 Write the mixed numbers for the party food that was eaten.

a 2 whole pizzas were eaten as well as 4 slices of another pizza, which was cut into 10 equal slices.

Mixed number = ☐

b 3 whole cakes were eaten as well as 2 slices of another cake, which was cut into 5 equal slices.

Mixed number = ☐

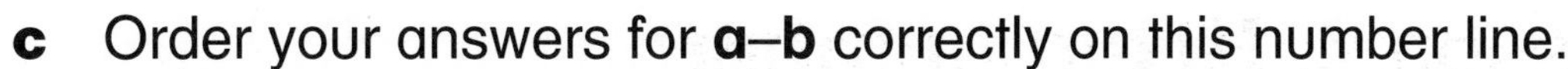

c Order your answers for **a–b** correctly on this number line.

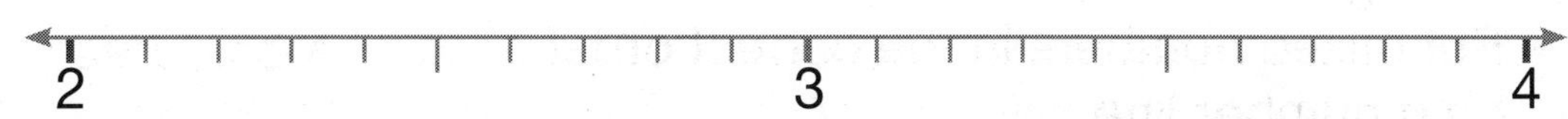

3 Draw an arrow from each mixed number to show where it belongs on the number line.

a $16\frac{1}{3}$ $17\frac{2}{3}$ $15\frac{1}{3}$ $15\frac{2}{3}$ $16\frac{2}{3}$

b $6\frac{1}{2}$ $6\frac{7}{10}$ $5\frac{2}{10}$ $5\frac{8}{10}$ $6\frac{3}{10}$

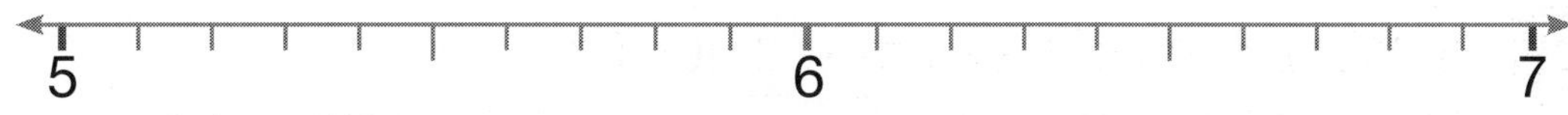

Challenge 3 Think about how many of each fraction there are in total in a mixed number.

Seven quarters is the same as $1\frac{3}{4}$, because there are four quarters in the whole and three in the fraction.

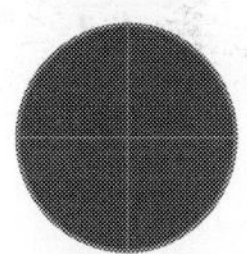
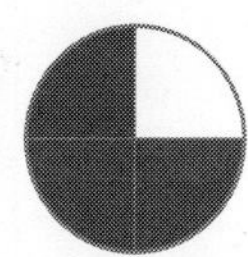

Write the mixed number and draw it as a diagram.

a Five thirds is the same as 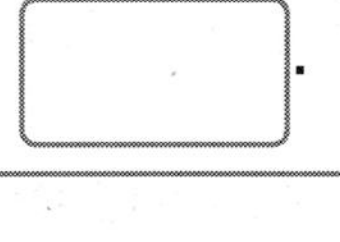.

b Ten quarters is the same as 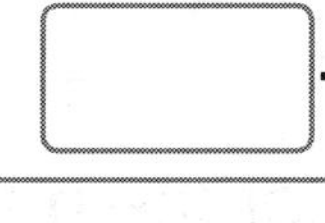.

c Seventeen eighths the same as 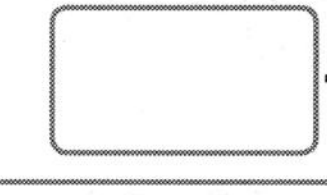.

Lesson 7: **Relating fractions to division**

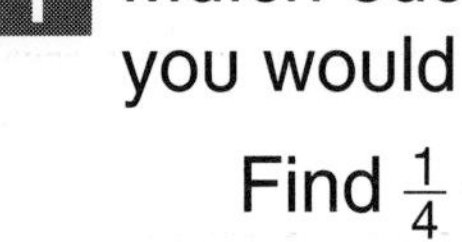

- Recognise links between fractions and division
- Say the division needed to work out a fraction calculation

Challenge 1 Match each question starter with the division calculation you would use to find the answer.

Find $\frac{1}{4}$ of... •	• divide by 5
Find $\frac{1}{3}$ of... •	• divide by 10
Find $\frac{1}{10}$ of... •	• divide by 4
Find $\frac{1}{5}$ of... •	• divide by 2
Find $\frac{1}{2}$ of... •	• divide by 8
Find $\frac{1}{8}$ of... •	• divide by 3

Challenge 2

1 Find different fractions of packs of colouring crayons.

Fill in the table to show the division questions you should use to find out the answers.

Number of crayons in the pack	Fraction needed	Division	Answer
30	$\frac{1}{2}$	30 ÷ 2	15
36	$\frac{1}{2}$		
52	$\frac{1}{4}$		
50	$\frac{1}{10}$		
55	$\frac{1}{5}$		
32	$\frac{1}{8}$		
42	$\frac{1}{3}$		
44	$\frac{1}{4}$		
50	$\frac{1}{2}$		
60	$\frac{1}{3}$		
40	$\frac{1}{10}$		

2 Work backwards from these division calculations to write the related fraction questions. Do not work out the answers.

Example: $56 \div 4 = \frac{1}{4}$ of 56

a $72 \div 8 =$ ________________ **b** $38 \div 2 =$ ________________

c $80 \div 5 =$ ________________ **d** $100 \div 10 =$ ________________

e $45 \div 3 =$ ________________ **f** $64 \div 2 =$ ________________

3 Choose three divisions in Question **2** and work out the answers.

Challenge 3

1 Georgia says: "To find a quarter of a number, as well as dividing by 4 I can also divide by 2 twice."

a Use **two different** numbers from the box below to test whether Georgia's idea works.

48 84 96 124 56

b Does Georgia's idea work? Yes / No

2 There is a way to find one tenth of a number without dividing by 10. It involves dividing by two different numbers.

Explain how to find one tenth without dividing by 10.

Number

Lesson 8: **Finding fractions of shapes and numbers**

- Find halves, quarters, thirds, fifths, eighths and tenths of shapes and numbers

You will need
- coloured pencils

1 Colour each shape to show the fractions.

a

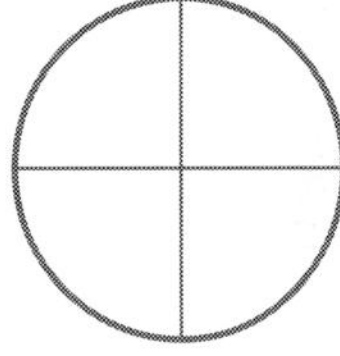

Show $\frac{3}{4}$.

b

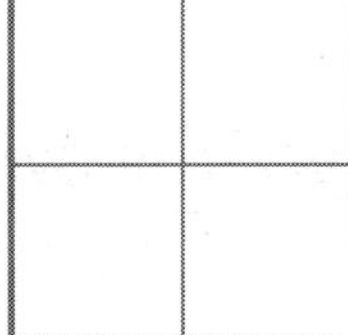

Show $\frac{1}{2}$.

c

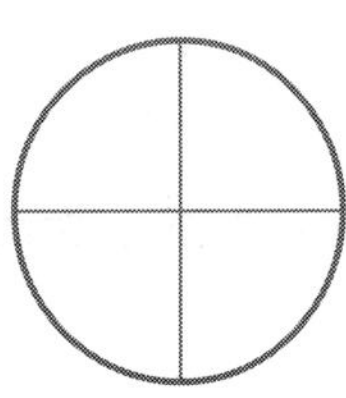

Show $\frac{1}{4}$.

d

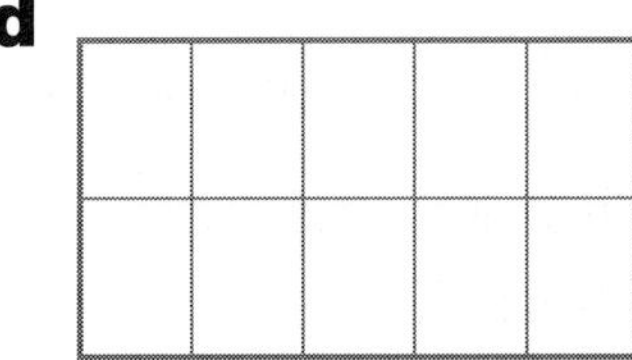

Show $\frac{2}{3}$.

2 Which three of the fractions you have coloured are more than $\frac{1}{2}$?

☐ and ☐

1 Kwame cuts three strips of paper into different lengths.

a The first strip is 48 cm long. He cuts it into eighths.

How long will each eighth be? ☐ cm

b His second strip of paper is a metre (100 cm) long. He cuts it into quarters.

How long will each quarter be? ☐ cm

c The last strip is 70 cm long. He cuts it into tenths.

How long will each tenth be? ☐ cm

2 What fraction of these shapes is shaded?

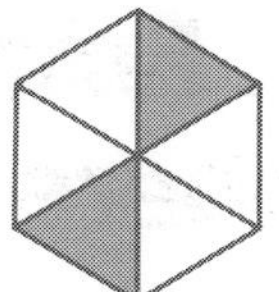

a Write your answer in sixths: ☐

b Write your answer in quarters: ☐

c Write your answer in eighths and quarters: ☐ or ☐

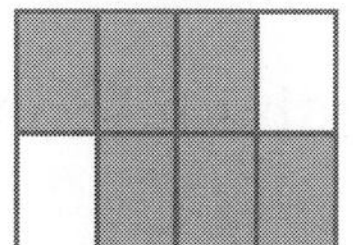

d Write your answer in tenths and fifths: ☐ or ☐

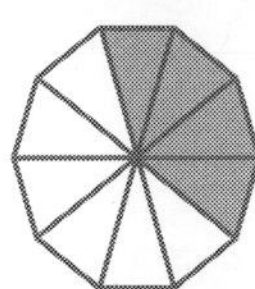

Challenge 3

1 a Write two fractions of number calculations that have the answer 26.

Example: $\frac{1}{2}$ of 52 = 26 $\frac{1}{4}$ of 104 = 26

b Write two fractions of number calculations that have the answer 21.

c Write two fractions of number calculations that have the answer 32.

2 Sometimes a fraction of a number question can result in an answer that is a decimal. For example:

$\frac{1}{2}$ of 15 = 7·5 $\frac{1}{10}$ of 52 = 5·2

Write two different fractions of number calculations that result in a decimal as the answer.

a ______________________

b ______________________

Lesson 1: **Adding three or four single-digit numbers**

- Add three or four single-digit numbers accurately
- Spot pairs of numbers that make addition quicker

You will need

- coloured pencils

Challenge 1

Find different pairs of numbers that total 10 and colour both circles the same colour.

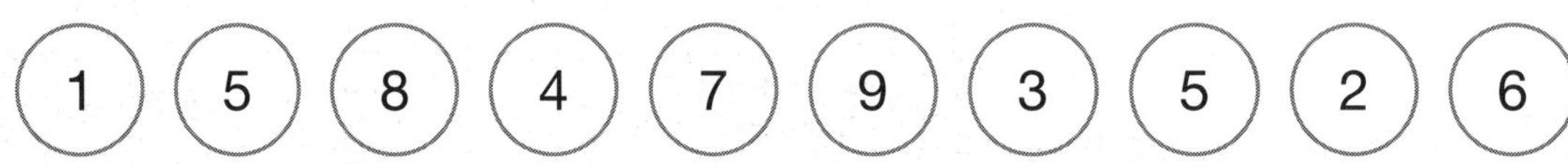

Challenge 2

1 In each of these sets of numbers, circle the two numbers you would add first. Look for numbers that are complements (numbers that make 10).

a 3 2 9 8 **b** 7 1 3 8 **c** 6 1 6 4

d 5 5 2 1 **e** 7 9 3 1 **f** 3 5 9 7

2 Write the totals of each group of numbers in Question **1**.

a ☐ **b** ☐ **c** ☐ **d** ☐ **e** ☐ **f** ☐

3 Not every group of numbers has a pair that makes 10. Work out the total of each group of numbers in your head.

Explain which numbers you added together first and why.

a 4 2 8 3 Total = ☐

____

b Total = ☐

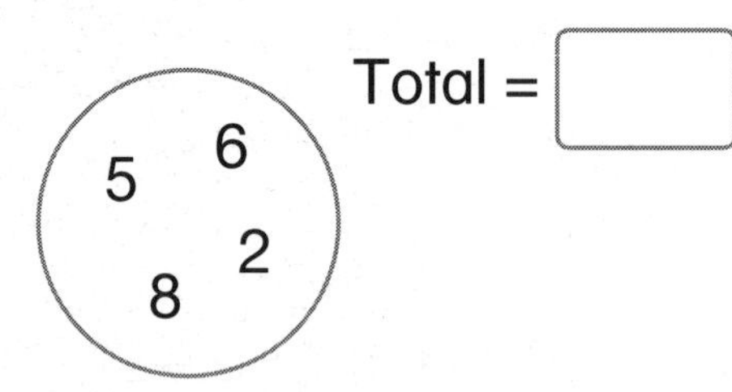

____

c 7 8 5 8 Total = ☐

____

d Total = ☐

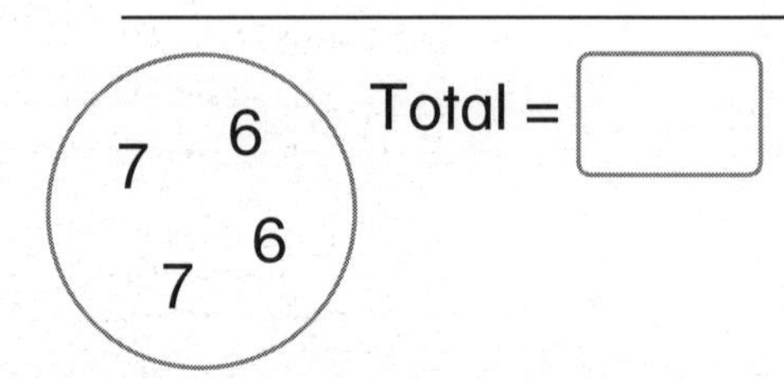

____

4 Check your answers to Question **3** by adding each set of numbers in a different order. Write down the order in which you add them.

a ________________

b ________________

c ________________

d ________________

1 You can look for complements when adding decimal numbers. Find decimals that equal 1 to help you add each set of numbers. Circle the decimals that equal 1 in each set.

a 0·7 0·4 0·3 **b** 0·5 0·2 0·8

c 0·3 0·6 0·4 **d** 0·9 0·5 0·5

2 Add each set of decimals in Question **1**, starting with the pair of complements that you circled. What are the totals?

a = ☐ **b** = ☐

c = ☐ **d** = ☐

3 Use your knowlege of doubles, near 10s and other facts to add these numbers. Explain your method.

a 4 4 4 4 = ☐ ________________

b 3 6 6 3 = ☐ ________________

c 9 9 9 9 = ☐ ________________

d 7 7 8 8 = ☐ ________________

Lesson 2: **Adding pairs of 2-digit numbers**

- Add pairs of 2-digit numbers
- Choose useful strategies to help add numbers

Challenge 1

1 Partition these 2-digit numbers.

Example:

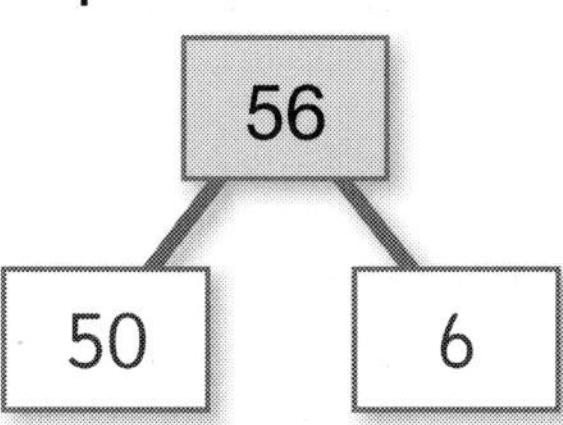

a 39

b 73

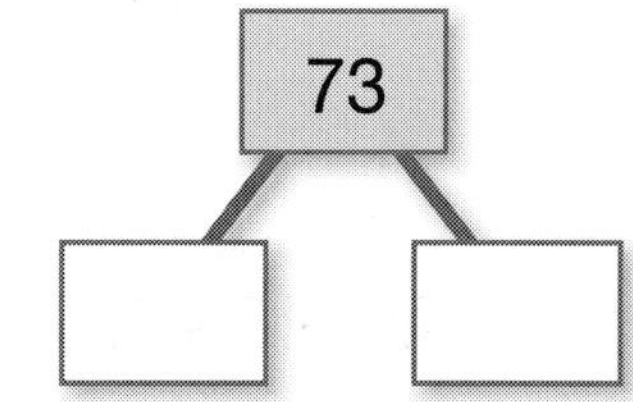

c 84

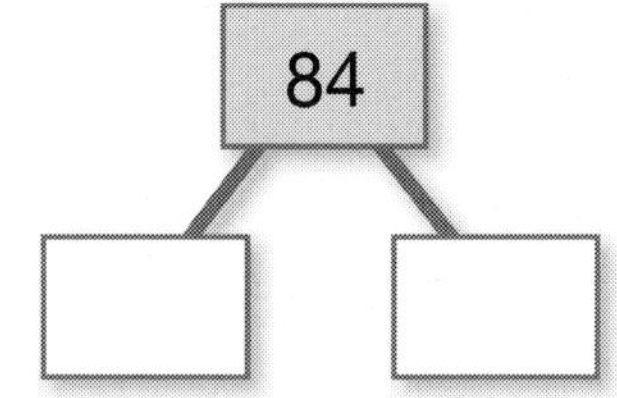

d 56

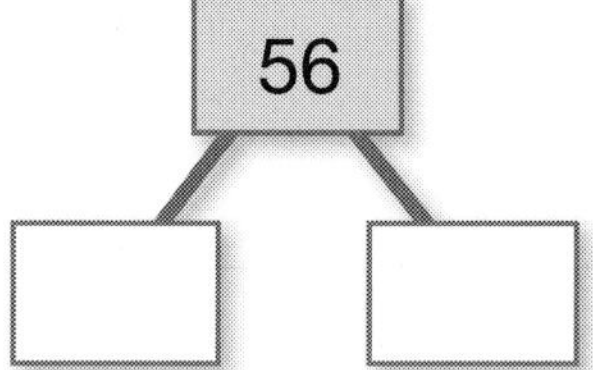

e 67

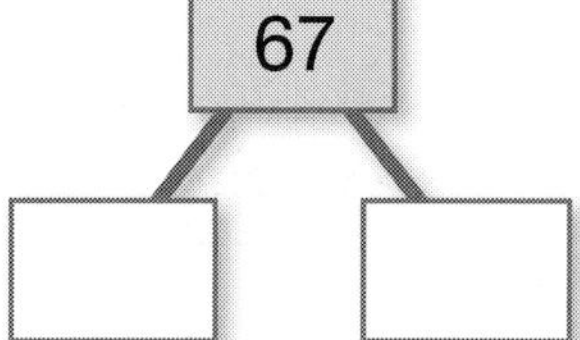

2 Add together.

a 67 + 46 = ☐ **b** 73 + 32 = ☐

c 56 + 53 = ☐ **d** 84 + 25 = ☐

Challenge 2

1 Use the empty number lines to add these pairs of numbers.
Hint: You might want to swap some of the numbers around.

a 57 + 65 = ☐ **b** 84 + 45 = ☐

c 38 + 67 = ☐ **d** 19 + 77 = ☐

2 Simran says: "I add pairs of 2-digit numbers by splitting up the second number in my head. First I add the 10s. Then I add the 1s.

If I'm working out 62 + 25, I split the 25 into 20 and 5. First I add the 20 to 62 to get 82. Then I add the 5 to get 87."

Use Simran's method to work out these calculations.

a 82 + 44 =

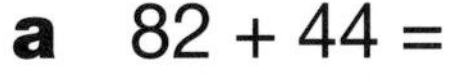

b 47 + 21 =

c 59 + 36 =

d 58 + 47 =

Challenge 3 Ellie spins a spinner and gets the digits 5, 7, 8 and 3.

She uses the digits to make different pairs of 2-digit numbers to add together.

a What is the largest total Ellie can make? ☐

Write the addition that makes this total. ☐ + ☐

b What is the smallest total Ellie can make? ☐

Write the addition that makes this total. ☐ + ☐

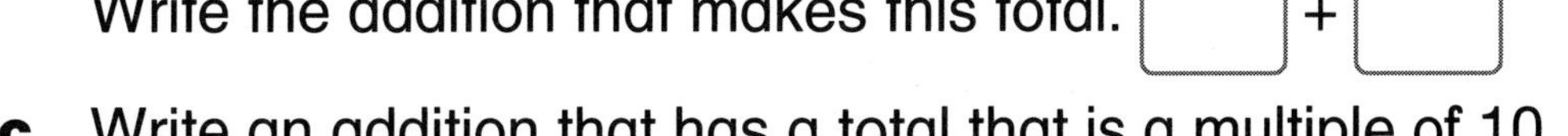

c Write an addition that has a total that is a multiple of 10.

☐ + ☐

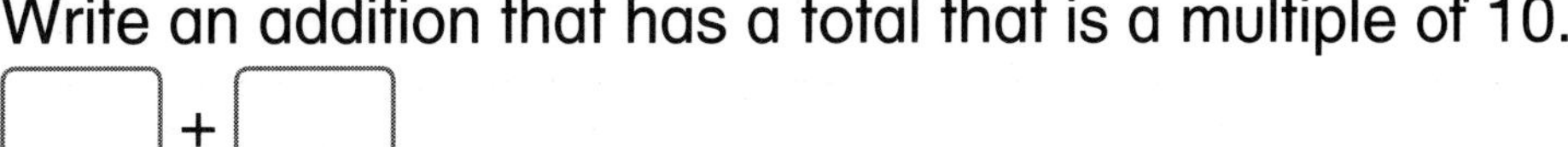

Number

Lesson 3: **Adding pairs of 3-digit numbers (1)**

- Use jottings to help add pairs of 3-digit numbers

You will need
- coloured pencil

Challenge 1

1 Add together.

a 528 + 101 = ☐ **b** 142 + 105 = ☐

c 213 + 102 = ☐ **d** 204 + 106 = ☐

e 652 + 107 = ☐ **f** 850 + 110 = ☐

2 Find different pairs of numbers that total 900 and colour both circles the same colour.

400 700 200 800 100 300 600 500

Challenge 2

1 Deon adds pairs of 3-digit numbers together. He uses a pencil and paper to jot down his thoughts. Look carefully at Deon's jottings. For each one, write the calculation he is carrying out.

a

651 → + 300, + 90, + 7

951
1041
(1048)

☐ + ☐ = ☐

b

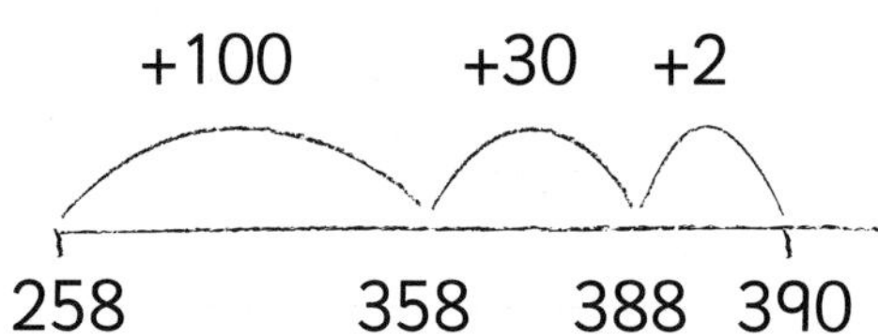

☐ + ☐ = ☐

c

~~422~~ ~~622~~ ~~682~~ (689)

☐ + ☐ = ☐

d

~~+ 399~~
+ 400
442 → 842
– 1
(841)

☐ + ☐ = ☐

2 Try to calculate the answers to these questions in your head, but use the space to write down any jottings to help. Remember, what you jot down is for your own benefit, so don't worry if no one understands it but you!

a 526 + 349 = ☐ **b** 838 + 425 = ☐

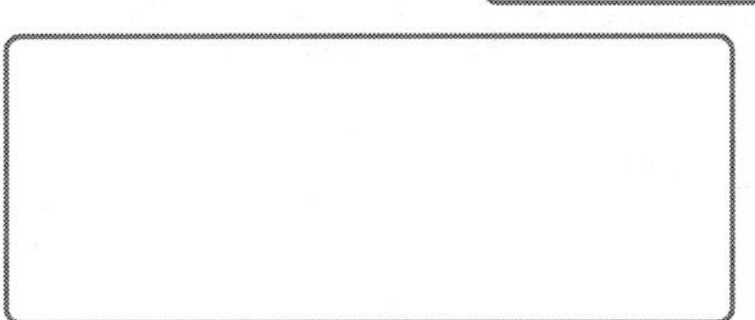

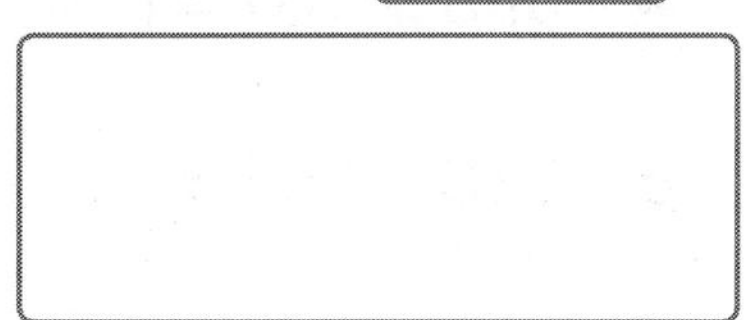

c 692 + 335 = ☐ **d** 787 + 249 = ☐

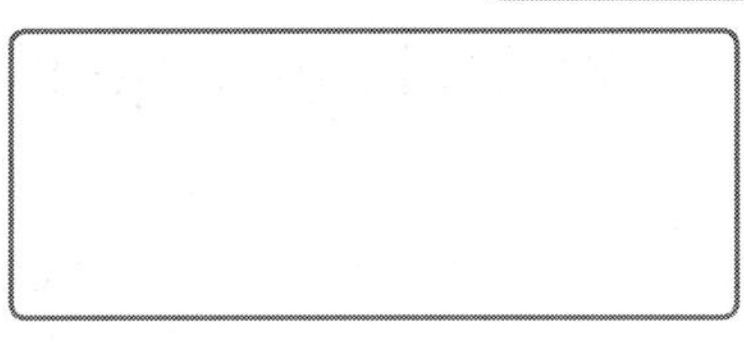

3 Make up a number story for each 3-digit addition calculation.

Example: 259 + 125 = 384

A bus has travelled 259 miles. It has another 125 miles to go until it reaches its destination. The whole journey is 384 miles long.

a 528 + 324 = 852 ______________________________

____

b 609 + 558 = 1167 ______________________________

____

Challenge **3** Nia and Reese wrote pairs of 3-digit numbers and calculated their totals.

- Nia split her smaller number into 100s, 10s and 1s and added each one separately.
- Reese noticed that his smaller number was near to 500, so he just added 500 and then adjusted the total.

Write a calculation that fits each learner's method.

a Nia's calculation could be: ☐

b Reese's calculation could be: ☐

Lesson 4: **Adding pairs of 3-digit numbers (2)**

- Use partitioning to help add pairs of 3-digit numbers

Challenge 1 Partition each 3-digit number into hundreds, tens and units.

Example: 5 3 8 = 500 + 30 + 8

a 645 = ___ + ___ + ___

b 294 = ___ + ___ + ___

c 321 = ___ + ___ + ___

d 979 = ___ + ___ + ___

e 513 = ___ + ___ + ___

Challenge 2

1 Partition each of these numbers into hundreds, tens and units, then find the total.

Example: 415 + 372 = 400 + 300 + 10 + 70 + 5 + 2
= 700 + 80 + 7
= 787

a 528 + 411 = ___
= ___
= ___

b 644 + 321 = ___
= ___
= ___

c 815 + 153 = ___
= ___
= ___

d 794 + 352 = ___
= ___
= ___

2 The school council is deciding what to spend its money on.

Here are the costs of the different projects it is considering.

Project	Cost
Restock the library with new books.	$224
Mend the cracks in the playground.	$467
Organise a school concert.	$153
Buy more musical instruments.	$375
Buy a new computer.	$886

a How much would it cost to mend the playground and have a school concert?

b What is the total cost of buying both a new computer and more musical instruments?

c Find the sum of the two cheapest projects.

1 Write two word problems where the answer is found by adding a pair of 3-digit numbers.

a ______________________________

b ______________________________

2 What are the answers to your questions?

a = ☐ **b** = ☐

Number

Lesson 5: **Subtracting pairs of 2-digit numbers**

- Subtract pairs of 2-digit numbers
- Choose useful strategies to help subtract numbers

Challenge 1

1 Partition these 2-digit numbers.

Example:

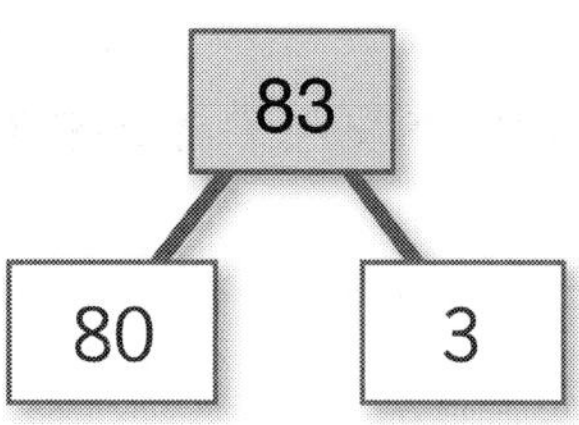

a

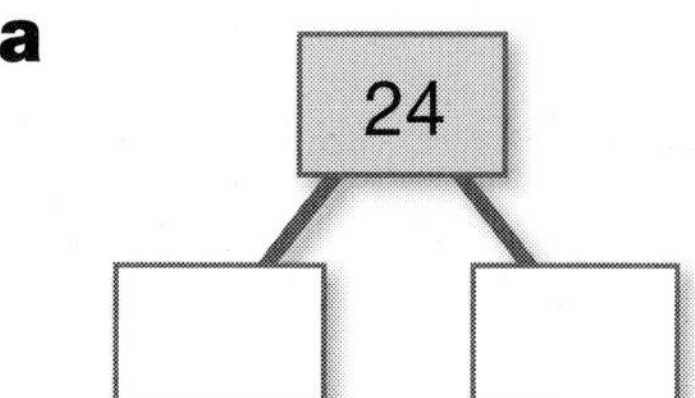

b

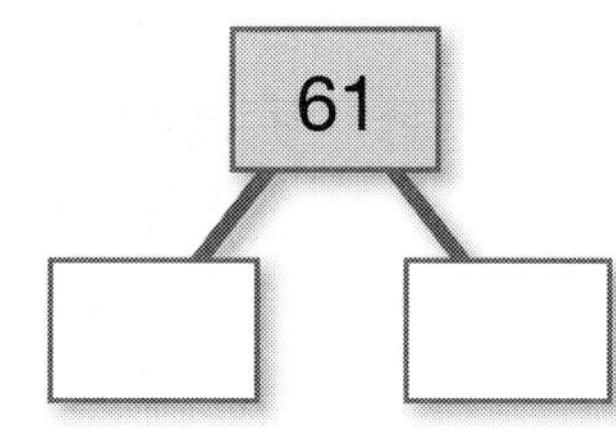

c 95

d

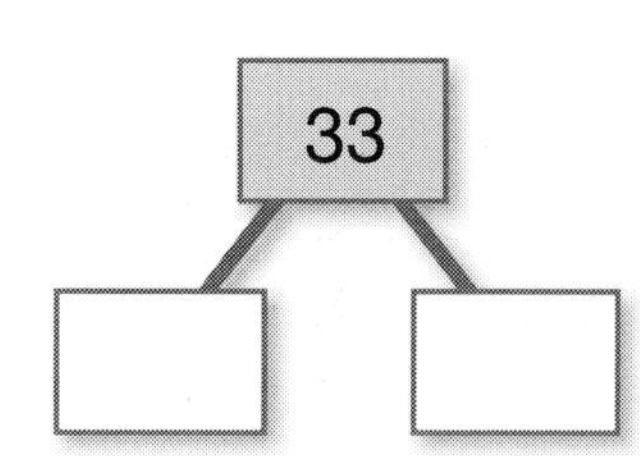

e

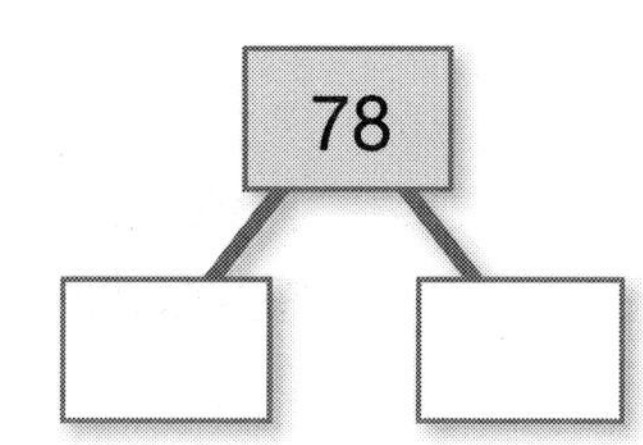

2 Complete.

a 29 – 19 = ☐ **b** 78 – 28 = ☐ **c** 33 – 13 = ☐

d 61 – 31 = ☐ **e** 95 – 40 = ☐

Challenge 2

1 Complete.

a 83 – 52 = ☐ **b** 37 – 23 = ☐ **c** 53 – 48 = ☐

d 96 – 39 = ☐ **e** 86 – 37 = ☐ **f** 52 – 26 = ☐

2 Connor says: "I subtract two 2-digit numbers by splitting up the second number in my head. First I subtract the tens. Then I subtract the units."

Use Connor's method to work out these calculations.

a 84 – 23 = ☐ **b** 96 – 15 = ☐ **c** 34 – 19 = ☐

d 42 – 27 = ☐ **e** 67 – 38 = ☐ **f** 75 – 46 = ☐

3 Write each calculation next to the strategy you would use to answer it. Then find the answer.

65 – 27   83 – 79   84 – 59

a The second number is very near to 60, so just subtract 60 and then adjust the answer.

b If you subtract the tens first, it will be 45. You can then subtract the units to find the answer.

c These numbers are close together, so start with the smaller number and count up to the larger number.

Challenge 3 Clara has the digit cards 8, 2, 7 and 5.

She uses the digits to make different pairs of 2-digit numbers to subtract from each other.

a What is the largest answer Clara can make?

Write the subtraction that makes this answer.

–

b What is the smallest answer Clara can make?

Write the subtraction that makes this answer.

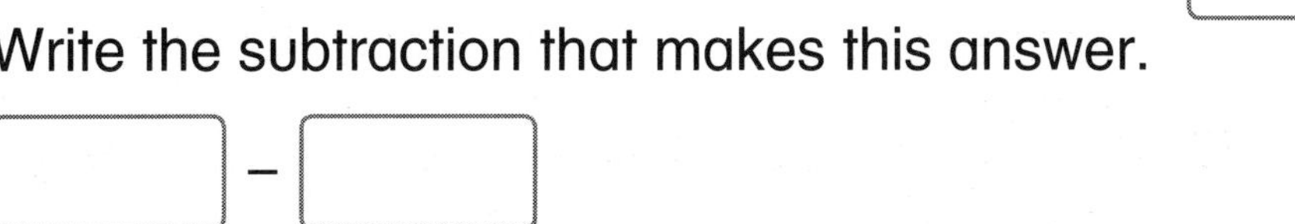

Number

Lesson 6: Subtracting a 2-digit number from a 3-digit number

You will need
- coloured pencil

- Use jottings to help subtract 2-digit numbers from 3-digit numbers

Challenge 1

1 What is 12 less than these numbers?

a 630 ☐ **b** 890 ☐ **c** 164 ☐

d 738 ☐ **e** 522 ☐ **f** 797 ☐

2 Find pairs of numbers that have a difference of 100 and colour both circles the same colour.

130 190 150 120 110 170

10 30 70 50 20 90

Challenge 2

1 Deon subtracts 3-digit numbers and 2-digit numbers. He uses a pencil and paper to jot down his thoughts.

Look carefully at Deon's jottings. For each one, write the subtraction that you think he has used to work it out.

a

– 7 – 50

532 539 589

☐ – ☐ = ☐

b

~~313~~ ~~283~~ 281

☐ – ☐ = ☐

c

423 → – 20 403

→ – 5 398

☐ – ☐ = ☐

d

~~– 49~~
– 50
804 ← 854
→ +1 805

☐ – ☐ = ☐

2 For each calculation, first round each of the second numbers and write an estimate.

Then, work out the answer. Show any jottings in the boxes.

Example: 562 – 48

Estimate = 562 – 50 = 512

a 258 cm – 42 cm

Estimate =

Answer =

b 522 cm – 98 cm

Estimate =

Answer =

Emma and Abdul have written 3-digit numbers and 2-digit numbers and calculated their differences by subtracting them.

- Emma split her smaller number into tens and units and subtracted each one separately.
- Abdul noticed that his two-digit number was near to 100, so he just subtracted 100 and then adjusted the total.

Write down a calculation that fits each student's method.

a Emma's calculation could be:

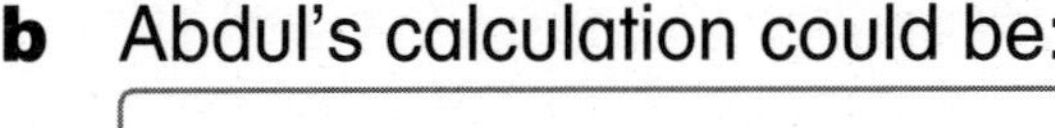

b Abdul's calculation could be:

Lesson 7: **Subtracting pairs of 3-digit numbers (1)**

- Use jottings to help subtract pairs of 3-digit numbers

Challenge 1 Use the number lines to subtract each pair of numbers and then complete the answer underneath.

a

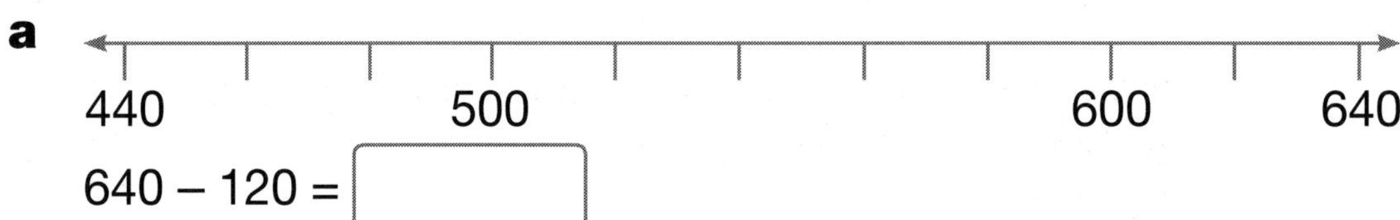

640 – 120 = ☐

b

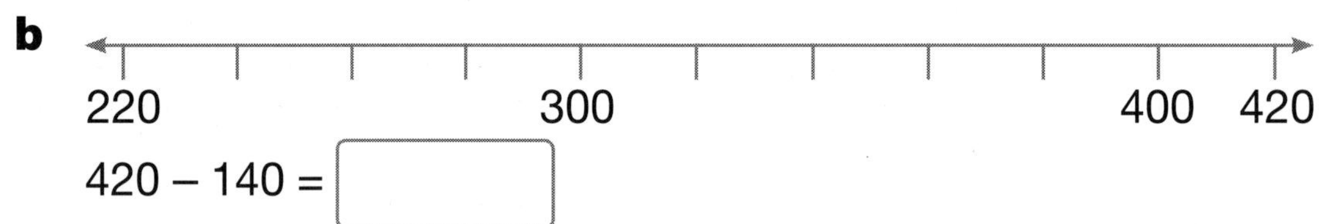

420 – 140 = ☐

c

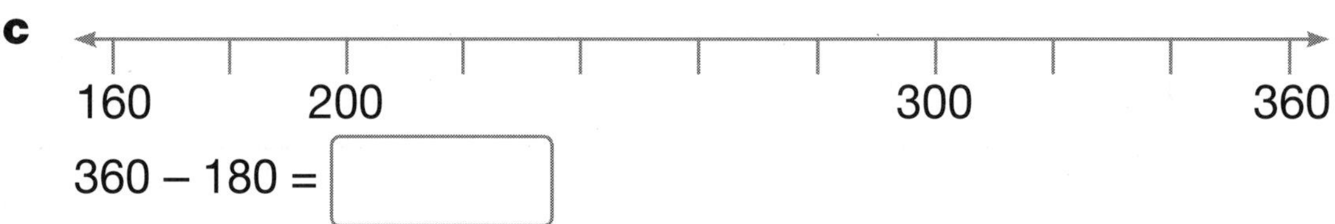

360 – 180 = ☐

Challenge 2

1 Use the blank number lines to subtract each pair of 3-digit numbers. Show your jottings.

a

392 – 265 = ☐

b

What is the difference between 777 cm and 518 cm?

☐

c

What is 357 subtracted from 466?

d

Your score in a computer game is 783 points.
It decreases by 399 points.
What is your new score?

e

What is 534 minus 256?

f

619 birds are migrating for the winter. 532 make it to their destination. How many got lost?

1 Write two word problems where the answer is found by subtracting a pair of 3-digit numbers. Try to vary the key words you use.

a ______________________________

____

b ______________________________

____

2 Write the answers to your questions.

a =   **b** =

Lesson 8: **Subtracting pairs of 3-digit numbers (2)**

- Use jottings to help subtract pairs of 3-digit numbers

Challenge 1

Use jottings to help you subtract these 3-digit numbers.

a 526 – 200 = ☐ **b** 452 – 300 = ☐

c 896 – 500 = ☐ **d** 678 – 400 = ☐

e 701 – 400 = ☐ **f** 563 – 300 = ☐

Challenge 2

1 Work out the answers to these subtractions. Use your preferred mental strategy and show any jottings in the box.

a 829 – 352 = ☐ **b** 702 – 449 = ☐

c 531 – 527 = ☐ **d** 615 – 299 = ☐

e 966 – 593 = ☐ **f** 621 – 612 = ☐

2 Some astronauts are all on year-long missions to the International Space Station. (Remember, there are 365 days in a year.)

They have all been aboard for different lengths of time.

a Use subtraction to find out how long each astronaut has got left before returning to Earth. Show any jottings in the box.

Astronaut	Number of days aboard so far	Calculation needed	Number of days left
Yuri	146	365 – 146	
Al	259		
Neil	358		
Krish	276		
Paula	102		
Dion	189		
Adi	277		
Fran	289		
Mo	156		

b Which astronaut has only one week left before they return to Earth? ______

c Which astronaut has just over 100 days left?

______

d Which astronauts have an even number of days remaining?

______

Carla, an astronaut on the International Space Station, is on a 625-day mission. She has been there for 483 days already.

Explain three different strategies to work out how long she has left. Remember to show any jottings.

Strategy 1:

Strategy 2:

Strategy 3:

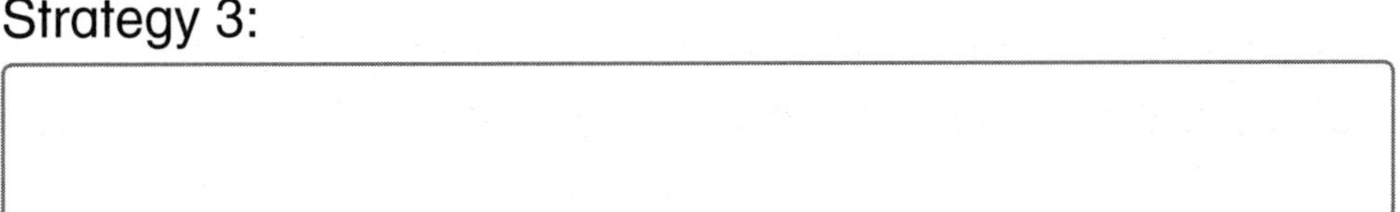

Number

Lesson 1: **Mental addition (1)**

- Choose useful mental strategies to add numbers

Challenge 1

Complete the calculations.

a 20 + 30 + 40 = ☐ **b** 30 + 50 + 70 = ☐

c 335 + 49 = ☐ **d** 229 + 99 = ☐

e 28 + 54 = ☐ **f** 79 + 79 = ☐

Challenge 2

1 Write each learner's name under the strategy you think will help them work out their answer in their heads.

I am finding the total of 40, 30 and 60.

Kai

I am adding 38 and 84 together.

Michael

Lauren

Tia

I need to know what I add to 450 to make 1000.

Strategy A: Think of multiples of 5 that make 100. If you know what pairs with 45 to make 100, you can work out the answer to your question.

____

Strategy B: Imagine that these were not multiples of 10 and were just single digits. If you know what the three digits are added together, it will help you answer your question.

____

Strategy C: Start with the larger number so you do not have so much to add. Add the tens first and then the units.

____

Strategy D: One of your numbers is very close to a multiple of 100. If you round it up to 300, you can add the two numbers very quickly. Then adjust your answer.

____

Challenge 3 Write two questions that will test the addition skills you have been practising during this lesson. Write the answers and then the strategies that you want your learners to use.

Question 1: ____

____

____

Question 2: ____

____

____

Answers:

1: [ ] 2: [ ]

Strategies:

1: ____

____

____

2: ____

____

____

Lesson 2: **Adding pairs of 3-digit numbers (3)**

- Use written methods to add pairs of 3-digit numbers

Challenge 1

1 Draw 2 more hundreds on each abacus and write the new total.

a 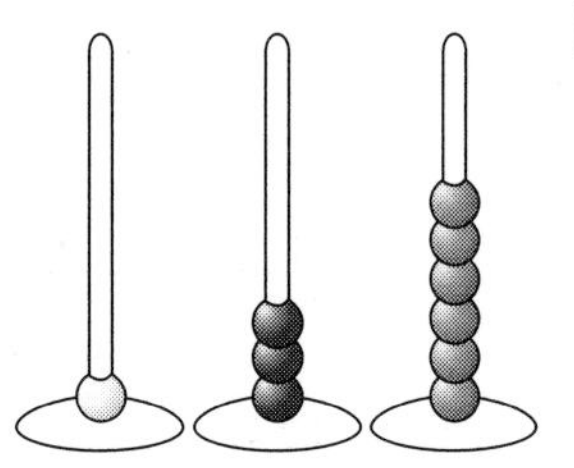

136 + 200 = ☐

b 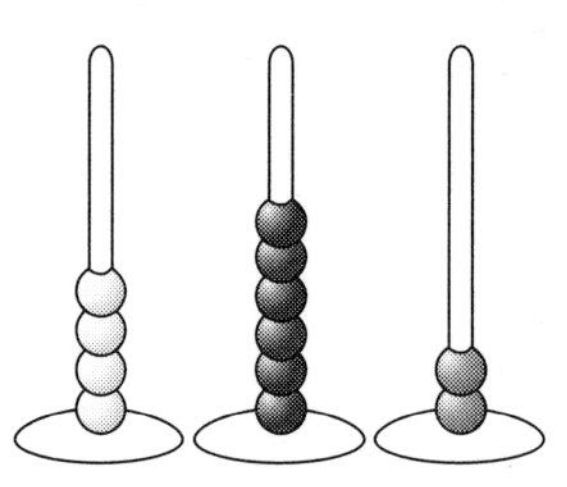

462 + 200 = ☐

c 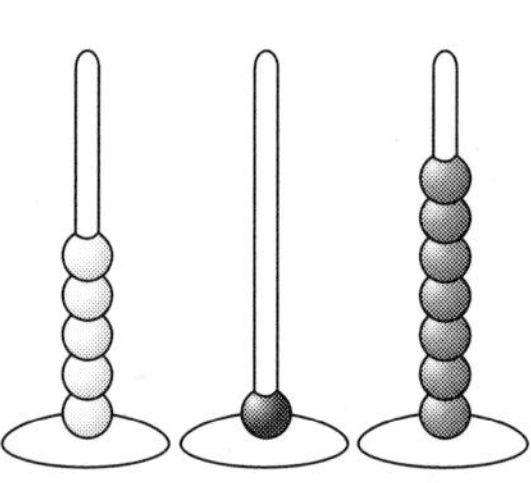

517 + 200 = ☐

2 Draw 1 more hundred and 3 more tens on each abacus and write the new total.

a 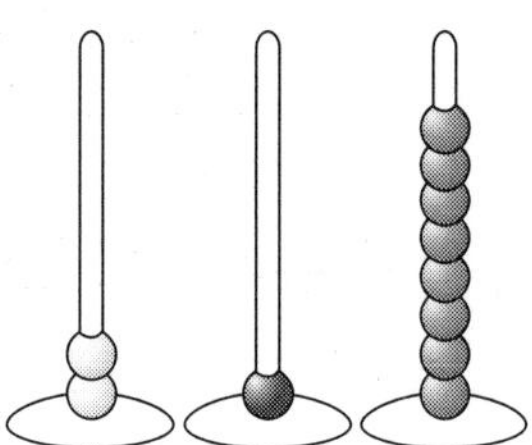

218 + 130 = ☐

b 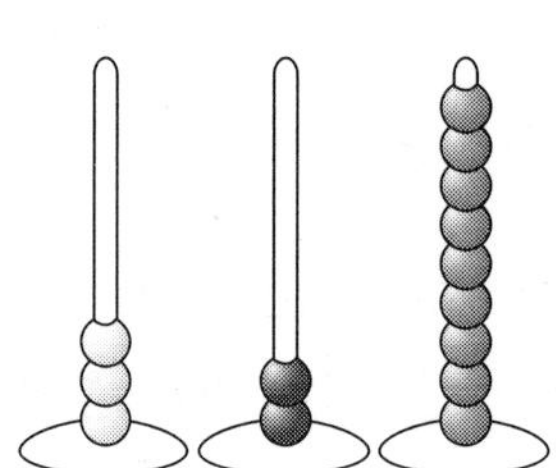

329 + 130 = ☐

c 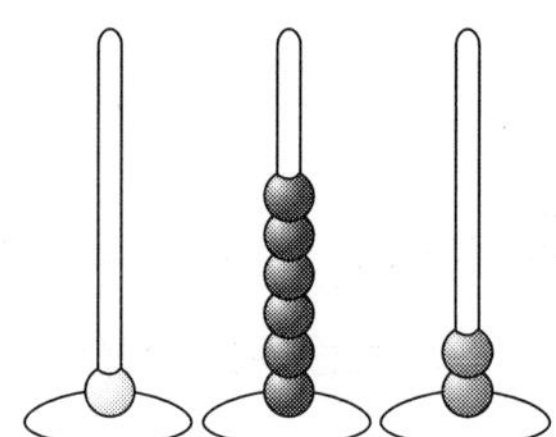

162 + 130 = ☐

Challenge 2

1 Use the written method to calculate each total.

Example:

568 + 134

	5	6	8
+	1	3	4
		1	2
		9	0
	6	0	0
	7	0	2

a 423 + 254

+			

b 535 + 361

+			

c 672 + 229

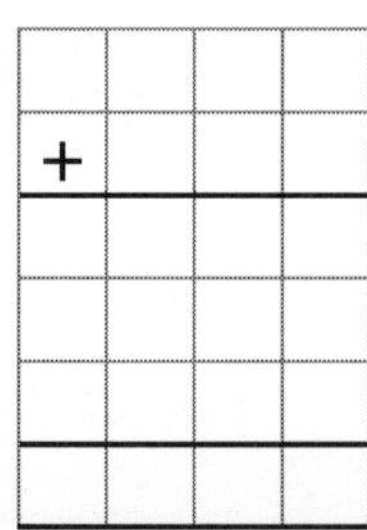

2 Estimate the answers, then work out the actual totals.

Example: 653 + 397
Estimate: 650 + 400 = 1050

Actual

	6	5	3
+	3	9	7
		1	0
	1	4	0
	9	0	0
1	0	5	0

a 598 + 399
Estimate:

Actual

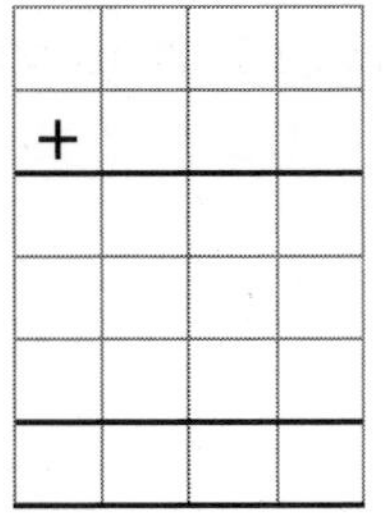

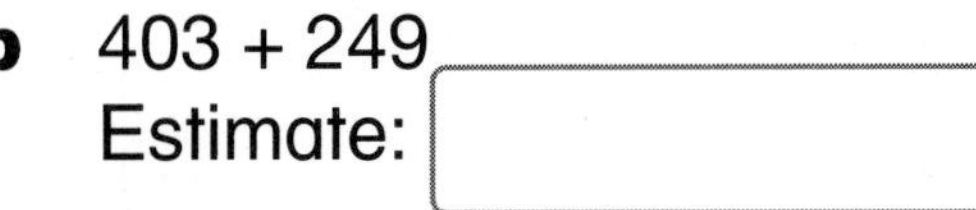

b 403 + 249
Estimate:

Actual

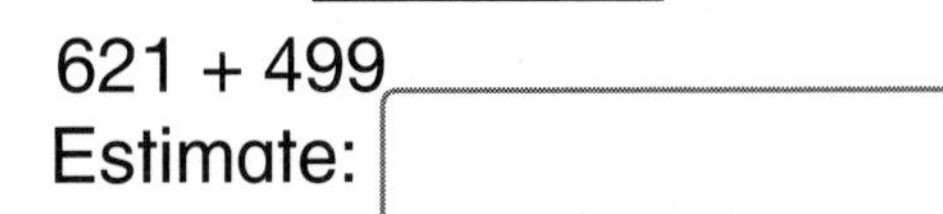

c 621 + 499
Estimate:

Actual

Challenge 3 Sofia has used a written method to work out these additions. However, she has made some mistakes.

Circle the part where you think Sofia has gone wrong. Show the correct method in the space to the right.

a

```
   625
+  432
   ---
     5
    40
   900
  4000
  ----
  4945
```

625 + 432

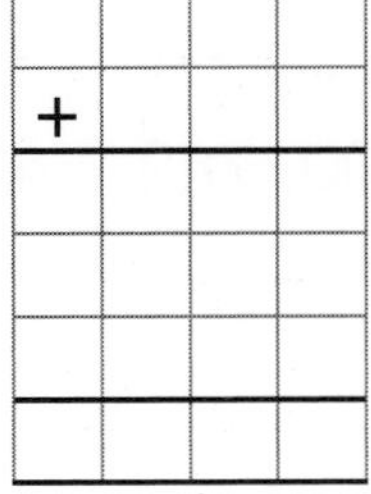

b

```
   462
+  227
   ---
     9
     8
   6
   ---
    23
```

462 + 227

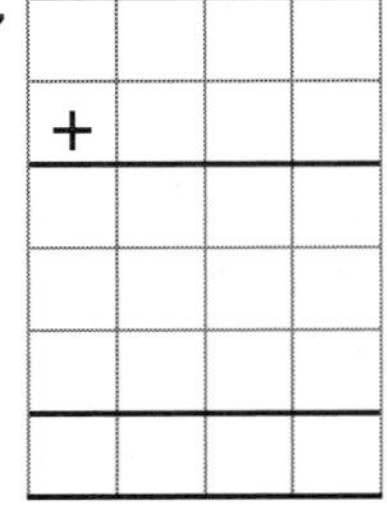

Lesson 3: **Mental subtraction (1)**

- Choose useful mental strategies to subtract numbers

Challenge 1

1 Work out the first subtraction in your head and use it to help answer the second.

a 8 – 2 = ☐ so 678 – 2 = ☐

b 7 – 5 = ☐ so 547 – 5 = ☐

c 9 – 1 = ☐ so 259 – 1 = ☐

d 8 – 3 = ☐ so 438 – 3 = ☐

2 Look carefully at the 3-digit numbers and their answers. Complete this sentence.

The _____ digit has changed in each of the 3-digit numbers.

Challenge 2

1 First estimate the answer by rounding one (or both) of the numbers. Then work out the actual answer.

Example: 398 cm is taken from a piece of string 769 cm long. What length is left?

Estimate: 770 – 400 = 370

Actual:
Round 398 to 400. 769 – 400 = 369.
Then add 2 to adjust: 369 + 2 = 371

a What is the difference between 478 kg and 199 kg? Estimate: ☐

Actual:

b What is $502 less than $985? Estimate: ☐

Actual:

Always read the question carefully. The next question contains the words 'added' and 'total', but it is actually a 'what is the difference between' question in disguise!

c A number added to 398 makes a total of 837. What is it? Estimate: ____

Actual:

2 Use whichever mental strategies you find helpful to answer these questions.

a How many more than 42 is 81? ____

b Subtract 9 from 803. ____

c 924 – 49 = ____ **d** 602 – ____ = 596

Challenge **3** Write two questions that will test the subtraction skills you have learned. Write the answers and the strategies that you want to use.

Question 1: ______________________________

____

Question 2: ______________________________

____

Answers: 1: ____ 2: ____

Strategies:

1: ______________________________

____

2: ______________________________

____

Lesson 4: **Subtraction involving 3-digit numbers**

- Use jottings to subtract from 3-digit numbers

Challenge 1

1 Cross off 5 beads from the tens column to subtract 50 from each number.

a

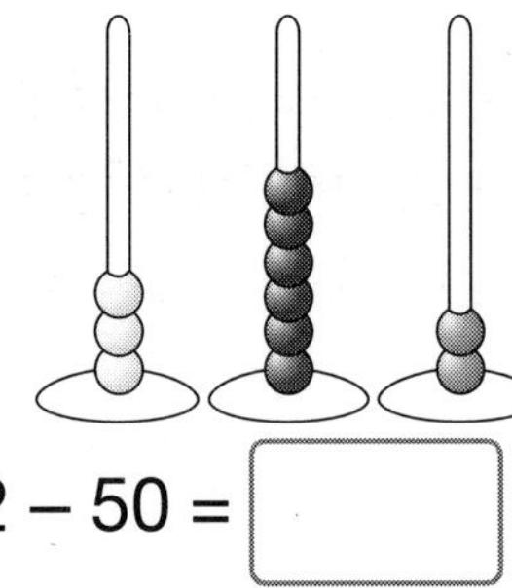

362 – 50 = ☐

b

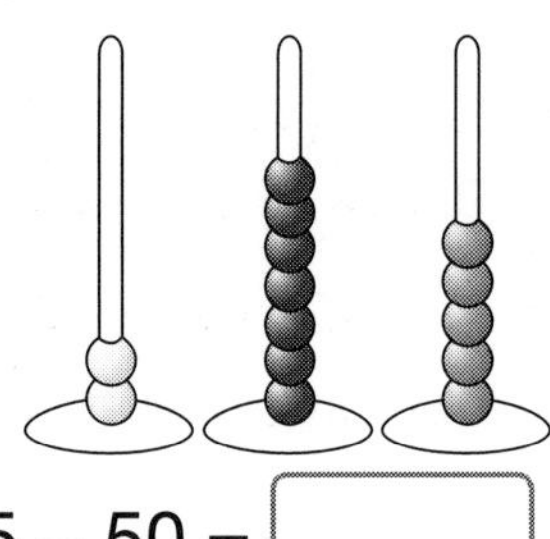

275 – 50 = ☐

c

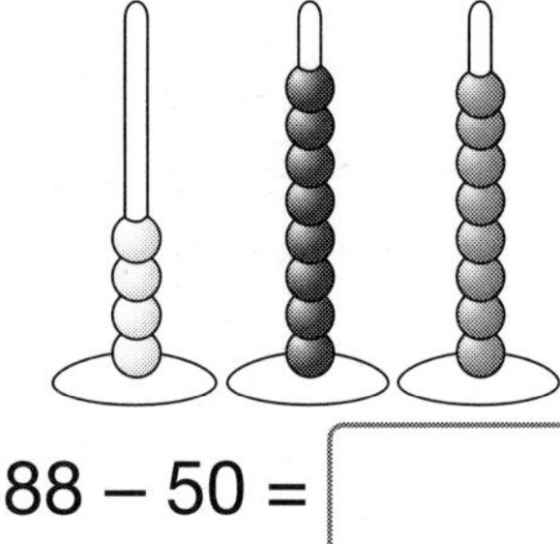

488 – 50 = ☐

2 Cross off 1 bead from the hundreds column to subtract 100 from each number.

a

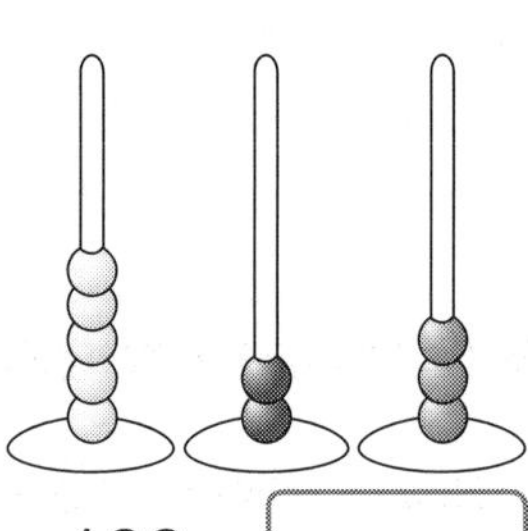

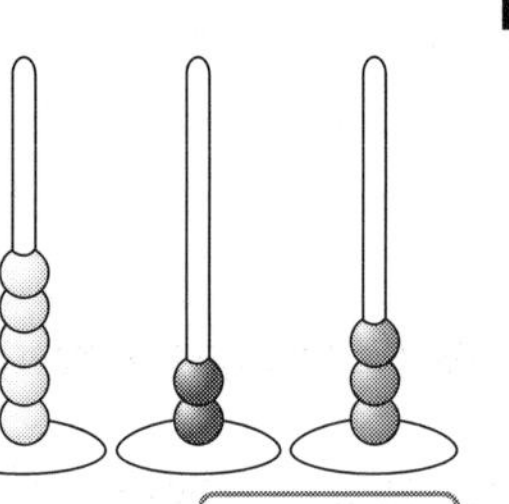

523 – 100 = ☐

b

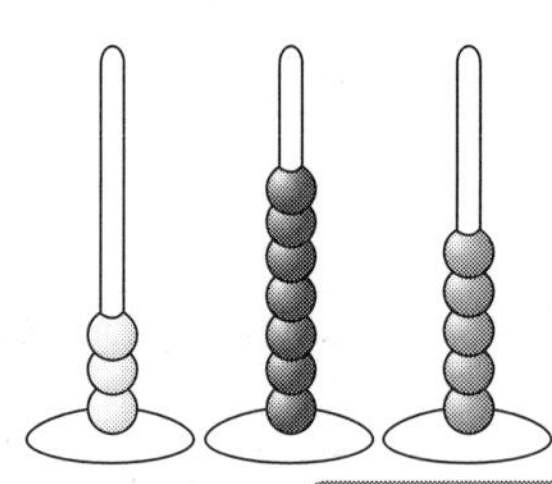

375 – 100 = ☐

c

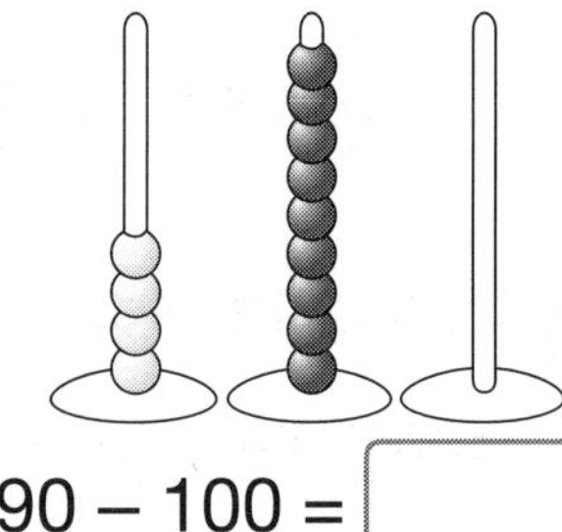

490 – 100 = ☐

Challenge 2

1 Use blank number lines to find the answers to these subtractions.

a

639 – 34 = ☐

b

271 – 96 = ☐

2

Georgia: I need to subtract 476 from 738.

Kara: I am working out the answer to 639 – 626.

Ben: I need to find the difference between 499 and 835.

Which strategy would you give each learner?

Strategy A: One of your numbers is near to a multiple of 100. Round it up to the nearest 100 and then subtract it, then adjust the answer. ______________

Strategy B: Use a blank number line or jottings to subtract the hundreds, then the tens and then the units. ______________

Strategy C: The numbers are both 3-digit numbers but they are actually close together. Don't subtract them. Count up from the smaller number to the larger number – it's a lot quicker!

____

3 Use the strategies to find the answer to each learner's question.

Georgia's answer = ☐ Kara's answer = ☐

Ben's answer = ☐

Challenge 3 Use subtraction to check which of the calculations are correct.

Example: 256 + 134 = 456 Backwards check: 456 – 134 = 322

correct/incorrect (circled: incorrect)

a 852 + 126 = 978 Backwards check: 978 – 126 = ☐

correct/incorrect ______________________________.

b 386 + 288 = 679 Backwards check: 679 – 288 = ☐

correct/incorrect ______________________________.

c 571 + 408 = 982 Backwards check: 982 – 408 = ☐

correct/incorrect ______________________________.

Number

Lesson 1: **Mental addition (2)**

- Choose appropriate mental strategies to add numbers

Challenge 1

1 Match each question with the fact that can help answer it.

What is 147 + 39? •	• 5 + 8 + 2 = 15
What is 50 + 80 + 20? •	• 6 + 4 = 10, so 600 + 400 = 1000
What do you add to 400 to get 1000? •	• 147 + 40 = 187
What is the total of 70, 20 and 70? •	• 7 doubled is 14, so 70 doubled is 140.

2 Use your knowledge of pairs that total 10 to complete these.

Example: 6 + 4 = 10, so [60] + [40] = 100

a 5 + 5 = 10, so [ ] + [ ] = 100

b 3 + 7 = 10, so [ ] + [ ] = 100

c 1 + 9 = 10, so [ ] + [ ] = 100

d 4 + 6 = 10, so [ ] + [ ] = 100

Challenge 2

1 In each rectangle, write a simple number fact that can be used to help answer the question. Then explain how you would use the fact to help.

a 45 + [ ] = 100

b 285 + 198 = [ ]

c [ ] + 250 = 1000

2 Use mental strategies to answer these questions.

a What is the sum of 80, 50 and 80?

b There are 1000 pages in a book. Jordan has read 350 of them. How many pages does he have left?

c How much is $542 and $79 altogether?

3 Look back at the calculations in Question **2**.

Choose any two and explain the method you used to find the answer. Choose questions where you used different methods.

Question number:

Strategy: ______________

Question number:

Strategy: ______________

Challenge 3

1 Kalim thinks of a pair of 2-digit numbers that equal 100. The first number has the digit 3 in the units place.

a What can you say about the second number?

____

b Write down all the possibilities that Kalim's numbers could be.

2 Lola thinks of a pair of numbers that equal 100. The first number has the digit 7 in the tens place and its units digit is not 0.

a What can you say about the second number?

____

b Use the same method that you used before to write down all the possibilities that Lola's number could be.

Lesson 2: **Mental addition (3)**

- Choose appropriate mental strategies to add pairs of 2-digit numbers
- Identify simple fractions with a total of 1

You will need
- coloured pencils

Challenge 1 Complete the calculations.

a $\frac{1}{2} + \square = 1$

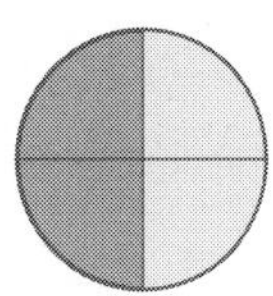

b $\frac{3}{5} + \square = 1$

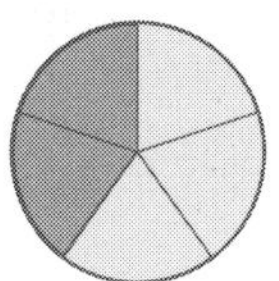

Challenge 2

1 Shade these shapes in two colours and write the addition that equals one whole.

Example: 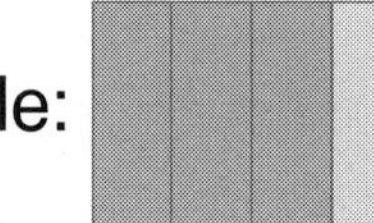 $\frac{3}{4} + \frac{1}{4} = 1$

a  $\square + \square = 1$

b  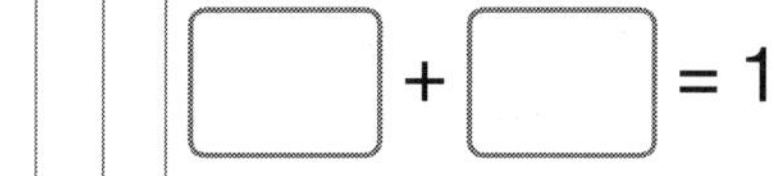 $\square + \square = 1$

c  $\square + \square = 1$

d 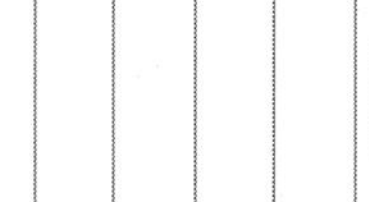 $\square + \square = 1$

2 Use two colours to shade these shapes in different ways and write the addition that equals one whole.

Example:
$\frac{2}{3} + \frac{1}{3} = 1$

a 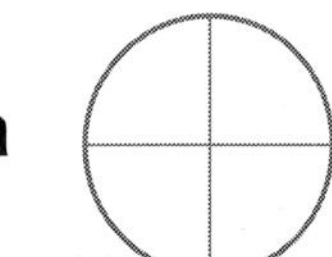 $\square + \square = 1$

b 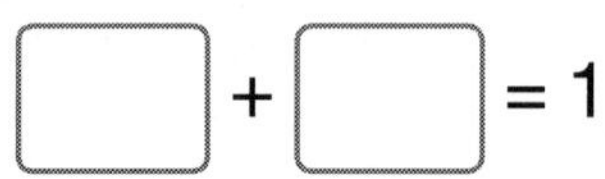 $\square + \square = 1$

c  $\square + \square = 1$

d  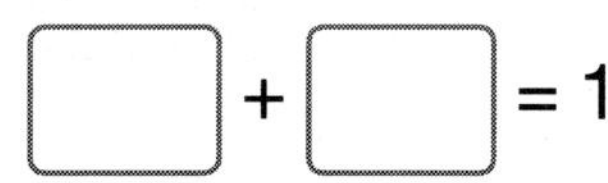 $\square + \square = 1$

3 a Clara cuts a cake into 8 equal slices. 3 slices are eaten by her friends. What fraction of the cake is left?

b James has \$39. His uncle gives him an extra \$47. How much does James now have?

c What is 56 km more than 88 km?

1 a Kyle says, "There are some pairs of fractions that have different denominators that add to one whole."
Use the large box to try to find examples of fractions with different denominators that equal one whole.

Is Kyle right?

2 Here is a way to find pairs of fractions with different denominators that equal one.

- Write a pair with the same denominator.
- Think of a fraction that is equivalent to one of the fractions.
- Rewrite the addition.

Use this method to write two different additions of fractions with different denominators that equal 1.

Example:

Original addition = $\frac{1}{2} + \frac{1}{2} = 1$ New addition = $\frac{2}{4} + \frac{1}{2} = 1$

a Original addition = New addition =

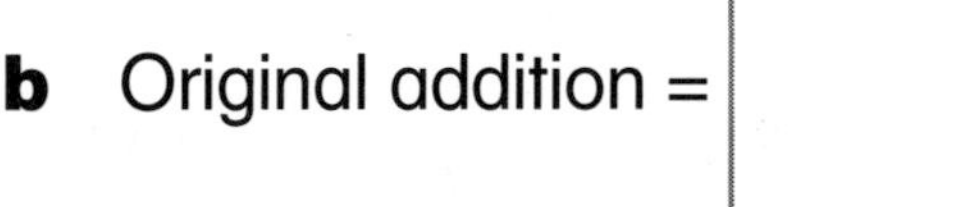

b Original addition =

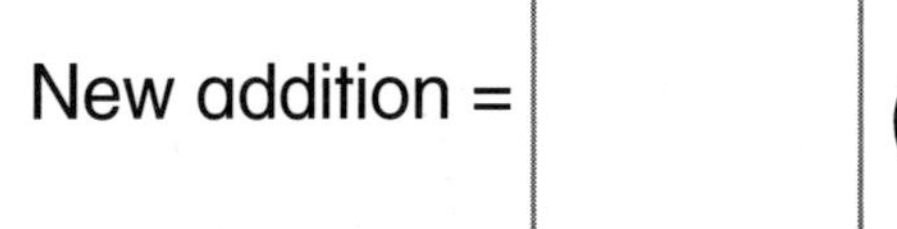

New addition =

Number

Lesson 3: Adding pairs of 3-digit numbers (4)

- Use written methods to add pairs of 3-digit numbers

You will need
- yellow, red and blue coloured pencils
- ruler

Challenge 1

1 Each 3-digit number increases by 103. Write the new numbers.

Example: 4 5 6 + 103 = 5 5 9

a 3 9 5 + 103 =

b 6 2 1 + 103 =

c 4 1 4 + 103 =

2 Each 3-digit number increases by 205. Write the new numbers.

a 2 0 4 + 205 =

b 1 8 2 + 205 =

c 7 5 1 + 205 =

Challenge 2

1 Complete these additions by writing the units, tens and hundreds totals underneath.

Example:

	5	3	8
+	2	5	3
		1	1
		8	0
	7	0	0
	7	9	1

a

	4	6	6
+	3	5	2

b

	5	7	2
+	3	2	7

c

	4	8	7
+	2	6	1

2 There is a shorter way to use this written method.

Colour the units additions yellow, the tens additions red and the hundreds additions blue to help you make connections between the methods.

Example:

	7	4	2
+	2	2	9
		1	1
		6	0
	9	0	0
	9	7	1

	7	4	2
+	2	2	9
	9	7	1
		1	

a

	3	4	8
+	3	7	3
		1	1
	1	1	0
	6	0	0
	7	2	1

	3	4	8
+	3	7	3
	7	2	1
	1	1	

b

	5	1	3
+	3	6	8
		1	1
		7	0
	8	0	0
	8	8	1

	5	1	3
+	3	6	8
	8	8	1
		1	

c

	6	7	6
+	5	5	7
		1	3
	1	2	0
1	1	0	0
1	2	3	3

	6	7	6
+	5	5	7
1	2	3	3
1	1	1	

d

	6	8	4
+	2	5	7
		1	1
	1	3	0
	8	0	0
	9	4	1

	6	8	4
+	2	5	7
	9	4	1
	1	1	

Challenge 3

1 Alicia is adding 3-digit numbers using the shorter method.

a She says, "The units in my numbers are 8 and 8 which adds to 16. I can't write two digits in the units column. What should I do?"

Explain what Alicia should do and why.

____

____

b Alicia then says, "The tens in my numbers are 5 tens add 3 tens which total 8 tens. My friend told me that I need to write 9 tens in that column instead. Why is this?"

____

____

2 Write the two calculations Alicia could be working out. One must have a 3-digit total and the other a 4-digit total.

a

b

Lesson 4: Adding pairs of 3-digit numbers (5)

- Use written methods to add pairs of 3-digit numbers

You will need
- ruler

Challenge 1

Draw a line to match each calculation with the correct answer.

421 + 110 •	• 675
501 + 146 •	• 437
623 + 134 •	• 757
143 + 152 •	• 295
522 + 153 •	• 531
206 + 231 •	• 647

Challenge 2

1 Complete these additions using the written method.

a 624 + 305 

b 539 + 322 

c 866 + 172 

d 896 + 712 

2 Read each of these word problems carefully.

a In a school there are 326 boys and 353 girls. How many children are there in the school altogether?

b Kian goes shopping with $672. He spends $157. How much money does he have left?

c Out of 425 customers in a café, 168 buy soft drinks. The rest buy coffee. How many customers buy coffee?

d In a recipe, 441 g of flour is mixed with 358 g of sugar. How is the mass of the mixture in total?

e The wind blows 289 coconuts to the ground. 167 of them crack when they hit the ground. How many are not cracked?

f There are 271 people watching camel racing. Later, the crowd increases by 369 people. How many people are watching the camel racing now?

Three out of the six word problems above are addition calculations.

Which questions are they? ☐, ☐ and ☐

3 Write out the three addition calculations from Question **2** and use the written method to work out the answers.

Challenge 3

1 Write four different calculations for this addition.

	?	?	?
+	?	?	?
	7	6	2
	1	1	

2 Write down two different calculations for this addition where every digit in the top two numbers is different.

	?	?	?
+	?	?	?
1	3	0	2
1	1	1	

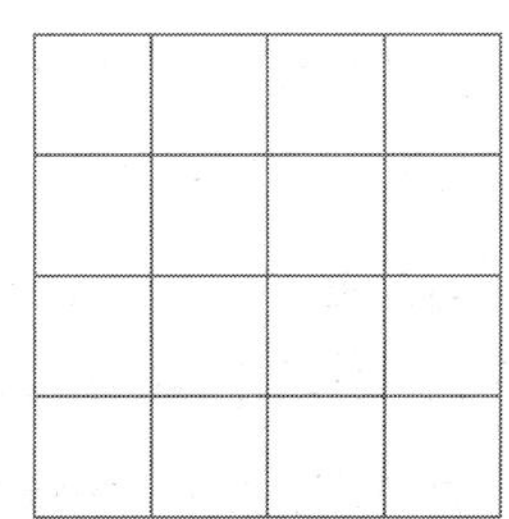

Number

Lesson 5: Mental subtraction (2)

- Choose appropriate mental strategies to subtract numbers

1 Draw a line to match each number to the multiple of 10 you would round it to.

59 •	• 70
71 •	• 60
49 •	• 50
92 •	• 90

2 Draw a line to match each number to the multiple of 100 you would round it to.

698 •	• 400
901 •	• 700
505 •	• 900
397 •	• 500

1 What is the difference between these near multiples of 100?

a 702 – 695 = ☐ **b** 804 – 798 = ☐

c 503 – 499 = ☐ **d** 608 – 595 = ☐

e 805 – 794 = ☐ **f** 505 – 487 = ☐

2 Choose one number from each grid to make different subtractions.

The numbers in the right-hand grid are all near multiples of 10 or 100, so use rounding to help find the answer.

523	846	614	640
907	687	831	952
548	508	792	773

38	199	49	403
202	32	298	197
71	497	302	398

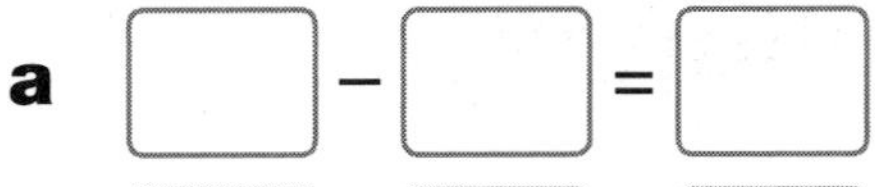

a ☐ – ☐ = ☐ b ☐ – ☐ = ☐

c ☐ – ☐ = ☐ d ☐ – ☐ = ☐

e ☐ – ☐ = ☐ f ☐ – ☐ = ☐

3 Explain how you would answer each of these questions.

a There are 428 vehicles in a car park. By late afternoon, 198 have gone. How many vehicles are left?

b There are 367 books in the school library. A parcel arrives, delivering another 69 books. How many books are there now?

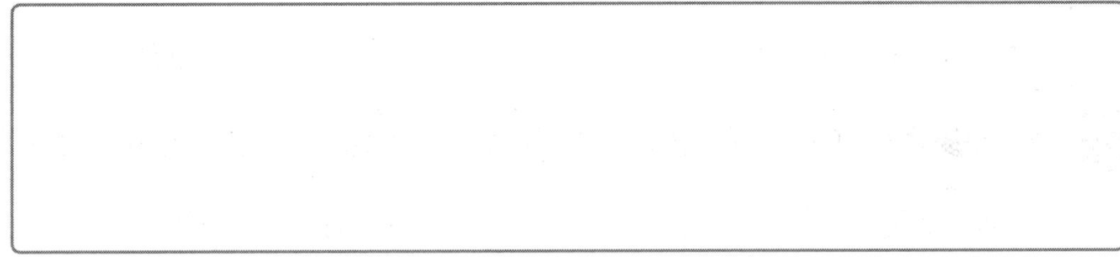

Challenge 3 Work out the answers to these subtractions and then make up a number story for each.

a 723 – 89 = ☐ **b** 406 – 392 = ☐

a ______________________________

____

____

b ______________________________

____

____

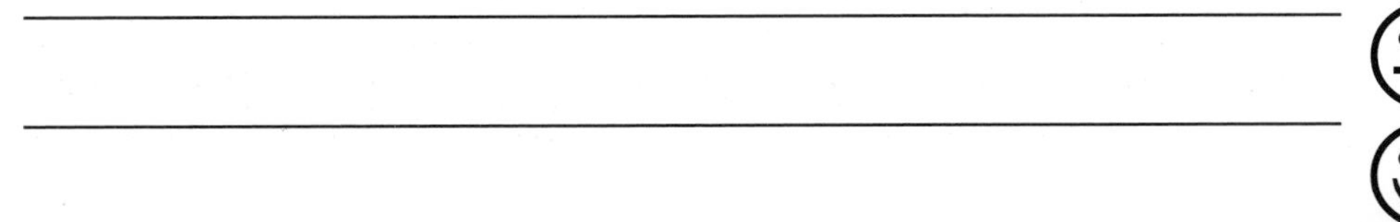

Number

Lesson 6: **Mental subtraction (3)**

- Choose appropriate mental strategies to subtract numbers

Challenge 1

Show these subtractions using the number lines.

a 503 – 6 = ☐

b 702 – 6 = ☐

c 304 – 5 = ☐

d 402 – 4 = ☐

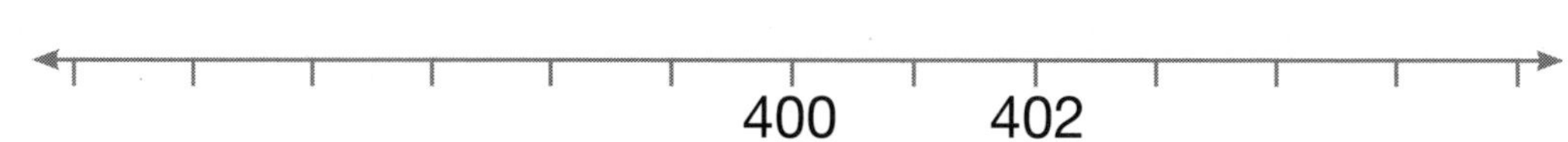

Challenge 2

1 Choose any strategy to work out these subtractions.

a 65 – 16 = ☐ **b** 56 – 18 = ☐

c 51 – 37 = ☐ **d** 64 – 28 = ☐

e 48 – 32 = ☐ **f** 82 – 54 = ☐

g 81 – 66 = ☐ **h** 90 – 37 = ☐

2 Choose one number from each grid to make different subtractions.

Hint: The numbers in the second grid are 2-digit numbers, so think about strategies that you know to help find the answer.

626	968	350	590
818	690	405	326
559	407	681	785

24	36	39	55
74	76	42	92
61	44	51	83

a ☐ − ☐ = ☐ **b** ☐ − ☐ = ☐

c ☐ − ☐ = ☐ **d** ☐ − ☐ = ☐

e ☐ − ☐ = ☐ **f** ☐ − ☐ = ☐

g ☐ − ☐ = ☐ **h** ☐ − ☐ = ☐

Fatima thinks of two numbers. She adds them together and her answer is 832.

She says, "One of the numbers I added is a 2-digit number and it ends in the digit 6."

a Explain how you could find examples of Fatima's numbers by using subtraction to help.

____

____

b Use subtraction to find all the possible pairs of numbers that Fatima could have thought of.

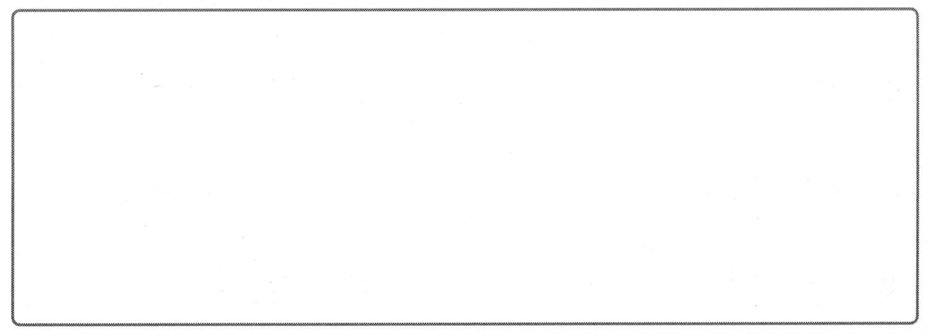

Number

Lesson 7: **Subtracting pairs of 3-digit numbers (1)**

- Use written methods to subtract pairs of 3-digit numbers

You will need
- ruler

Challenge 1

Practise the written method by subtracting these 2-digit numbers.

Remember to subtract the units first and then the tens.

Example:

	4	8
–	2	1
	2	7

a

	5	4
–	2	3

b

	6	7
–	1	4

c

	7	3
–	5	1

d

	5	9
–	3	8

e

	6	8
–	2	5

Challenge 2

1 Use the written method to subtract these numbers.

a 561 – 241

b 655 – 432

c 897 – 145

d 782 – 310

2 In these calculations, you will need to regroup the top number before you start subtracting each column.

a 738 – 429

b 523 – 381

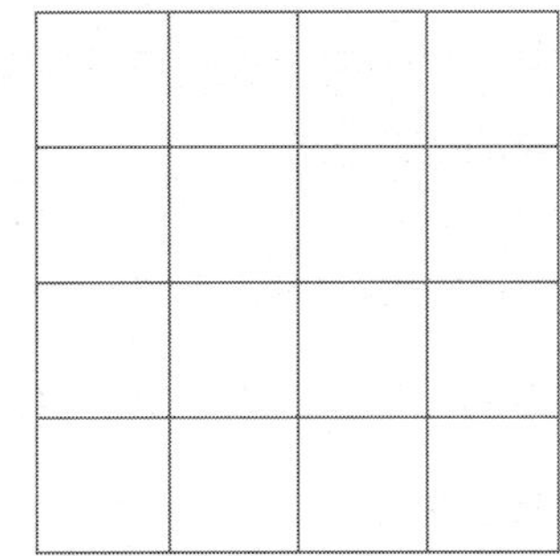

3 Explain when to regroup the top number in a subtraction. Give an example.

____

____

____

Challenge **3** Zak is subtracting 3-digit numbers using the written method.

a He says, "The units in my numbers are 1 and 5. I can't subtract 5 from 1? What should I do?"

Explain what Zak should do and why.

____

____

____

b Zak then says, "The tens in my numbers did show 4 tens subtract 2 tens, but now they show 3 tens subtract 2 tens. Has one ten disappeared?"

Explain to Zak where the 'missing' ten has gone. (If you are not sure, look back to Question 1a.)

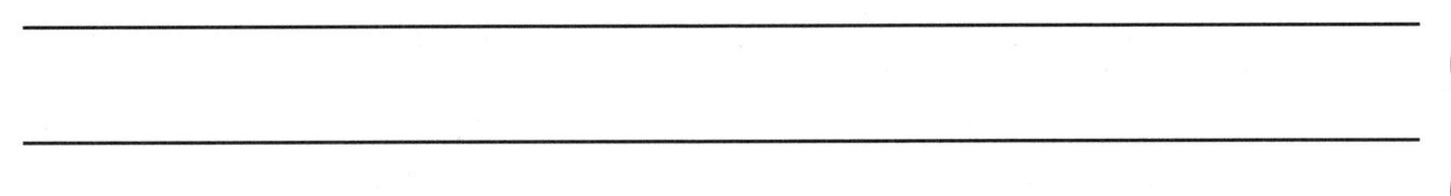

Lesson 8: **Subtracting pairs of 3-digit numbers (2)**

- Use written methods to subtract pairs of 3-digit numbers

You will need
- ruler

Challenge 1

Choose any of the numbers from the circles and write them underneath each 2-digit number to make different subtractions.

Example:

	6	8
−	2	1
	4	7

21 32 24

31 33 42 12

Remember to subtract the units first and then the tens.

a

	6	5
−		

b

	8	7
−		

c

	5	8
−		

d

	9	6
−		

e

	7	7
−		

f

	8	9
−		

1 Read each of these word problems carefully.

a Harriet has $762 in her savings. She takes out $459. How much does she have left?

b A piece of string is 500 cm long. A length of 169 cm is cut from it. What length is the piece of string now?

c There are 593 photos on the school computer. Your teacher uploads another 235. How many photos are on the computer now?

d Ryan weighs two pieces of fruit. The mass of his pineapple is 907 g. The mass of his orange is 156 g. What is the difference between the two masses?

e There are 356 children and 518 adults in a shopping mall. How many people are there altogether?

f A shop sells 738 newspapers on Monday. On Tuesday it only sells 562 newspapers. How many more did it sell on Monday?

Four out of the six word problems are subtraction calculations.

Which questions are they? ☐, ☐, ☐ and ☐.

2 Write out the four subtraction calculations from Question **1** and use the written method to work out the answers.

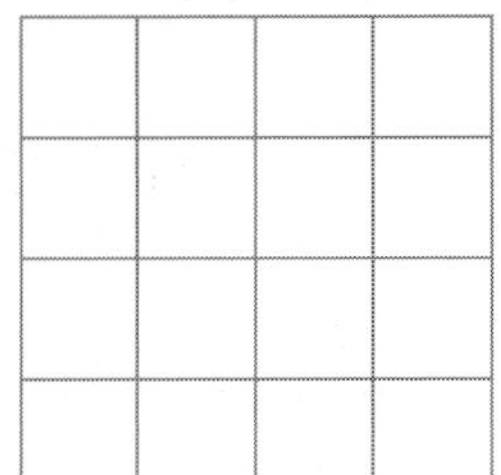
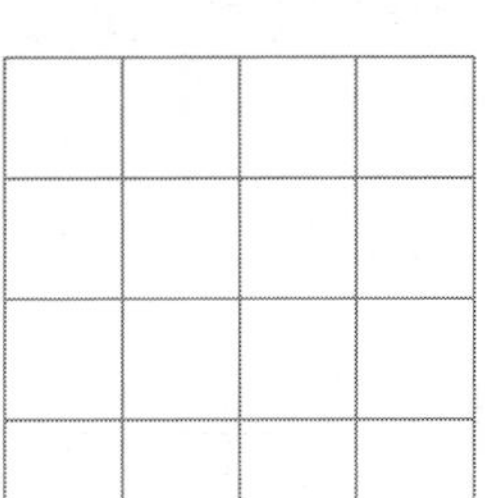
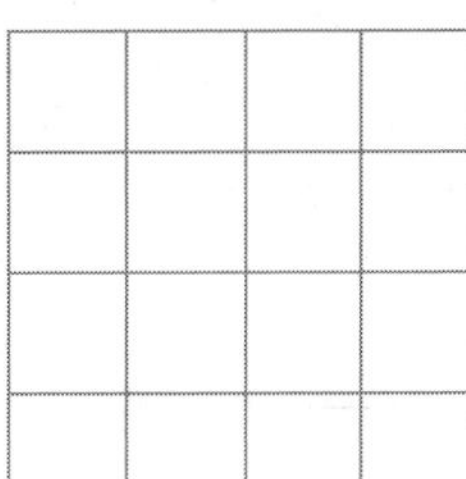

1 Write three different calculations for this subtraction.

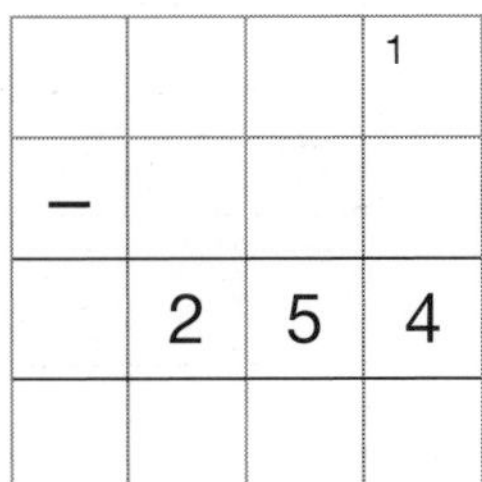

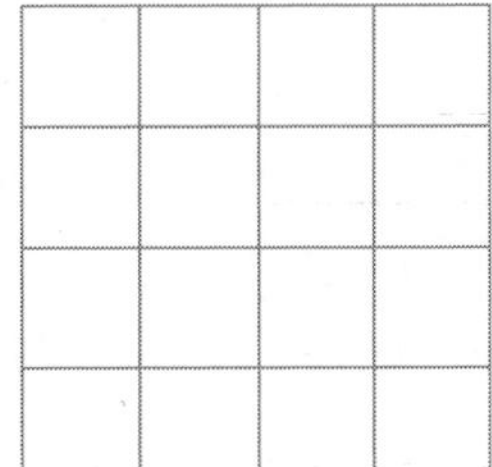

2 Write two different calculations for this subtraction where every digit in the top two numbers is different.

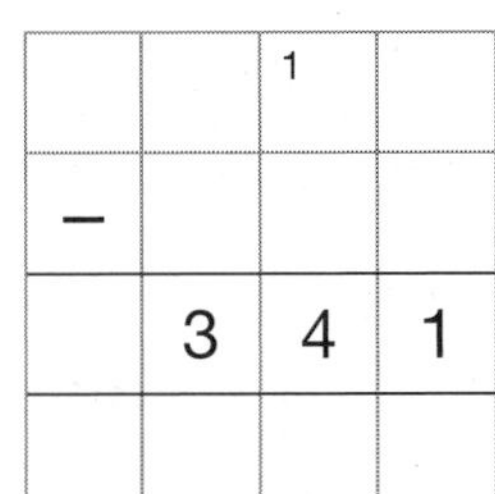

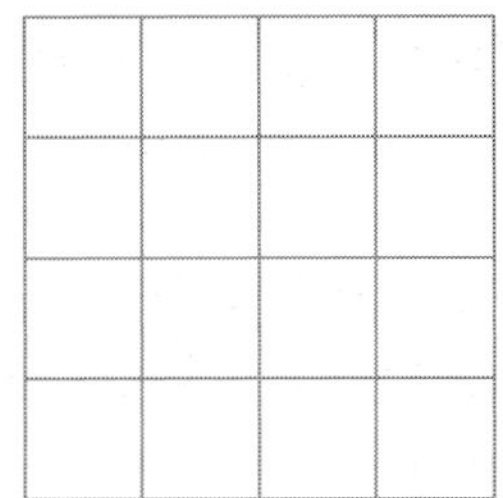
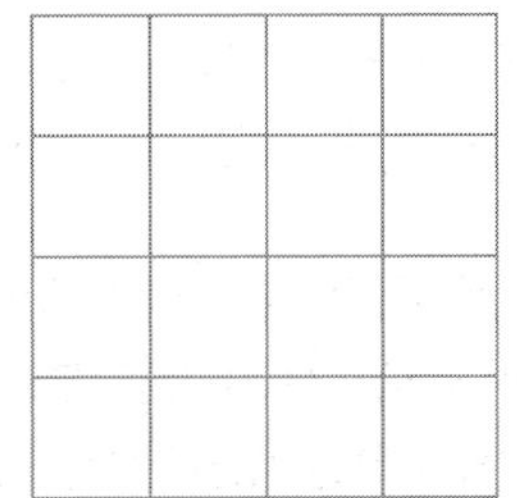

Lesson 1: Multiplication and division facts (1)

- Know multiplication and division facts for 2×, 3×, 4×, 5×, 6×, 9× and 10× tables
- Recognise multiples of 2, 3, 4, 5 and 10

You will need
- coloured pencil

Challenge 1 Write the multiplication for each array, then write the answer.

a ☐ × ☐ = ☐

b ☐ × ☐ = ☐

c ☐ × ☐ = ☐

d ☐ × ☐ = ☐

Challenge 2

1 a Colour each multiple of 2.

13 20 18 15 12 9 8 6

b Colour each multiple of 10.

85 72 40 28 30 60 97 90

c Colour each multiple of 5.

35 50 76 62 75 92 40 12

2 Write each multiple into the correct space on the Carroll diagram.

12 19 32 16 27 24 13 30

	Multiple of 4	Not a multiple of 4
Multiple of 3		
Not a multiple of 3		

Number

3 a Use your knowledge of each times-table to complete the multiplication square.

b Colour three of the facts in the square that you think you need to try to remember.

c How will you try to remember these facts?

____

____

×	3	8	4	7	6
2					
9					
6					
3					
10					
5					
4					

Challenge 3

Satpal says that there are twice as many division facts for 10 as there are for 5, because the number 10 is twice as large as the number 5.

10 ÷ 10 = 1
10 ÷ 5 = 2
10 ÷ 2 = 5
10 ÷ 1 = 10

5 ÷ 5 = 1
5 ÷ 1 = 5

a Use the box below to test Satpal's idea with other numbers that are twice as large as one another.

b Did you find any more examples that fit Satpal's statement?

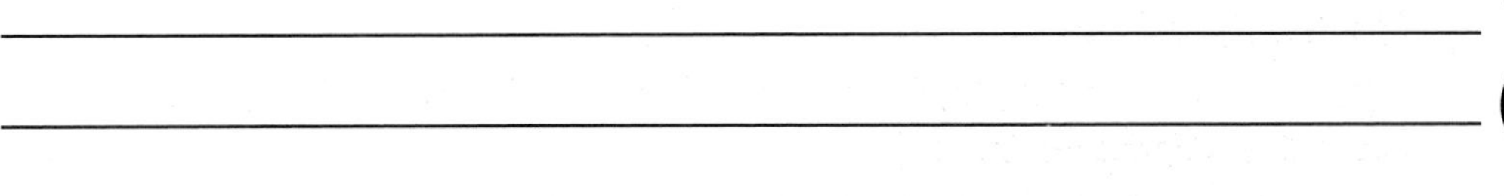

Lesson 2: **6× and 9× multiplication and division facts**

- Know multiplication and division facts for 6× and 9× tables

Challenge 1 Continue each sequence.

a 3, 6, 9, ☐, ☐, ☐, ☐, ☐, ☐, ☐

b 6, 12, 18, ☐, ☐, ☐, ☐, ☐, ☐, ☐

c 9, 18, 27, ☐, ☐, ☐, ☐, ☐, ☐, ☐

Challenge 2

1 Write each multiple into the correct space on the Venn diagram.

42 27 18 30 54 81 48 36 63

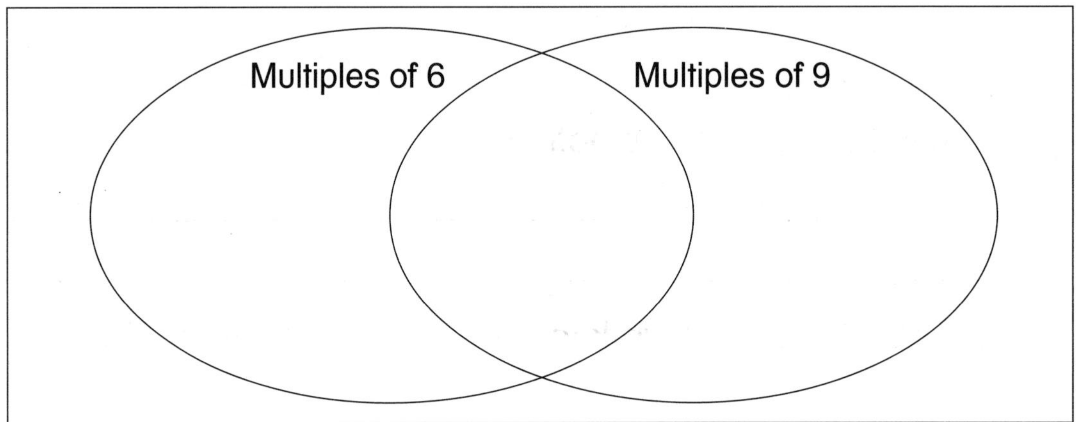

2 Complete these calculations.

a ☐ × 9 = 54

b 5 × 6 = ☐

c 3 × 9 = ☐

d ☐ ÷ 6 = 6

e How many 9s are there in 72? ☐

f What do you multiply 6 by to get 24? ☐

g What is 9 doubled? ☐

h What is 42 split into 6? ☐

3 Rachel spins two spinners and multiplies the numbers to find the product. One of her spinners shows 6.

a What do both spinners show if their product is 18?

[ ] and [ ]

b What do both spinners show if their product is 30?

[ ] and [ ]

Challenge 3

1 Take multiples of 9 and add their digits together.

What pattern do you notice?

____

____

2 Does the pattern work for numbers greater than 90?

How does the pattern still work?

____

____

____

Lesson 3: **7× and 8× multiplication and division facts**

- Know multiplication and division facts for 7× and 8× tables
- Find the easier way to multiply by reversing multiplications

Challenge 1

1 Continue each sequence.

a 4, 8, 16, ☐, ☐, ☐, ☐, ☐, ☐, ☐

b 7, 14, 21, ☐, ☐, ☐, ☐, ☐, ☐, ☐

c 8, 16, 24, ☐, ☐, ☐, ☐, ☐, ☐, ☐

2 Draw a line to match each multiplication fact with its answer.

3 × 7   2 × 8   4 × 7   3 × 8   5 × 7   4 × 8

35   21   32   28   16   24

1 Write the numbers into the correct spaces in the Carroll diagrams.

a 63 22 37 28 41 14 70 49 56 11

	Even numbers	**Not even numbers**
Multiples of 7		
Not multiples of 7		

b 78 62 32 18 64 72 42 58 40 56

	Larger than 50	**Not larger than 50**
Multiples of 8		
Not multiples of 8		

2 Write these calculations another way.

Example: 5 × 7 is the same as 7 × 5

a 4 × 8 is the same as ☐

b ☐ is the same as 6 × 8

3 Show how you can use 5× and 2× tables facts to help with your 7× tables. Example: 4 × 7 = (4 × 5) + (4 × 2) = 20 + 8 = 28

a 5 × 7 =
(☐ × 5) + (☐ × 2)
= ☐ + ☐
= ☐

b 3 × 7 =
(☐ × 5) + (☐ × 2)
= ☐ + ☐
= ☐

c 6 × 7 =
(☐ × 5) + (☐ × 2)
= ☐ + ☐
= ☐

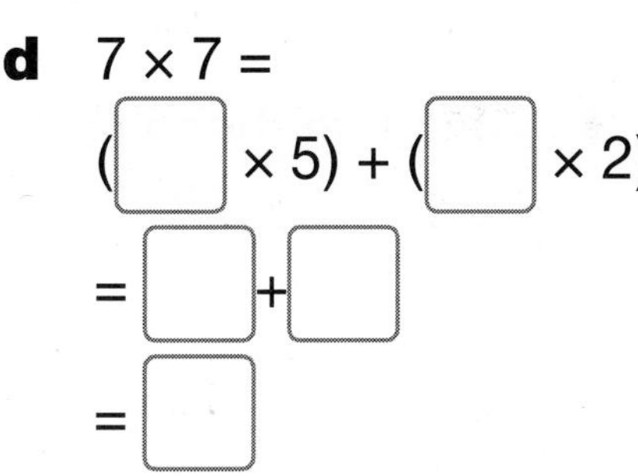

d 7 × 7 =
(☐ × 5) + (☐ × 2)
= ☐ + ☐
= ☐

Challenge 3 Each new number begins with a tens digit that is the same as the units digit of the previous number and is only made with multiples of 4.

32, 24, 40, 04, 48, 80

a Make a similar number chain using only multiples of 8.

The longest chain I can make is:

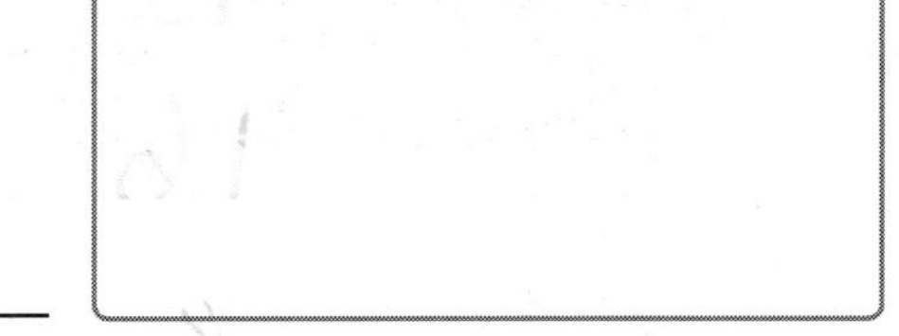

____

b Make a similar number chain using a multiple of 7, followed by a multiple of 8, then a multiple of 9, and so on.

The longest chain I can make is:

____

____

Number

Lesson 4: **Multiplying multiples of 10 to 90**

- Multiply multiples of 10 up to 90 by a single-digit number

Challenge 1 Draw a line to match each multiplication with a times-table fact that you think might be able to help.

Example: 60 × 5 matches with 6 × 5

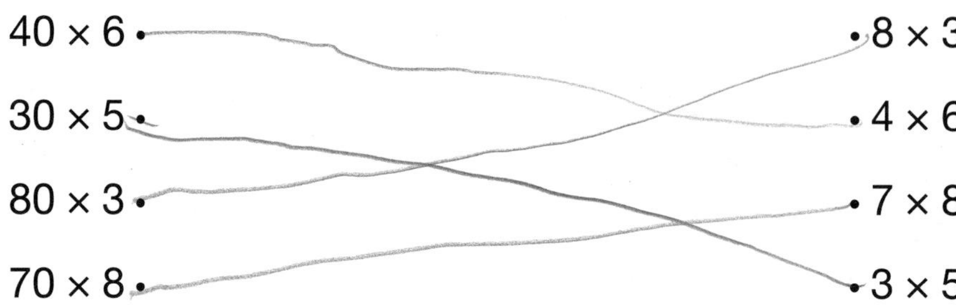

Challenge 2 **1** Complete these calculations.

a 7 × 5 = 35 so 70 × 5 = 350

b 6 × 4 = 24 so 60 × 4 = 240

c 2 × 9 = 18 so 20 × 9 = 180

d 8 × 3 = 24 so 80 × 3 = 240

e 5 × 8 = 40 so 50 × 8 = 400

f 4 × 4 = 16 so 40 × 4 = 160

g 3 × 2 = 6 so 30 × 2 = 60

h 7 × 8 = 56 so 70 × 8 = 560

2 a Put a tick (✓) or a cross (✗) next to each question to show whether it is correct or not.

30 × 6 = 180 ✓	50 × 4 = 200 ✓	60 × 5 = 320 ✗
50 × 5 = 260 ✗	30 × 8 = 240 ✓	90 × 9 = 850 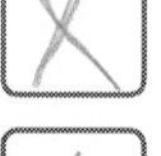

Number

b For each wrong answer, write the calculation and the correct answer.

50 × 5 = 250	60 × 5 = 300	90 × 9 = 810

Challenge 3

1 Use times-tables facts to help you answer.

Example: 5 × 3 can be used to help answer 500 × 3.

Use these numbers to make six different multiplications:

400 6 300 8 600 5 900 4

6	×	300	=	1,800	5	×	8	=	40
400	×	4	=	1,600	6	×	600	=	3,600
8	×	900	=	7,200	4	×	300	=	1,200

140 × 3 = 420

2 Use times-tables facts to help you answer.

For example: 120 × 5.

a Use these numbers to make six different multiplications:

140 3 210 5 120 6 150 4

140	×	3	=	420	5	×	6	=	30
150	×	4	=	600	3	×	4	=	12
210	×	3	=	630	5	×	3	=	15

Lesson 5: **Multiplying a 2-digit number (1)**

- Use partitioning to multiply a 2-digit number by a single-digit number

Challenge 1

Split the 2-digit numbers into their tens and units.

Example:

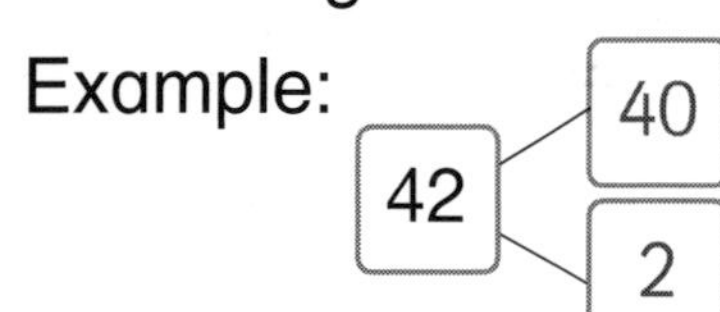

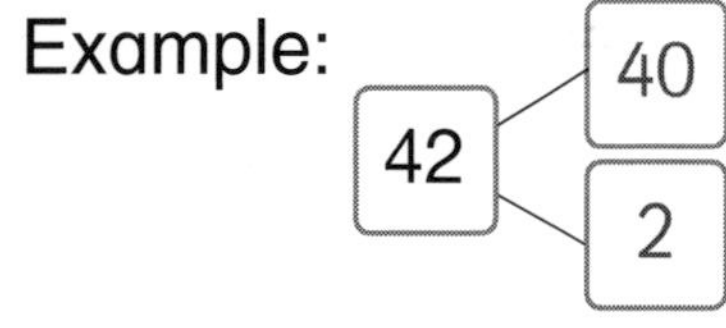

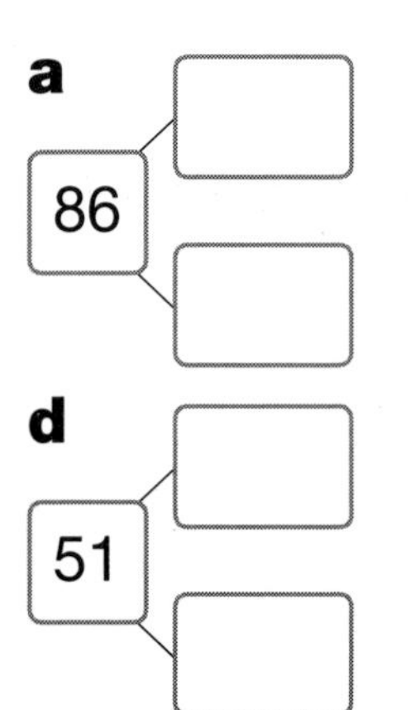

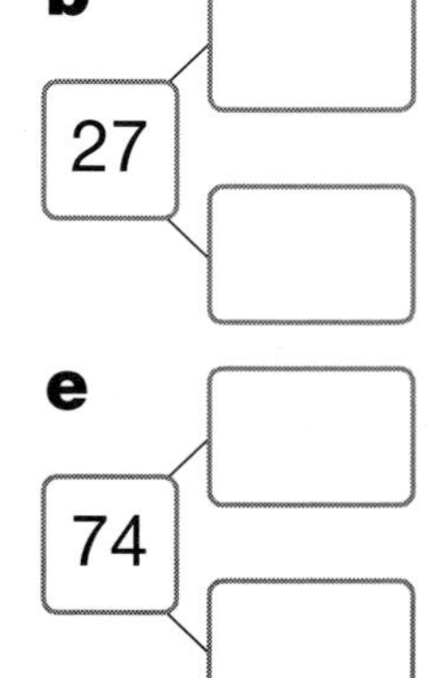

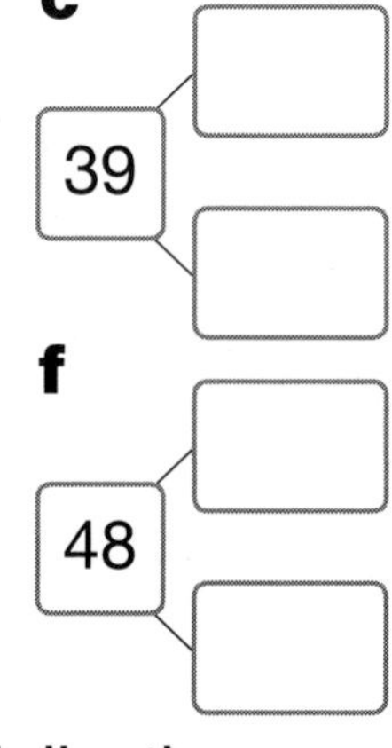

Challenge 2

1 Use the partitioning method to work out these multiplications.

Example: 42 × 3 = 40 × 3 + 2 × 3
= 120 + 6
= 126

a 35 × 4
= ☐ + ☐
= ☐ + ☐
= ☐

b 13 × 6

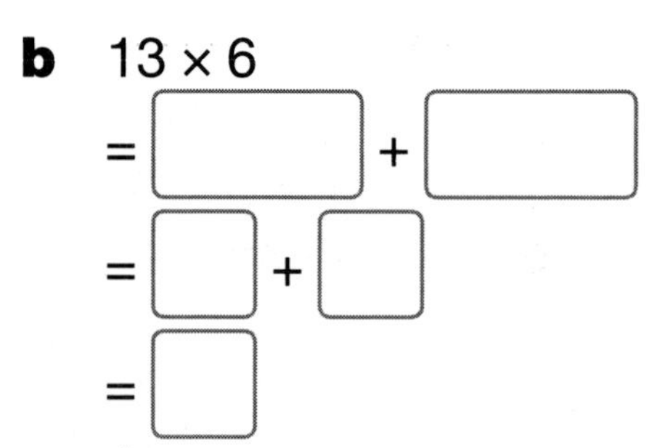

c 28 × 5
= ☐ + ☐
= ☐ + ☐
= ☐

d 57 × 3

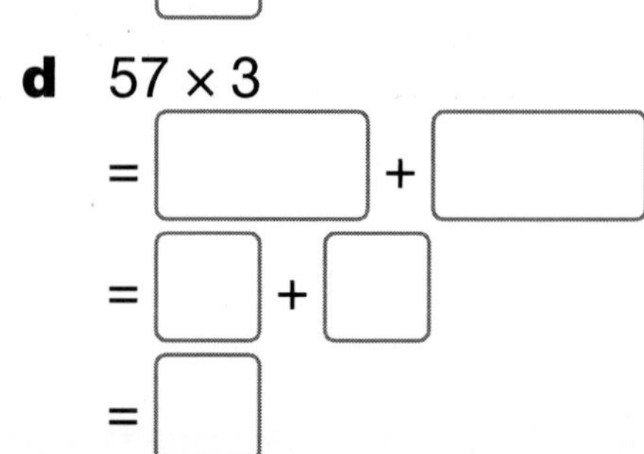

Student's Book page 53

2 Before working out the answers to these calculations, round one (or both) of the numbers and estimate what the answer will be.

a 49 × 6 Estimate = ☐
49 × 6
= ☐ + ☐
= ☐ + ☐
= ☐

b 32 × 6 Estimate = ☐
32 × 6
= ☐ + ☐
= ☐ + ☐
= ☐

c 19 × 7 Estimate = ☐
19 × 7
= ☐ + ☐
= ☐ + ☐
= ☐

d 51 × 8 Estimate = ☐
51 × 8
= ☐ + ☐
= ☐ + ☐
= ☐

3 Explain how to use partitioning to multiply any 2-digit number by a single-digit number.

____

____

____

Challenge 3 Use any three digits to make as many different totals as you can. You must make your totals by multiplying 2-digit numbers by single-digit numbers using partitioning to help.

Write your chosen digits here: ☐ ☐ ☐

Complete your multiplications in the space below.

Number

Lesson 6: **Multiplying a 2-digit number (2)**

- Use the grid method to multiply a 2-digit number by a single-digit number

Challenge 1

Partition the numbers in the grids.

Example: 16 × 5

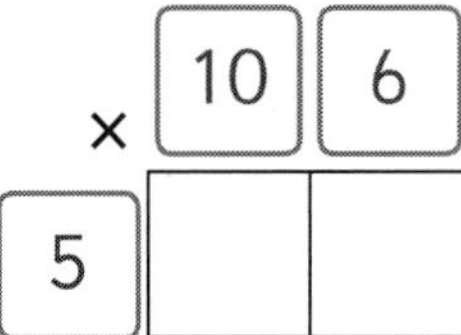

×	10	6
5		

a 18 × 4

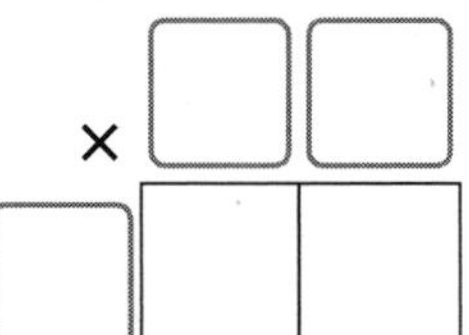

b 24 × 5

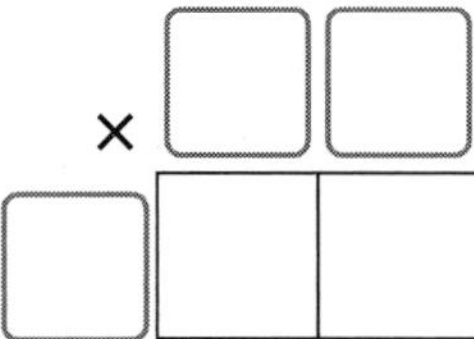

c 17 × 8

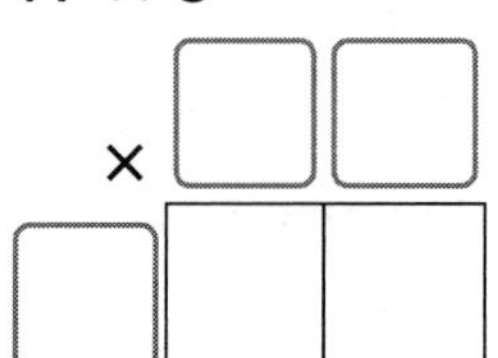

d 21 × 6

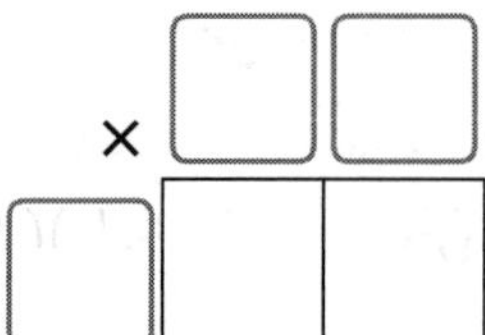

Challenge 2

1 Use the grid method to work out these multiplications.

Example: 21 × 6

×	20	1
6	120	6

120 + 6 = 126

a 25 × 4

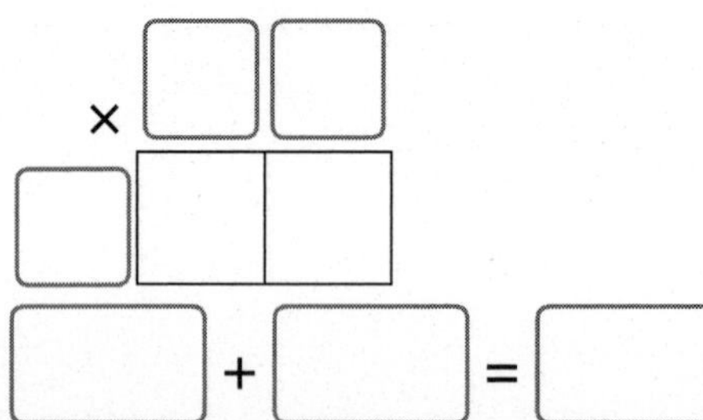

b 36 × 5

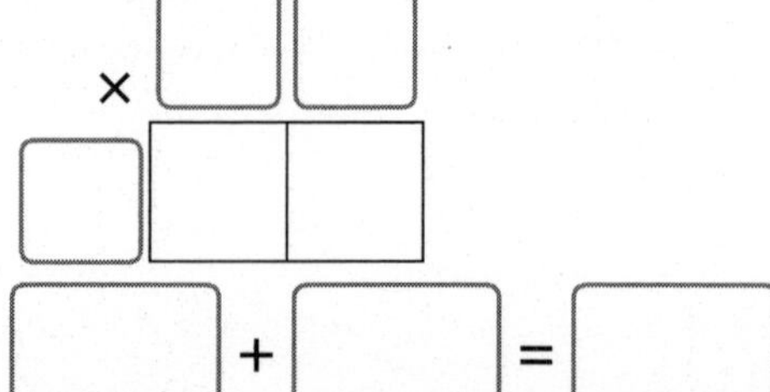

c 26 × 4

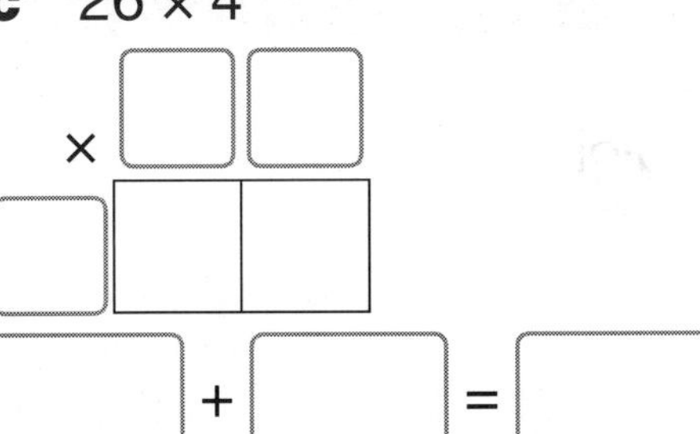

d 43 × 6

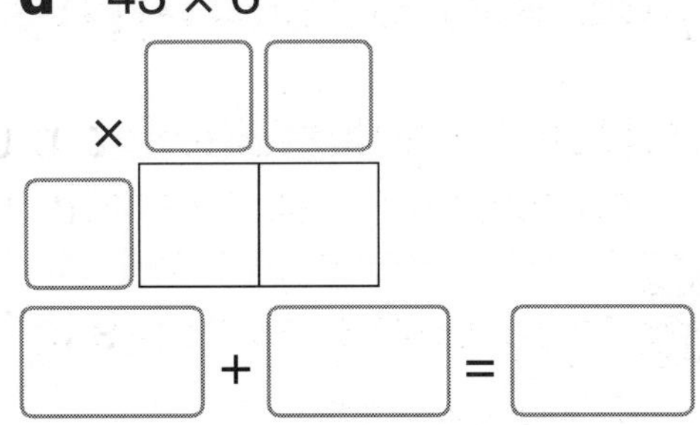

2 First round the numbers and estimate, then use the grid method to calculate.

a 29 × 4 Estimate =

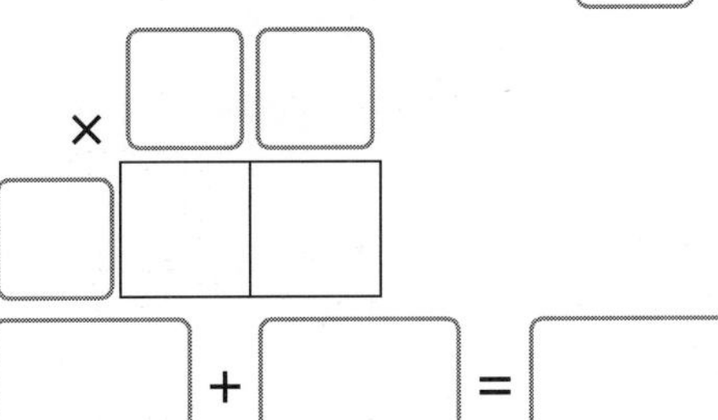

b 39 × 3 Estimate =

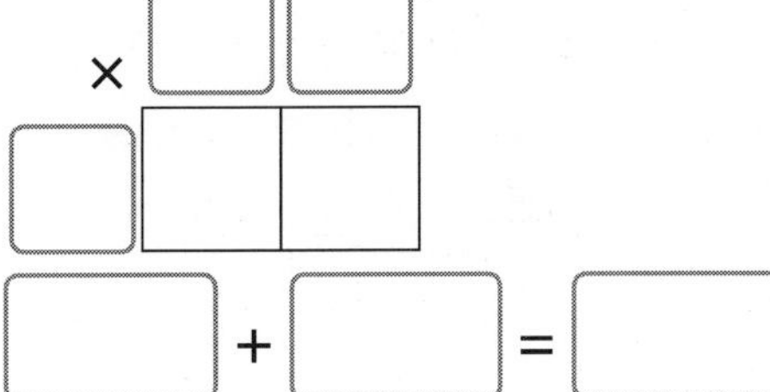

1 Use these number cards to write two different word problems where a 2-digit number is multiplied by a single-digit number.

a ______________________

____

____

b ______________________

____

____

2 Use the grid method to solve your word problems.

Number

Lesson 7: **Dividing a 2-digit number (1)**

- Divide a 2-digit number by a single-digit number

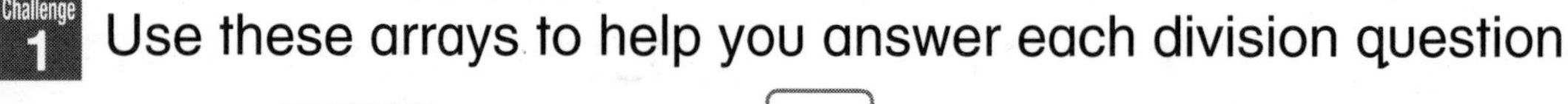

Challenge 1 Use these arrays to help you answer each division question.

a 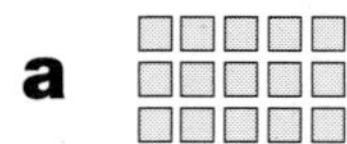 $15 \div 3 = \square$

b $24 \div 6 = \square$

c $18 \div 6 = \square$

d  $42 \div 7 = \square$

Challenge 2

1 Use the empty number lines to work out the answers to these division questions.

Example:

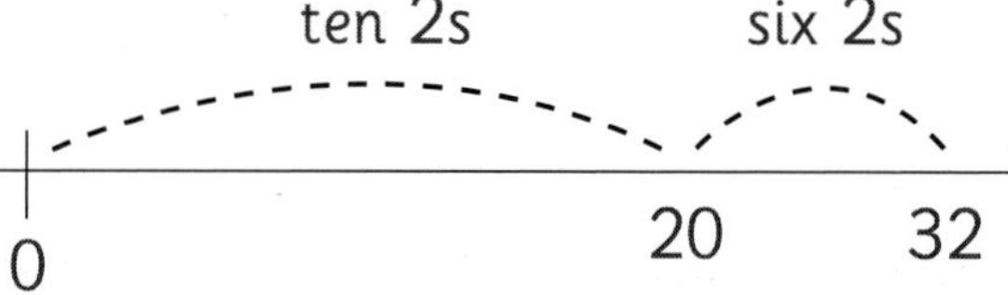

$32 \div 2 = 16$

a 0 $38 \div 2 = \square$

b 0 $45 \div 3 = \square$

c 0 $84 \div 6 = \square$

d 0 $80 \div 5 = \square$

2 Use the clues to work out the division each person is answering.

I know that ten 2s are 20 and seven 2s are 14. I can then work out the answer

I worked out the answer by counting ten 5s and then another four 5s.

a $\square \div \square = \square$ **b**  $\square \div \square = \square$

1 A gardener has 72 flower bulbs to plant in rows of the same length.

Name all the possible ways she can plant the flowers.

Number of rows	Number of bulbs in each row	Number of flowers altogether (must equal 72)
2	36	72

2 A gardener needs to plant 60 seeds into pots. Each pot has to have the same amount of seeds.

Use this table to help record the different possibilities.

Number of pots	Number of seeds in each pot	Number of flowers altogether (must equal 60)

Lesson 8: **Dividing a 2-digit number (2)**

• Divide a 2-digit number by a single-digit number

You will need

• coloured pencils

Challenge 1 Shade the circles in different colours to help find each answer.

a ○○○○○○○○○○○○○○○○○○

How many 2s are in 18? ☐

b ○○○○○○○○○○○○○○○○○○○○

How many 5s are in 20? ☐

c ○○○○○○○○○○○○

How many 4s are in 12? ☐

Challenge 2

1 For each of these division questions, use two multiplication facts to help find the answer.

Example: 48 ÷ 4

10 × 4 = 40

2 × 4 = 8

So 48 ÷ 4 = 12

a 60 ÷ 4

☐ × 4 = ☐

☐ × 4 = ☐

So 60 ÷ 4 = ☐

b 80 ÷ 5

☐ × 5 = ☐

☐ × 5 = ☐

So 80 ÷ 5 = ☐

c 78 ÷ 6

☐ × 6 = ☐

☐ × 6 = ☐

So 78 ÷ 6 = ☐

d 42 ÷ 3

☐ × 3 = ☐

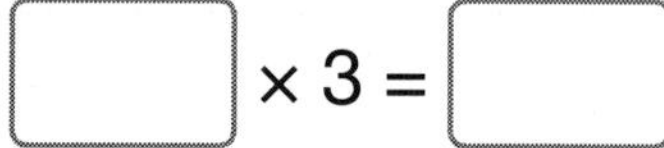

☐ × 3 = ☐

So 42 ÷ 3 = ☐

2 Explain how you would find the answer to these division questions.

a How many 3s are in 51?

____

____

____

b How many 4s are in 76?

____

____

____

c How many 5s are in 75?

____

____

____

Challenge 3

1 Write six multiplication facts where a number between 20 and 30 is multiplied by a single digit number, for example: $22 \times 4 = 88$.

☐ × ☐ = ☐ ☐ × ☐ = ☐

☐ × ☐ = ☐ ☐ × ☐ = ☐

☐ × ☐ = ☐ ☐ × ☐ = ☐

2 Use your multiplication facts to write six division facts where the answer is between 20 and 30.

☐ ÷ ☐ = ☐ ☐ ÷ ☐ = ☐

☐ ÷ ☐ = ☐ ☐ ÷ ☐ = ☐

☐ ÷ ☐ = ☐ ☐ ÷ ☐ = ☐

Number

Lesson 1: Multiplication and division facts (2)

- Know multiplication facts up to 10 × 10 and the related division facts
- Recognise multiples of 2, 3, 4, 5 and 10

Challenge 1

1 Count on or back in 4s and complete the sequences.

a 4, 8, ☐, ☐, ☐, 24, ☐, 32, ☐, ☐

b 40, 36, ☐, ☐, ☐, 20, ☐, ☐, 8, ☐

2 Count forward or back in 3s and complete the sequences.

a 3, 6, ☐, ☐, 15, 18, ☐, ☐, ☐, ☐

b 30, 27, ☐, ☐, ☐, ☐, 12, 9, ☐, ☐

3 Count forward or back in 6s and complete the sequences.

a 6, 12, 18, ☐, ☐, ☐, ☐, 48, ☐, ☐

b 60, 54, 48, ☐, ☐, ☐, ☐, ☐, ☐, ☐

Challenge 2

1 Complete these multiplication targets.

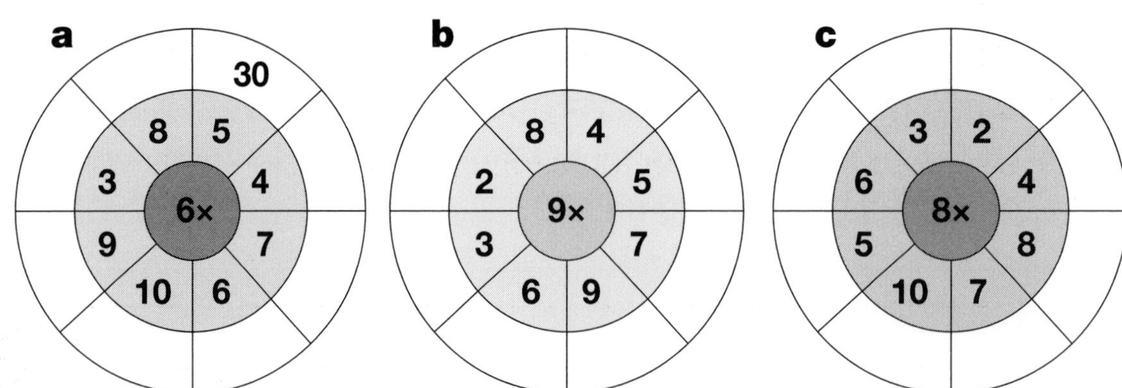

2 Complete these targets.

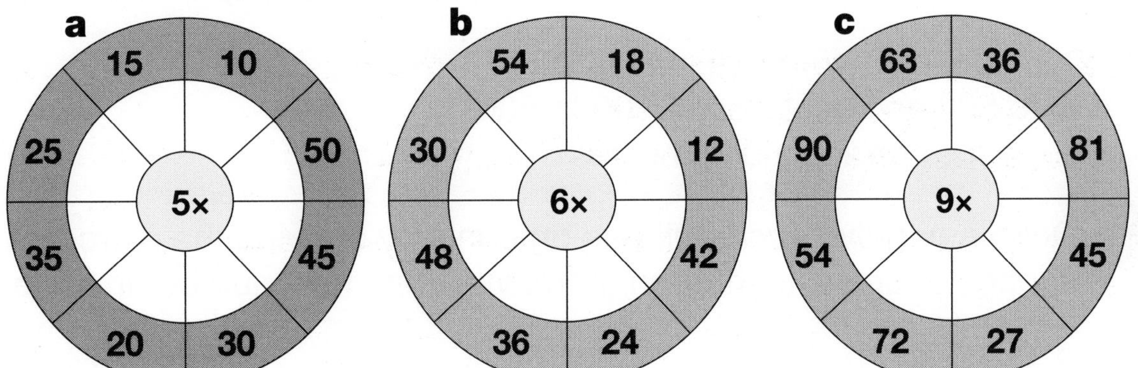

3 Circle the question in each pair that seems easiest to work out. Then write the answer.

a 5 × 8 or 8 × 5? ☐ **b** 6 × 7 or 7 × 6? ☐

c 7 × 5 or 5 × 7? ☐ **d** 9 × 3 or 3 × 9? ☐

e 8 × 4 or 4 × 8? ☐ **f** 4 × 9 or 9 × 4? ☐

Challenge **3**

Class 4 are having a reading competition.

- Khaled reads every day for six days.
- Liam reads every day for a week.
- Molly reads every day for nine days.
- one person read 7 pages every day
- one person read 8 pages every day
- one person read 5 pages every day

What are the possible totals for each person?

Khaled: ____________________

____

Liam: ____________________

____

Molly: ____________________

____

Lesson 2: **Doubling and halving (1)**

- Double 2-digit numbers, multiples of 10 to 500 and multiples of 100 to 5000
- Know the corresponding halves

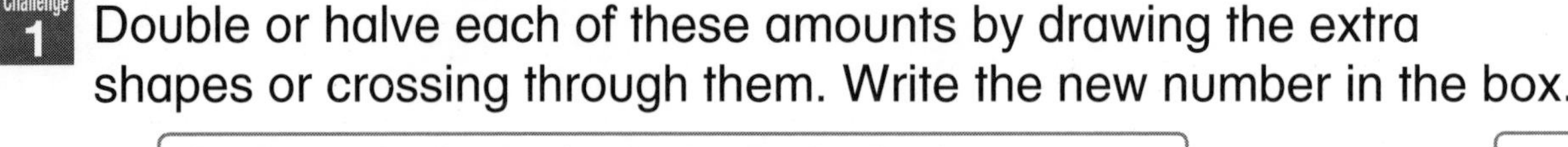

Challenge 1

Double or halve each of these amounts by drawing the extra shapes or crossing through them. Write the new number in the box.

a 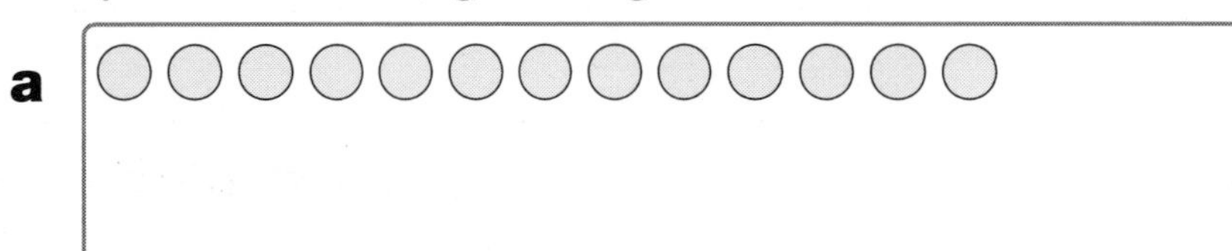 Double 13 = ☐

b  Halve 24 = ☐

Challenge 2

1 Double the tens and then the units of each of these to find the answer.

Example: What is double 45?

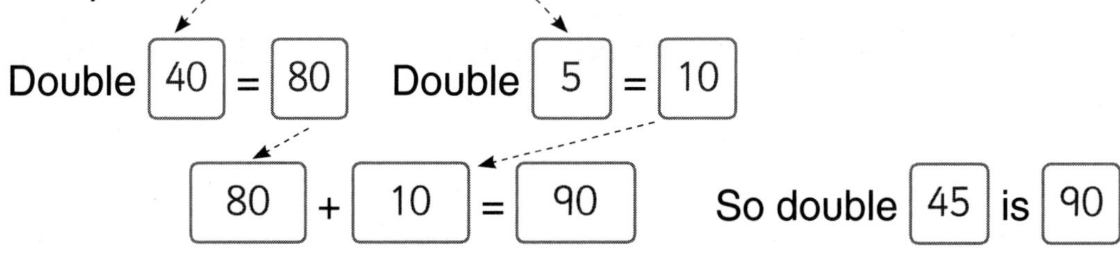

a What is double 36?

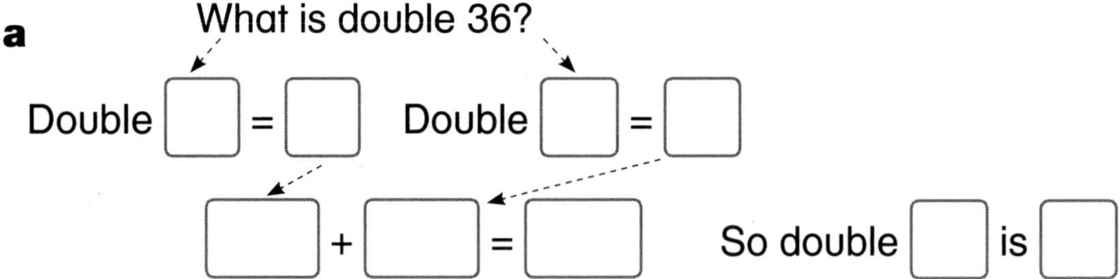

b What is double 49?

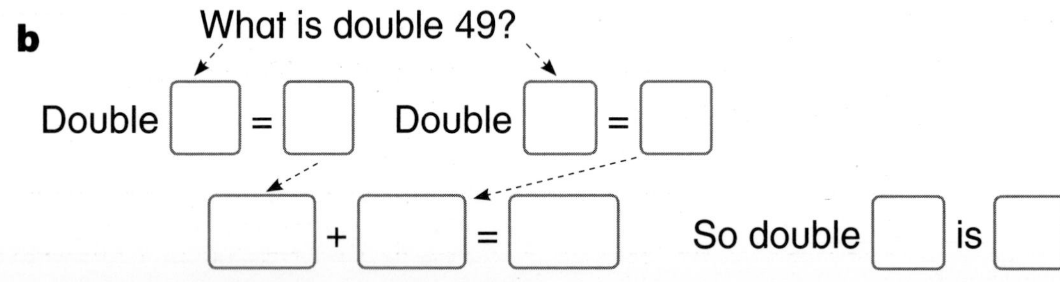

2 Complete each row.

Number	Double the number	Double 10 times the number	Double 100 times the number
11	Double 11 = 22	Double 110 = 220	Double 1100 = 2200
15			
	Double 26 = 52		
		Double 390 = 780	
			Double 1300 = 2600

3 Halve these numbers.

a Half 76 = ☐ **b** Half 38 = ☐ **c** Half 94 = ☐

d Half 880 = ☐ **e** Half 550 = ☐ **f** Half 1200 = ☐

1 Complete the table to show how numbers change when they are doubled three times.

Number	Double once	Double twice	Double three times
6	12	24	48
3			
8			
5			
10			
12			
14			

2 Look at the first and the last numbers in each row. What do you notice?

____

____

Lesson 3: **Multiplying and dividing by 10 (1)**

- Multiply and divide 3-digit numbers by 10

Challenge 1 Multiply by 10.

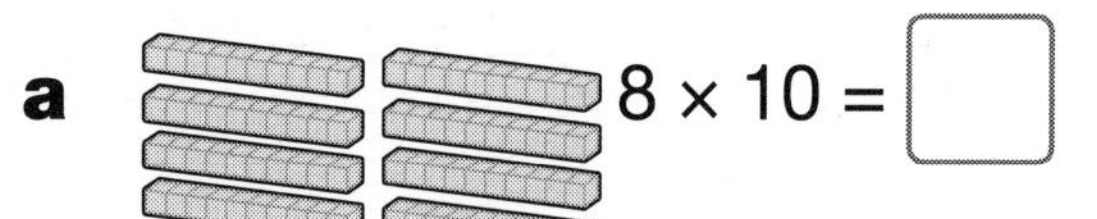

a 8 × 10 = ☐ **b** 10 × 10 = ☐

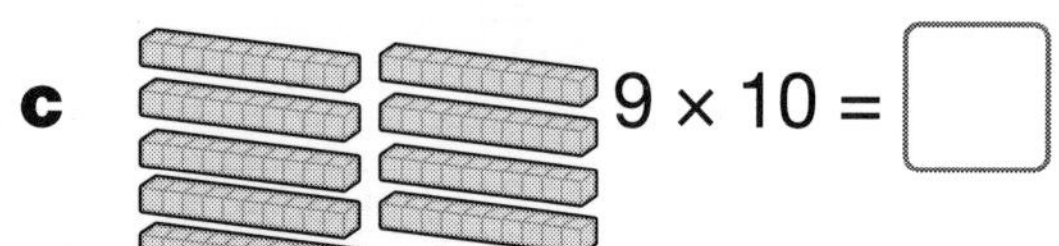

c 9 × 10 = ☐ **d** 12 × 10 = ☐

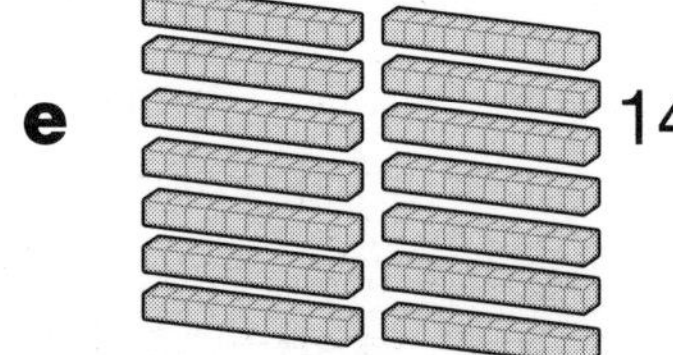

e 14 × 10 = ☐

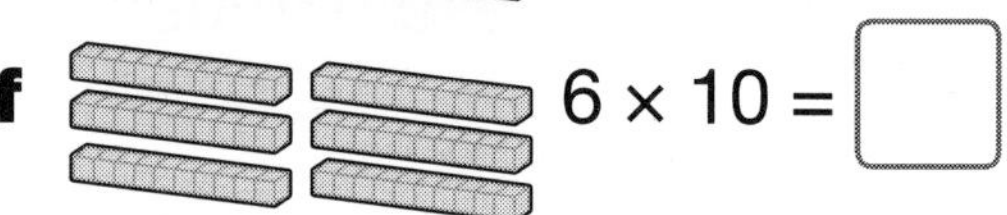

f 6 × 10 = ☐

Challenge 2

1 Draw arrows to show what happens when a 3-digit number is multiplied by 10.

Example:

Th	H	T	U
	5	2	4
5	2	4	0

524 × 10 = 5240

a

Th	H	T	U
	7	2	9

☐ × 10 = ☐

b

Th	H	T	U
	4	6	7

☐ × 10 = ☐

c

Th	H	T	U
	8	4	0

☐ × 10 = ☐

d

Th	H	T	U
	1	0	5

☐ × 10 = ☐

2 Complete these calculations. Example: 562 ÷ 10 = 56·2

a 141 ÷ 10 = ☐ **b** 592 ÷ 10 = ☐

c 926 ÷ 10 = ☐ **d** 653 ÷ 10 = ☐

e 897 ÷ 10 = ☐ **f** 323 ÷ 10 = ☐

g 462 ÷ 10 = ☐ **h** 944 ÷ 10 = ☐

i 820 ÷ 10 = ☐ **j** 240 ÷ 10 = ☐

Why are the answers to **i** and **j** whole numbers?

____

____

Use 8, 2, 0 and 4 to make 3-digit numbers.

a Write ten possible 3-digit numbers.

b Multiply each of your 3-digit numbers by 10.

c Divide each of your 3-digit numbers by 10.

Number

Lesson 4: **Multiplying and dividing by 10 (2)**

- Multiply and divide 3-digit numbers by 10

You will need
- 0–9 digit cards

Challenge 1

Use digit cards to help you find the answers.

a 2 4 × 10 = ☐ ☐ ☐

b 1 2 × 10 = ☐ ☐ ☐

c 2 3 × 10 = ☐ ☐ ☐

d 1 9 × 10 = ☐ ☐ ☐

e 1 6 × 10 = ☐ ☐ ☐

f 1 4 × 10 = ☐ ☐ ☐

Challenge 2

1 Complete the table to show how these numbers change when they are multiplied or divided by 10.

÷ 10		× 10
	841	
	230	
	781	
	445	
	501	
	573	
	996	
	205	
	770	
	323	

2 Describe what happens to the value of the digits in the number 624 when it is divided by 10.

____

____

Challenge 3

1 Harper takes three digit cards and makes three different 3-digit numbers from them. She multiplies the numbers by 10.

Her first answer is between 5000 and 6000.

Her second answer is between 8000 and 9000

Her third answer is between 2000 and 3000.

a What do you think Harper's digit cards were?

☐, ☐ and ☐

b Write down three calculations that match the clues.

Calculation for first answer: ☐ × 10 = ☐

Calculation for second answer: ☐ × 10 = ☐

Calculation for third answer: ☐ × 10 = ☐

2 Harper takes three different digit cards and makes three different 3-digit numbers. She divides the numbers by 10.

Her first answer is between 30 and 40.

Her second answer is between 10 and 20.

The sum of the digit cards is 8.

a What do you think Harper's digit cards were?

☐, ☐ and ☐

b Write down two calculations that match the clues.

Calculation for first answer: ☐ ÷ 10 = ☐

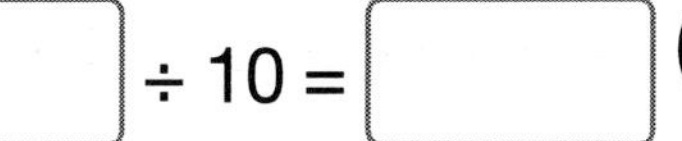

Calculation for second answer: ☐ ÷ 10 = ☐

Lesson 5: **Multiplying a 2-digit number (3)**

- Multiply a 2-digit number by a single-digit number

Challenge 1

1 Write how you could partition each of these numbers.

Example: 28 can be split into [20] and [8].

a 49 can be split into [ ] and [ ].

b 51 can be split into [ ] and [ ].

c 67 can be split into [ ] and [ ].

d 32 can be split into [ ] and [ ].

2 Work out the multiplications and write the answers in each grid. Then, add the numbers in the grid to get your answer.

a

×	10	3
2		

[ ] + [ ] = [ ]

b

×	10	5
2		

[ ] + [ ] = [ ]

c

×	10	2
3		

[ ] + [ ] = [ ]

Challenge 2

1 Use the partitioning method to work out these multiplications.

Example: 32 × 5

= [30 × 5] + [2 × 5]

= [150] + [10]

= [160]

a 54 × 6

= [ ] + [ ]

= [ ] + [ ]

= [ ]

Number

b 63×3

= ___ + ___

= ___ + ___

= ___

c 78×4

= ___ + ___

= ___ + ___

= ___

2 Use the grid method to work out these multiplications.

Example: 26×7

×	20	6
7	140	42

140 + 42 = 182

a 35×6

×

___ + ___ = ___

b 23×8

×

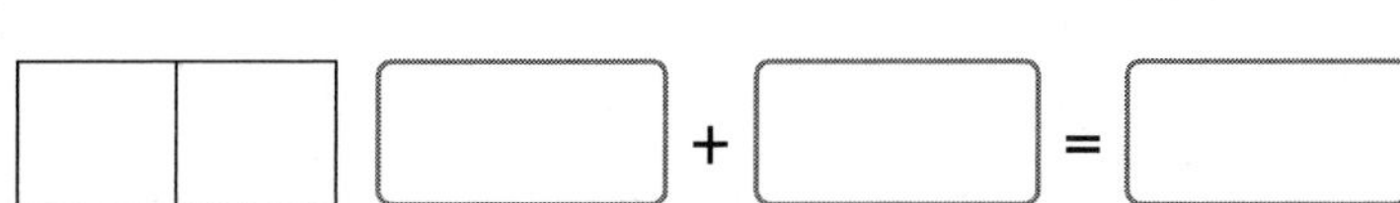

c 55×4

×

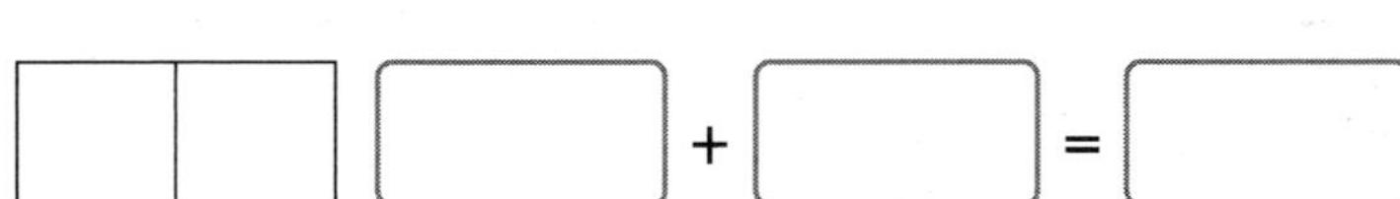

3 Do you prefer to use partitioning or the grid method? Why?

____

____

Write down two multiplications that could be represented by the letters. Use either partitioning or the grid method to show your working.

a AB × C = DEF **b** GH × G = JKL **c** PP × P = QQ

Number

Lesson 6: **Multiplying a 2-digit number (4)**

- Multiply a 2-digit number by a single-digit number

You will need
- coloured pencil

Complete each part of the multiplication and then add both numbers together to find the answer.

a 12 × 2

10 × 2 = △

2 × 2 = ○

△ + ○ = □

b 14 × 2

10 × 2 = △

4 × 2 = ○

△ + ○ = □

c 12 × 5

10 × 5 = △

2 × 5 = ○

△ + ○ = □

d 13 × 3

10 × 3 = △

3 × 3 = ○

△ + ○ = □

1 Use your preferred method to work out the answers to these multiplications.

a 18 × 9

b 38 × 5

c 47 × 4

d 58 × 3

Number

2 Work backwards by multiplying the numbers to find the number being divided. Show your working.

a A number divided by 2 is 64. What is the number?

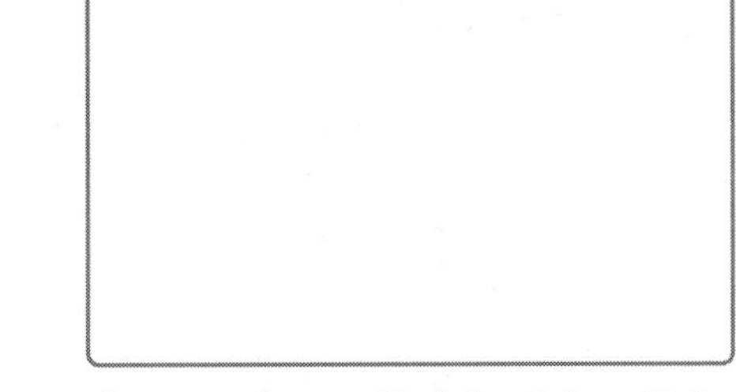

b A number divided by 3 is 73. What is the number?

c A number divided by 5 is 44. What is the number?

d A number divided by 9 is 37. What is the number?

Challenge **3** Harry makes four multiplications using numbers from this grid.

Each of his multiplications are 2-digit numbers multiplied by single-digit numbers.

When he colours in the numbers he has used, it makes a symmetrical pattern in the grid.

Write four multiplications that Harry could have chosen and colour the grid to show your symmetrical pattern.

8	18	27	9
47	68	95	34
3	61	72	9
38	6	7	47
8	5	6	5

Number

Lesson 7: **Dividing a 2-digit number (3)**

- Divide a 2-digit number by a single-digit number

Challenge 1 Use these arrays to help you answer each division question.

a 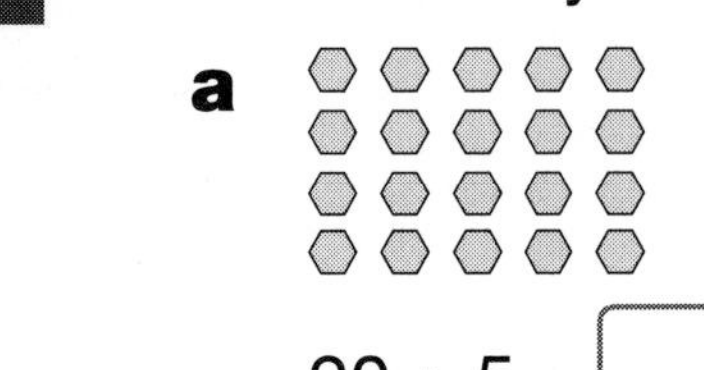

20 ÷ 5 = ☐

b

32 ÷ 4 = ☐

c

35 ÷ 5 = ☐

d 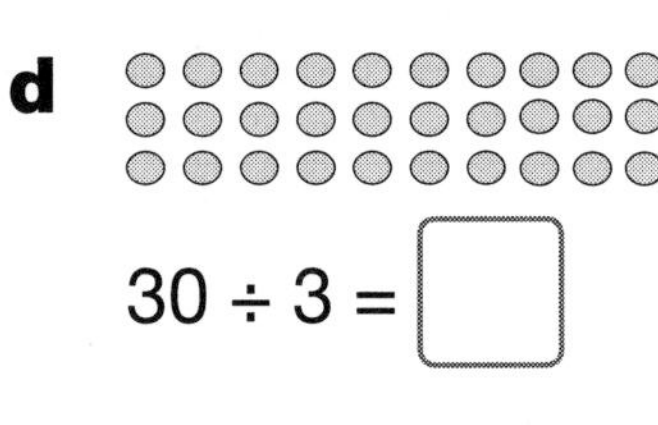

30 ÷ 3 = ☐

e

18 ÷ 9 = ☐

f

12 ÷ 2 = ☐

Challenge 2 **1** Work out these divisions.

Example: 36 ÷ 2
36 – 6 = 30 (minus 3 twos)
30 – 30 = 0 (minus 15 twos)
= 18

a 57 ÷ 3

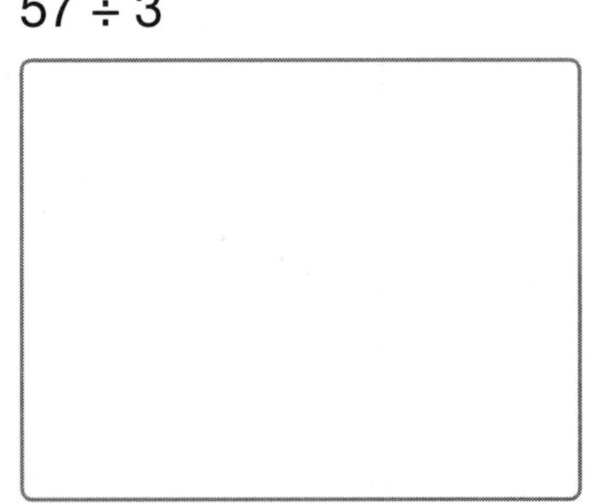

b 52 ÷ 4

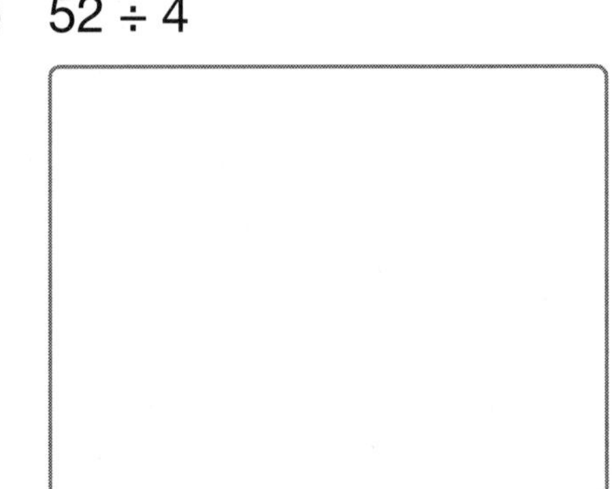

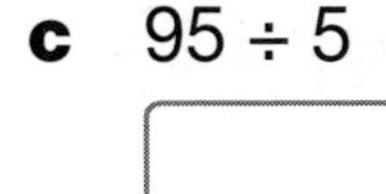

c 95 ÷ 5

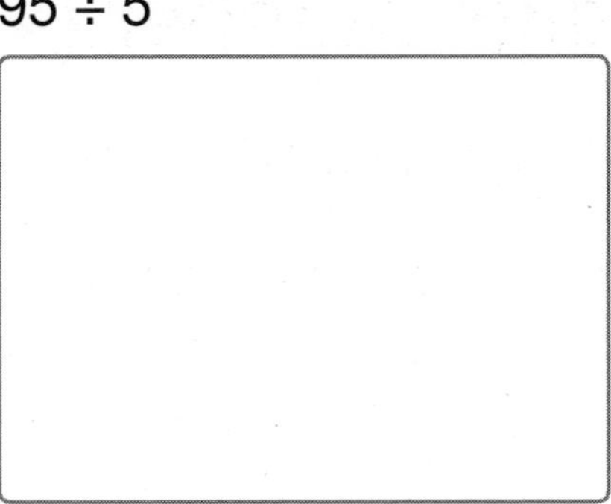

d 72 ÷ 6

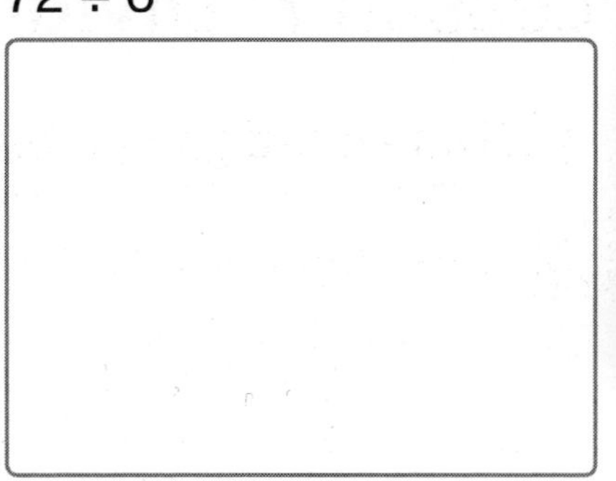

2 Check three of your division answers from Question **1** by working backwards and using multiplication to help.

Challenge **3** Toby, Olivia and Krishna are dividing 2-digit numbers by single-digit numbers.

Toby's answer is 15. Olivia's answer is 18. Krishna's answer is 14. What could their division questions be?

Krishna

Lesson 8: **Dividing a 2-digit number (4)**

- Divide a 2-digit number by a single-digit number
- Round up or down after division

You will need
- coloured pencils

Challenge 1

Shade the circles in different colours to help find each answer.

a ○○○○○○○○○○○○○○○○○○○○

How many 2s are in 20? ☐

b ○○○○○○○○○○○○○○○○○○○○
○○○○○ How many 5s are in 25? ☐

c ○○○○○○○○○○○○○○○○○○

How many 3s are in 18? ☐

Challenge 2

1 These word problems do not have numbers in them, but you should be able to tell what to do if there is a remainder. Write 'Round up' or 'Round down' for each problem.

Example: There are ________ biscuits to be put into packets. Each packet holds ________ biscuits. How many full packets can you make? Round down

a A baker is making cakes. Each cake tray has space for ________ cakes. The baker has made enough mixture to bake ________ cakes altogether. How many full cake trays will she have?

☐

b A class of ________ children is told to work in groups of ________.Some children may need to work in a smaller group. How many groups will there be?

☐

2 Solve each of these word problems. Decide whether to round the answer up or down to actually answer the problem.

a Tinaya has to take 5 ml of cough medicine every day. The bottle contains 67 ml of medicine. How many days' worth of medicine does Tinaya have?

b A farmer needs to build a fence 55 metres long. Fencing is sold in 3 metre reels. How many reels must the farmer buy?

Challenge 3

1 Ryan divides a mystery number by 2 and says that he has a remainder of 1. Jessica says that Ryan's mystery number must have been odd.

Is Jessica right? ☐ Explain your answer.

____

____

2 Ryan divides a mystery number by 5 and says that he has a remainder of 3. Jessica says that there are only two possible digits that Ryan's mystery number must end with.

What are the digits? ☐ or ☐ Explain how Jessica knows this.

____

____

____

____

Lesson 1: **Multiplication and division facts (3)**

Number

- Know multiplication facts up to 10 × 10 and the related division facts

Challenge 1

1 Write one multiplication and one division fact for each multiplication fact triangle.

a 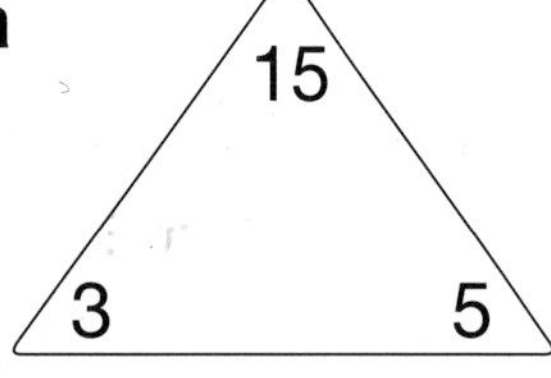

3 × 5 = 15
15 ÷ 3 = 5

b 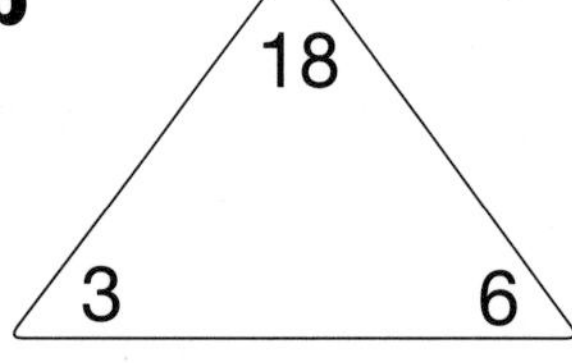

6 × 3 = 18
18 ÷ 6 = 3

c 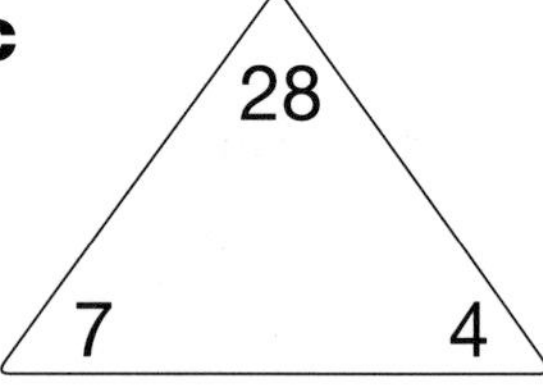

7 × 4 = 28
28 ÷ 7 = 4

2 Complete these blank multiplication triangles with facts you think you need to practise.

a 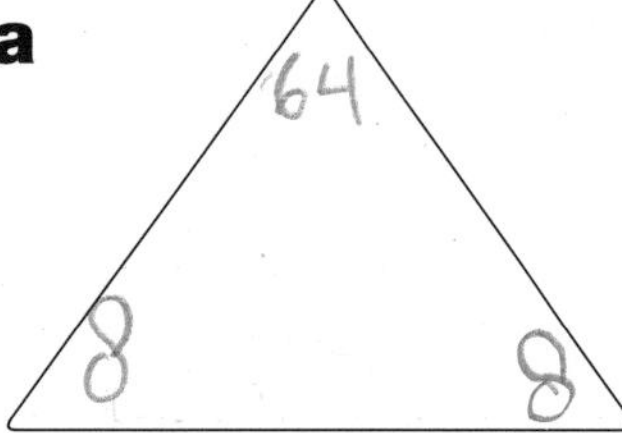

b 

c 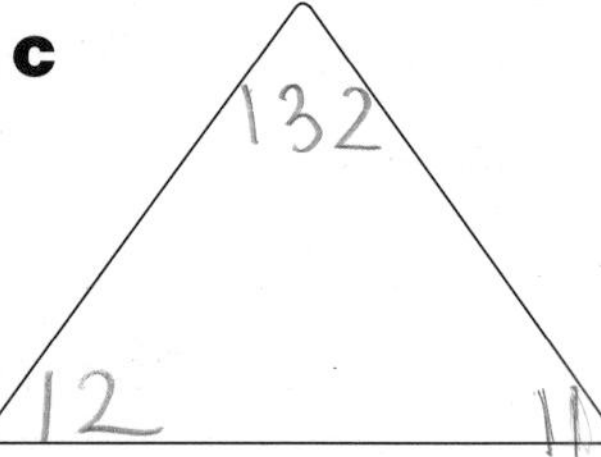

Challenge 2

1 There are several ways you could complete these multiplication fact triangles. Write two ways for each.

a 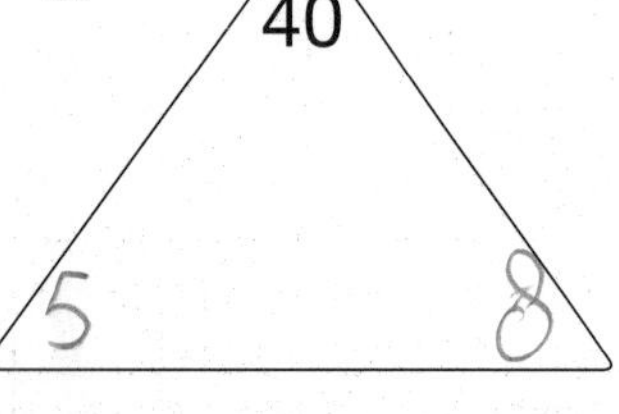

b 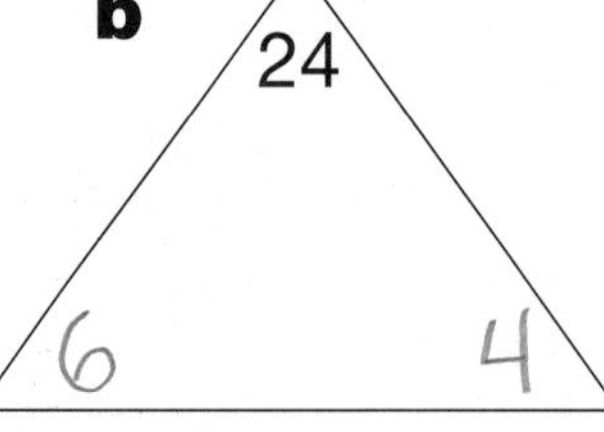

c 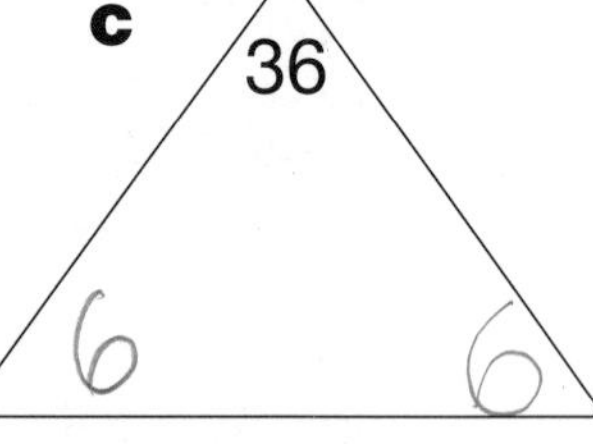

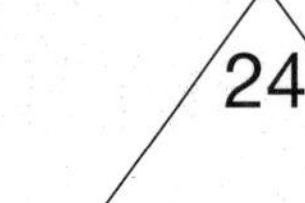

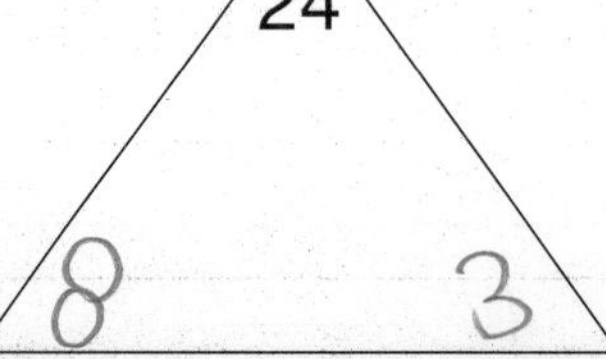

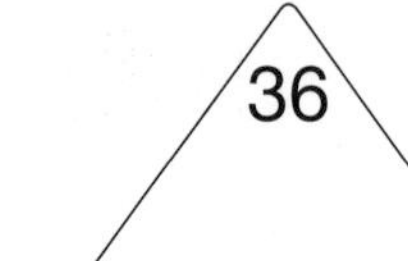

2 Write the numbers 2 to 10 in each of the circles below (in any order), then complete the calculations you have made.

(8) × 7 = 56	(12) × 9 = 108	(6) × 8 = 48
(7) × 6 = 42	(8) × 8 = 64	(12) × 6 = 72
(8) × 7 = 56	(8) × 5 = 40	(9) × 9 = 81

3 Write the numbers 2 to 10 in each of the circles below (in any order), then complete the calculations you have made.

24 ÷ (6) = 4	49 ÷ (9) = 7	36 ÷ (6) = 6
16 ÷ (8) = 2	45 ÷ (5) = 9	9 ÷ (3) = 3
64 ÷ (8) = 8	35 ÷ (7) = 5	100 ÷ (10) = 10

Challenge 3 These are parts of a full multiplication square (up to ×10). Complete the blank squares.

Example:

12	18	24
	21	

a

30	35	40	45

b

20		
24	28	32

c

28	32		
	36	42	48

d

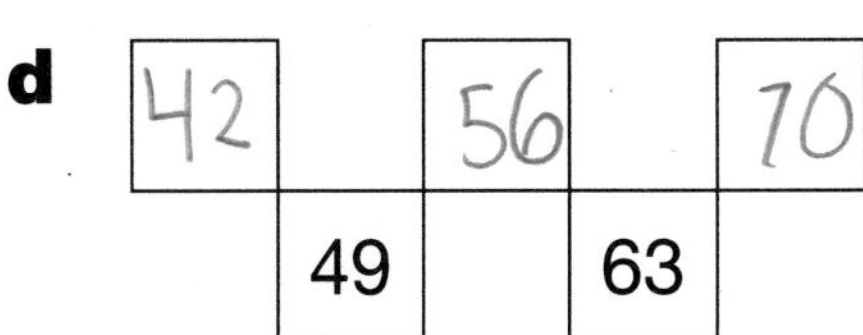

e

				64
45			72	
	60	70		90

Number

Lesson 2: Doubling and halving (2)

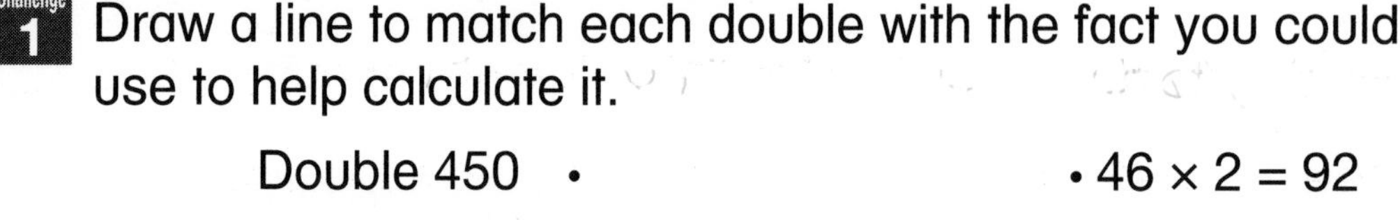

Challenge 1

Draw a line to match each double with the fact you could use to help calculate it.

Double 450 •	• 46 × 2 = 92
Double 210 •	• 48 × 2 = 96
Double 4800 •	• 21 × 2 = 42
Double 2300 •	• 45 × 2 = 90
Double 390 •	• 39 × 2 = 78
Double 4600 •	• 23 × 2 = 46

Challenge 2

1 Answer these questions.

a Double 34 = ☐ **b** Half of 90 = ☐

c Half of 4600 = ☐ **d** Double 39 = ☐

e Double 90 = ☐ **f** Double 3900 = ☐

2 Use partitioning to double or halve these 2-digit numbers.

Example:

56 doubled = [50 × 2] + [6 × 2]
= 100 + 12
= 112

56 halved = [50 ÷ 2] + [6 ÷ 2]
= 25 + 3
= 28

a 54 doubled
= ☐ + ☐
= ☐ + ☐
= ☐

b 67 doubled
= ☐ + ☐
= ☐ + ☐
= ☐

c 78 halved

= [ ] + [ ]

= [ ] + [ ]

= [ ]

d 84 halved

= [ ] + [ ]

= [ ] + [ ]

= [ ]

Challenge 3 Use partitioning to double and halve these 3-digit numbers.

Double each of your numbers by doubling the hundreds, the tens and the units, and then adding the totals together.

Halve the numbers by doing the opposite.

Example: 152 doubled [100 × 2] + [50 × 2] + [2 × 2]

= [200] + [100] + [4]

= [304]

a [267] doubled

= [ ] + [ ]

= [ ] + [ ]

= [ ]

b [516] doubled

= [ ] + [ ]

= [ ] + [ ]

= [ ]

c [586] halved

= [ ] + [ ]

= [ ] + [ ]

= [ ]

d [752] halved

= [ ] + [ ]

= [ ] + [ ]

= [ ]

Number

Lesson 3: **Multiplying a 2-digit number (5)**

- Multiply a 2-digit number by a single-digit number

Challenge 1

Solve each problem. Use the boxes to show your working.

a There are five chicks in a nest. Each chick eats three worms a day. How many worms do the adults need to bring every day?

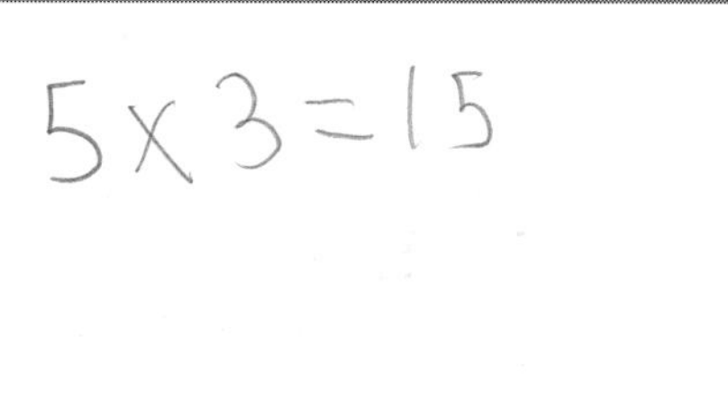

5 x 3 = 15

15 worms

b There are six bunches of bananas in a crate. Each bunch has four bananas on it. How many bananas are there altogether?

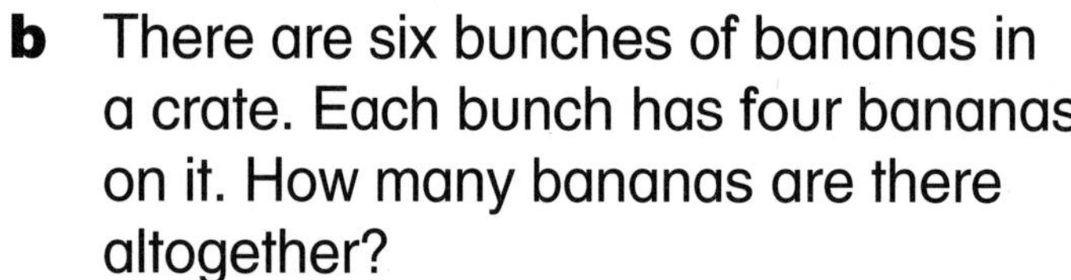

6 x 4 = 24

24 bananas

c It takes Isla eight minutes to walk around the school building. She walks around the building five times. How long does it take her?

8 x 5 = 40

40 minutes

Challenge 2

1 Circle the operation you would use to solve each problem.

a What is the difference in length between a piece of wood 52 cm long and a piece 9 cm long? + − × ÷

b How many 9 cm pieces of wood can you cut from a piece 52 cm long? + − × ÷

c Nine pieces of wood 52 cm long are put together end to end. How long will they be in centimetres? + − × ÷

d A piece of wood 9 cm long is glued onto the end of a piece 52 cm long. How long is the piece of wood now? + − × ÷

2 Solve these word problems. Show your working.

a Last week a mechanic changed all 4 tyres on 58 cars. How many tyres did he change?

58 × 4 = 216 — 216 tires

b There are 26 luggage spaces on a bus. Each space has room for three bags. How many bags fit altogether?

26 × 3 = 78 — 78 bags

c Nia saves $6 a week. How much money will she have after saving for 38 weeks?

38 × 6 = 228 — 228 dollars

Challenge 3 Each of these word problems is a two-step problem. Write down each step and then calculate the answer.

a There are nine trees in a field. Each tree has 34 birds in it. There is a loud noise and 100 birds fly away. How many birds are left?

34 × 9 = 306; 306 − 100 = 206 — 206 birds

b A shopkeeper sold seven rugs for $89 each. He then lost $
How much money did he have left?

89 × 7 = 623; 623 − 30 = 593 — 593 dollars

Lesson 4: **Dividing a 2-digit number (5)**

- Divide a 2-digit number by a single-digit number

Challenge 1 Solve each problem. Use the boxes to show your working.

a Eighteen camels are taking people and bags across the desert. Half of them have people on them. How many do not?

[ ] camels

b There are 42 children in the school choir. At practice, the chairs are put in rows of six. How many rows should there be?

[ ] rows

c 45 pencils are shared equally between nine children. How many pencils will they have each?

[ ] pencils

Challenge 2

1 Circle the operation you would use to solve each problem.

a What is the total of $76 and $4? + − × ÷

b $76 shared between four friends. + − × ÷

c Joe saves $4 a week. How much will he have in 76 weeks? + − × ÷

2 One of the problems in Question **1** was a division problem. What is the answer to it?

[ ]

3 Solve these word problems. Show your working.

a Some shelves each hold seven books. How many shelves are needed to hold 93 books?

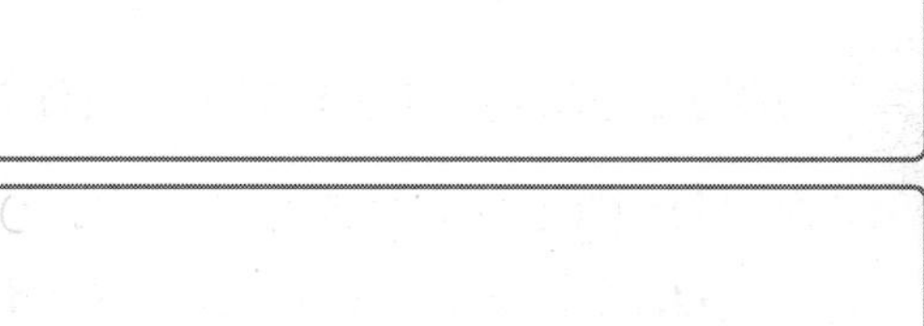

b There are 24 hours in a day. Krish spends $\frac{1}{3}$ of a day sleeping. How many hours does he sleep for?

c 81 ÷ 6   69 ÷ 4   56 ÷ 3
One of these calculations equals 18 r2. Which is it?

Challenge 3 Using only the digits on these number cards, make the following 'two-digit number divided by single-digit number' calculations.

1 2 3 4 5 6

a Make a division where there is a remainder of 1.

b Make a division where the answer is less than 10.

c Make a division where the answer is more than 20.

d Write a word problem where the answer has to be rounded up.

Lesson 5: **Multiplying and dividing 2-digit numbers**

- Multiply and divide a 2-digit number by a single-digit number

Challenge 1 Solve each problem.

a Spiders have eight legs.How many legs do three spiders have? 24 legs

b Kasey writes out each of her spelling words four times to learn them. She has 10 different words to learn.
How many words does Kasey write out? 40 words

c Maryam has 36 sweets. She splits them into six equal piles to share with her friends.
How many sweets will they have each? 6 sweets

d How many wheels are on nine bicycles? 18 wheels

Challenge 2 **1** Solve these word problems. Show your working.

Hint: Remember, if you divide and there is a remainder, you may need to round the answer up or down.

a A stall holder has 57 minutes until opening time. In this time, he needs to spend equal time doing three things:

- unpacking the fruit,
- displaying the fruit
- cleaning his stall.

How long should he spend on each job?

b A large amount of lemons are shared into 12 bags with eight lemons in each bag. How many lemons are there altogether?

12 × 8 = 96   96 lemons

c Apples are put in trays of six. There are 93 apples altogether. How many trays are needed?

16 apples

d Figs cost $6 per pack. The owner of a restaurant buys 17 packs. How much does she pay?

17 × 6 = 102   102 dollars

Challenge 3 Choose any two of the numbers from the grid and multiply or divide them.

2	14	30
25	3	12
10	28	4

a How many of the numbers between 1 and 10 can you make?

10 × 4 = 40   3×4=12   2×4= 8   3×2=6   7×7=49   10 × 3 = 30   10 × 2 = 20

b How many of the numbers between 11 and 20 can you make?

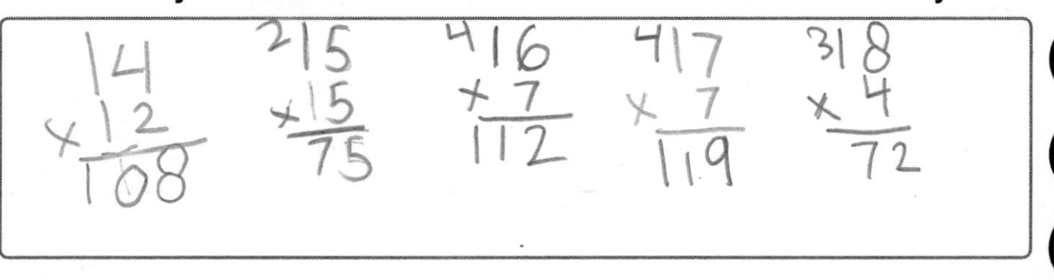

14 × 12 = 108   15 × 15 = 75   16 × 7 = 112   17 × 7 = 119   18 × 4 = 72

Number

Lesson 6: **Ratio and proportion (1)**

- Understand and write simple statements about proportion

You will need
- ruler

Challenge 1 Circle the correct word in each pair so that the statements are true.

a

The house is **half / twice** as tall as the tree.

The tree is **half / twice** as tall as the house.

b

The chicken is a **half / quarter** of the height of the zebra.

The elephant is **half / double** the height of the zebra.

Challenge 2

1 Nia has cut different lengths of grey and white paper. She takes one of each colour and compares them. Complete the statements underneath each pair of strips.

Example:

Two grey strips fit into one white strip.

The grey strip is $\frac{1}{2}$ of the length of the white strip.

a

☐ grey strips fit into one white strip.

The grey strip is ☐ of the length of the white strip.

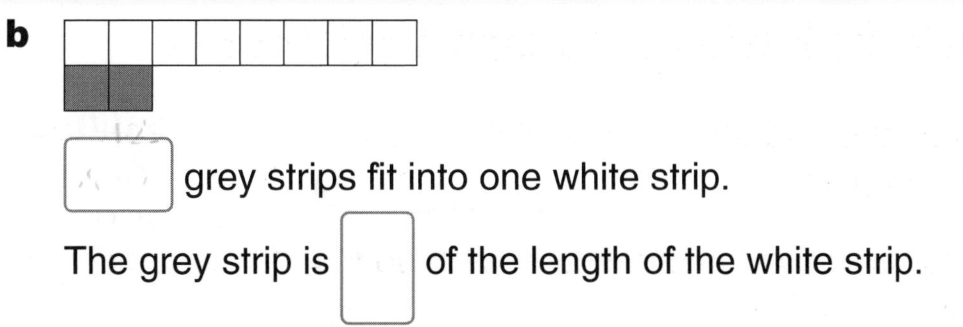

b ☐ grey strips fit into one white strip.

The grey strip is ☐ of the length of the white strip.

2 Five children have different-sized chocolate bars. They each eat a number of squares of their bar.

a Complete the table to show how much each person has eaten as a proportion of the whole bar.

Name	Number of squares in the whole bar	Number of squares eaten	Proportion of the bar eaten
Asim	10	5	$\frac{5}{10}$ or $\frac{1}{2}$
Ben	4	1	
Crista	12	6	
Dan	9	3	
Emma	20	2	

b Complete these statements about the table.

__________ ate one third of the squares in their bar.

__________ ate one tenth of their bar. __________ and

__________ ate a different number of squares but still ate the same proportion of their chocolate bar.

Challenge 3

1 A song is 36 minutes long. A second song is $\frac{1}{4}$ as long. How long is the second song? ☐ minutes long

2 A room is 12 metres long. 6 metres is covered in carpet. What proportion of the room is covered in carpet?

☐ of the room is covered in carpet

Number

Lesson 7: **Ratio and proportion (2)**

- Use simple fractions to show and work out proportion

You will need
- ruler
- sheet of paper

Challenge 1

Measure each of these images and then draw them at $\frac{1}{2}$ their original height and width on a sheet of paper.

a

b

c

d

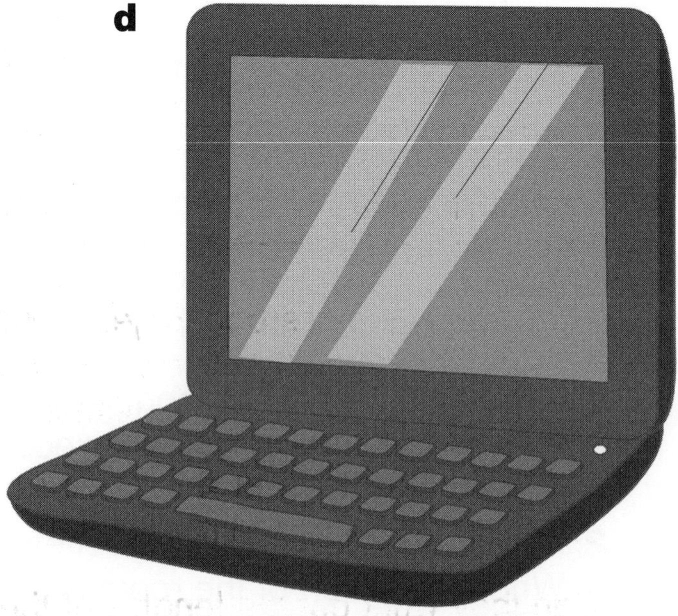

1 a A diamond is 7 mm wide in a photograph.
The photograph is labelled 'half actual width'.

How wide is the diamond in real life? ☐ mm

b A flower is 6 cm tall in a diagram.
The diagram is labelled 'quarter actual height'.

How tall is the flower in real life? ☐ cm

2 Ahmed is using chalk to draw a plan of his classroom, on the playground. To draw it in proportion, he decides to draw the plan $\frac{1}{2}$ of the actual length and width.

Complete the table to show the size of Ahmed's plan.

	Real-life measurement	**Size on Ahmed's drawing**
Length of classroom	8 m	4 m
Width of classroom	6 m	
Table length	1 m	
Whiteboard width	3 m	
Maths book length	26 cm	
Window height	58 cm	
Pencil length	16 cm	

Measure some classroom objects and then divide the measurements by 10 to find out what size they should be when you draw them at a $\frac{1}{10}$ of their actual height or width.

- Draw the objects on a sheet of paper and pass your sketches to a friend to measure.
- Can they work out the lengths of the objects in real life by multiplying the measurements by 10?

Lesson 8: **Ratio and proportion (3)**

- Begin to understand and use ratio to describe simple relationships

You will need
- coloured pencils

Challenge 1

1 Complete each sentence.

a ■□□□

For every 1 grey square, there are ☐ white squares.

b ■■■□□

For every ☐ grey squares, there are ☐ white squares.

c ■■□

For every ☐ grey squares, there is ☐ white square.

2 Shade the squares to match the descriptions.

a □□□□□

For every 1 white square, there are 4 shaded squares.

b □□□□□□□□□□

For every 3 white squares, there are 7 shaded squares.

c □□□

For every 1 white square, there are 2 shaded squares.

Challenge 2

1 Use two different colours to shade each set of circles and show each ratio.

a A ratio of 1 to 3 ○○○○

b A ratio of 3 to 7 ○○○○○○○○○○

c A ratio of 2 to 6 ○○○○○○○○

d A ratio of 2 to 3 ○○○○○

e A ratio of 3 to 5 ○○○○○○○○

2 These diagrams show the number of girls and boys in different groups. What is the ratio of girls to boys in each group?

a There are ☐ girls for every ☐ boy.

The ratio is ☐ to ☐

b There are ☐ girls for every ☐ boys. The ratio is ☐ to ☐

c There are ☐ girls for every ☐ boys. The ratio is ☐ to ☐

d There are ☐ girls for every ☐ boys.The ratio is ☐ to ☐

3 If the ratio of girls to boys in a group is 1 to 6, how many people do you think are in the group? ☐

Challenge **3** Isaac has a bag of coloured counters. It contains 3 blue counters, 5 red counters, 1 green counter and 2 yellow counters.

a What is the ratio of blue counters to yellow counters? ☐

b What is the ratio of green counters to red counters? ☐

c What fraction of the bag are red counters? ☐

d What fraction of the bag are blue counters? ☐

Lesson 1: **Different polygons**

- Identify, describe, visualise, draw and classify a variety of 2D shapes and find real-life examples of them

You will need
- ruler

Challenge 1

1 Name these polygons.

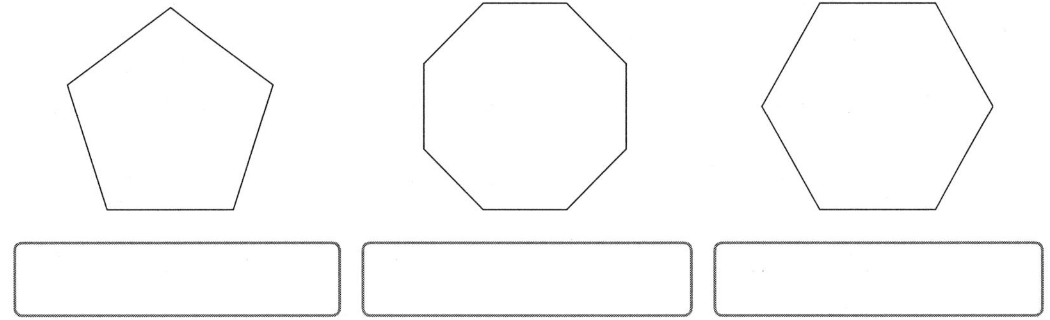

2 Why are these shapes regular?

Challenge 2

1 Here are three heptagons.

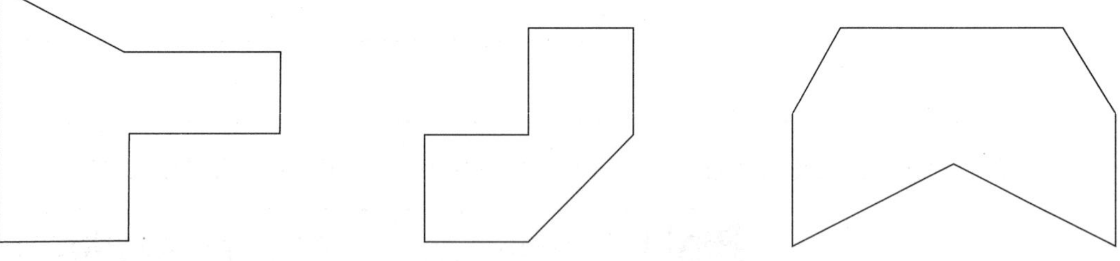

a Write two ways in which they are similar.

b Write two ways in which they are different.

2 Draw two different quadrilaterals below.

a Write three ways in which they are similar.

___

___

___

b Write three ways in which they are different.

___

___

___

Challenge 3 Draw a heptagon in each section of this Carroll diagram.

	Right angles	**No right angles**
Symmetrical		
Not symmetrical		

Geometry

Lesson 2: Quadrilaterals

- Identify, describe, visualise, draw and classify a variety of quadrilaterals and find real-life examples of them

You will need
- ruler

1 Name these quadrilaterals.

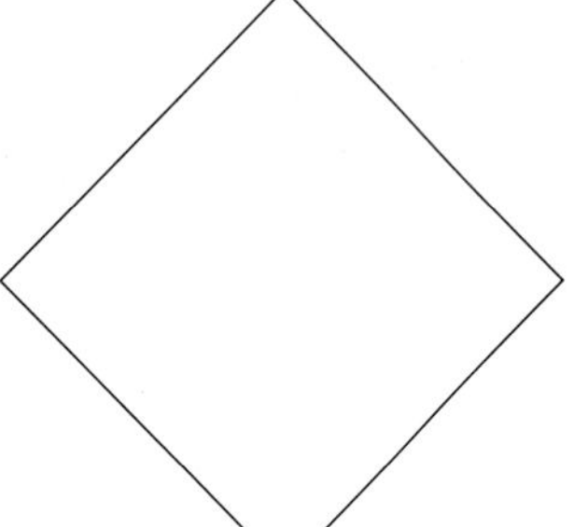

_______________ _______________

2 Explain why a square is a rectangle.

____

____

1 Draw an irregular quadrilateral below.

Write its properties, stating why it is irregular.

____

____

____

2 Draw two different trapeziums.

Describe their properties.

____

____

____

Challenge **3** Draw a quadrilateral in each section of this Carroll diagram.

	Parallel sides	**No parallel sides**
Right angles		
No right angles		

Lesson 3: **Classifying polygons**

- Identify, describe, visualise and draw a variety of polygons and classify them

You will need
- ruler

1 Draw two shapes in this Carroll diagram.

Regular	Not regular

2 Label this Carroll diagram.

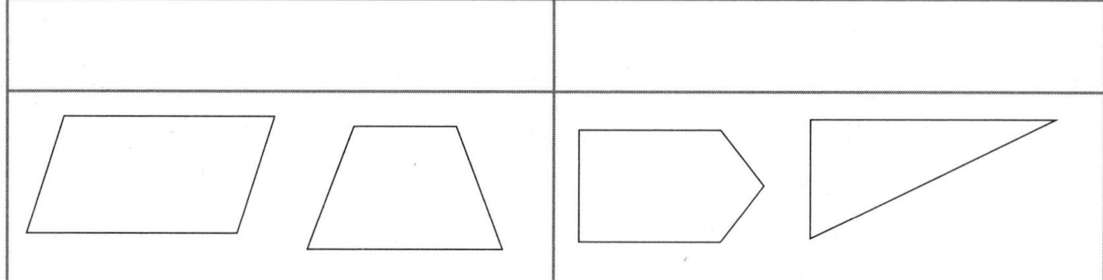

1 a Label the ovals in this Venn diagram.

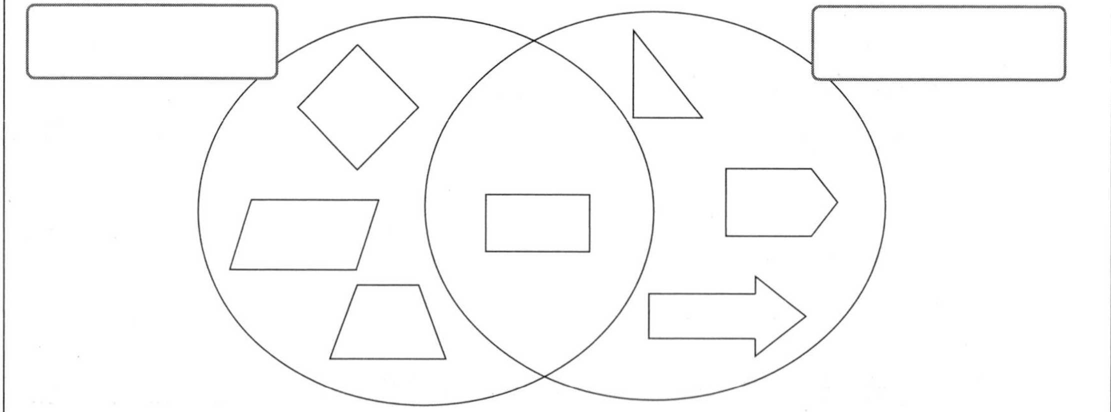

b Draw a shape that would be placed outside of the two ovals in the Venn diagram. Explain why it does not fit in any of the three regions formed by the intersecting ovals.

____

____

Student's Book page 75

2 Draw a different polygon in each section of this Carroll diagram.

	Parallel sides	No parallel sides
Quadrilaterals		
Not quadrilaterals		

Challenge 3 For each statement, write whether it is sometimes, always or never true. Explain your answer, using drawings if you wish.

a 'Regular shapes are symmetrical.' ______________

b 'Shapes can have right angles.' ______________

c 'Irregular shapes are not symmetrical.' ______________

Lesson 4: **Drawing polygons**

- Identify, describe, visualise and draw a variety of polygons
- Identify 2D shapes in drawings and pictures

You will need
- ruler

Challenge 1

1 Draw a regular quadrilateral.

2 Draw an irregular quadrilateral.

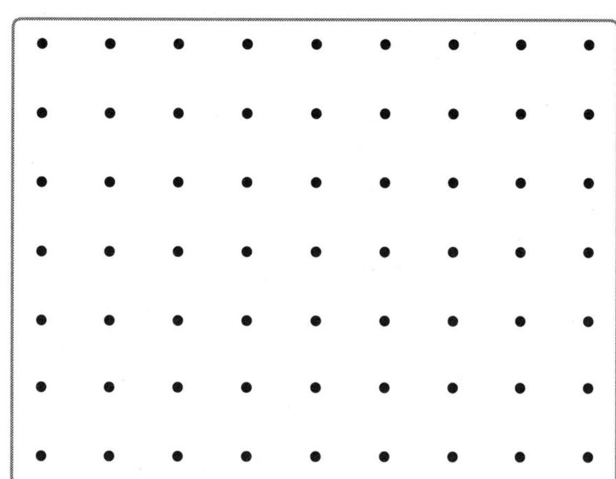

Challenge 2

1 a Add two lines to these three to draw a polygon.

b What is the name of the shape? ______________________

2 a Add two lines to these four to draw a polygon.

b What is the name of the shape? ______________________

3 a Draw two different polygons.

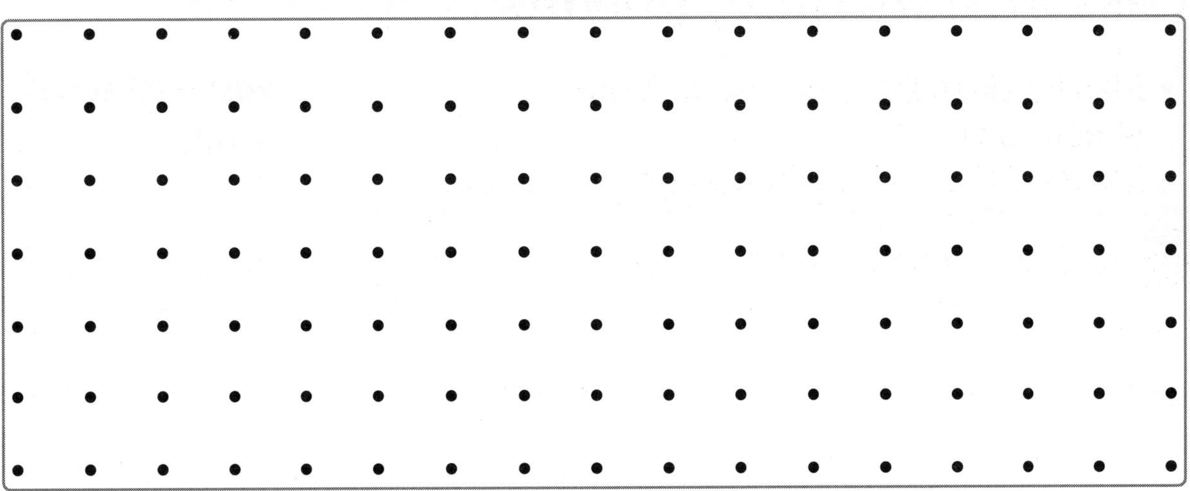

b Write one way in which they are similar and one way in which they are different.

____

____

1 Explain why you cannot add a line to these lines, to draw a quadrilateral.

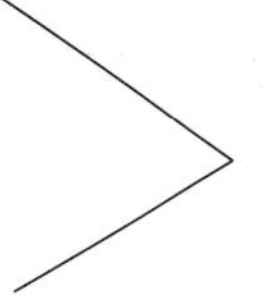

____

____

____

2 If you drew two more lines to the shape in Question **1**, what shape could you make?

____

Draw the shape in the box.

Lesson 5: **Identifying lines of symmetry**

- Identify lines of symmetry in 2D shapes and in the environment

You will need
- ruler

Challenge 1 Draw all the lines of symmetry on these shapes.

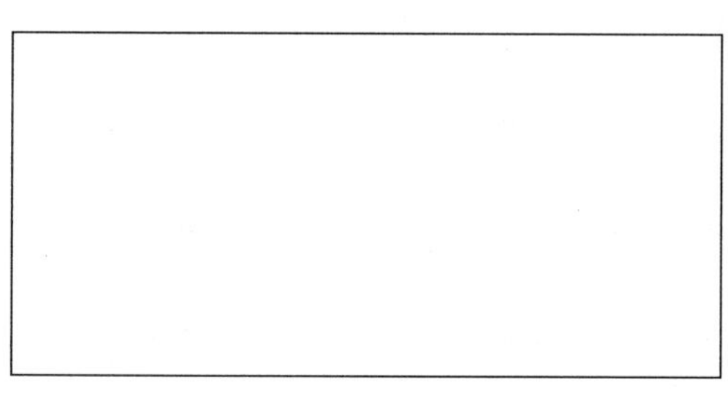

Challenge 2

1 Inside each shape write the number of lines of symmetry it has.

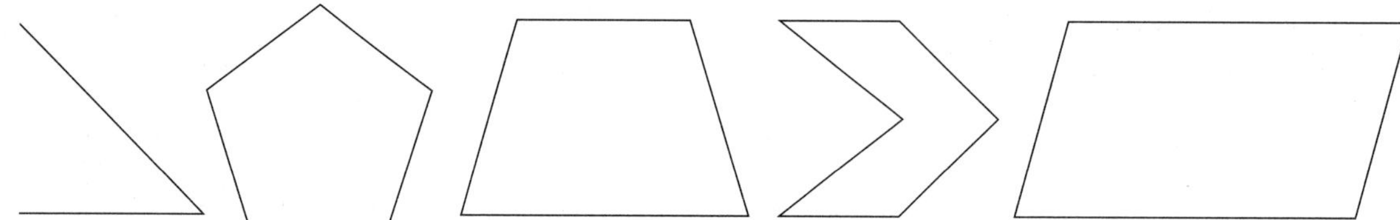

2 Explain why this shape is not symmetrical.

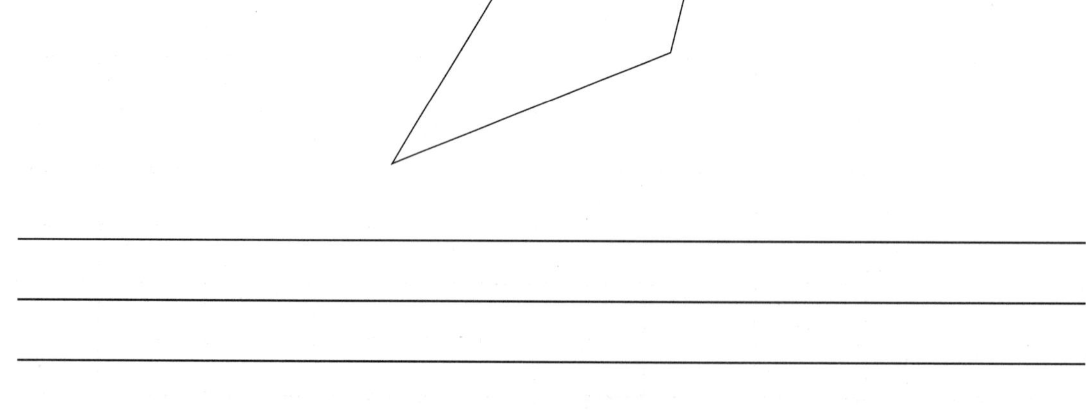

____

____

____

____

3 In the box below, draw a trapezium and a kite that each have one line of symmetry.

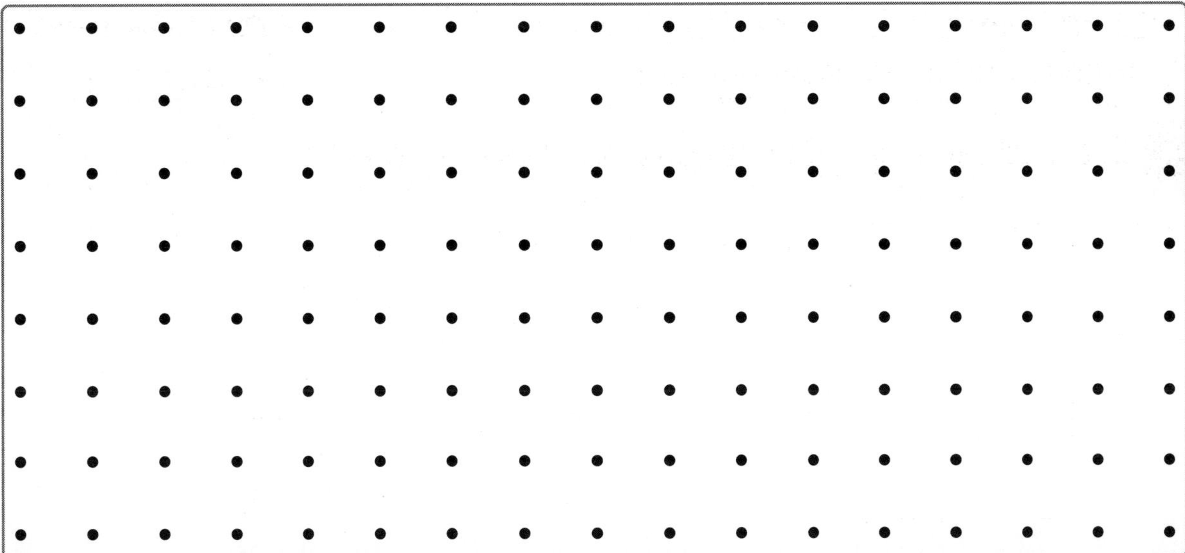

Challenge **3** Draw a shape made up from six squares that has two lines of symmetry.

Geometry

Lesson 6: **Completing symmetrical figures and patterns**

- Complete symmetrical figures and patterns

You will need
- ruler
- mirror

Challenge 1

Place your mirror on the mirror line. Write the shapes you can see.

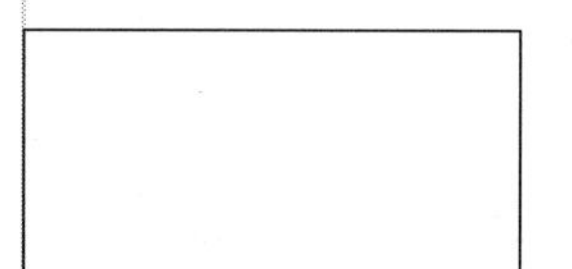

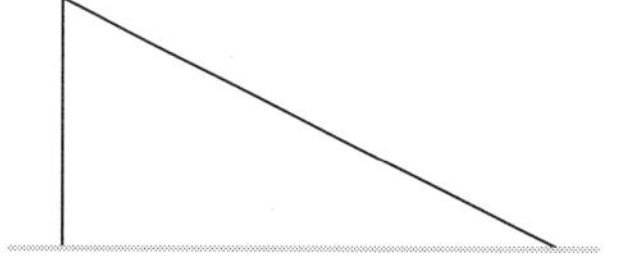

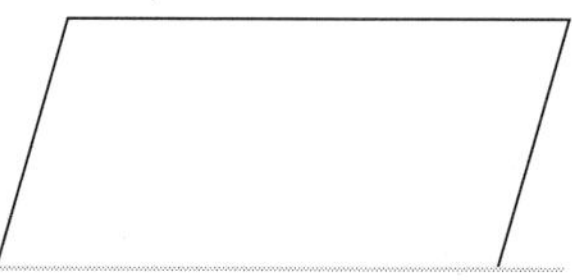

____________________ ____________________ ____________________

Challenge 2

1 Reflect and draw each shape across the mirror line. Name the shapes you have made.

a shape ______________________________

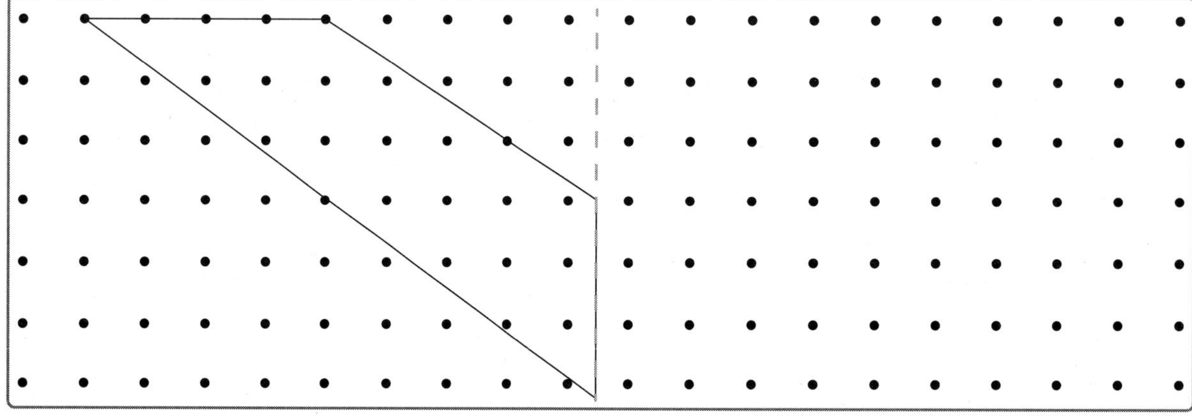

b shape ______________________________

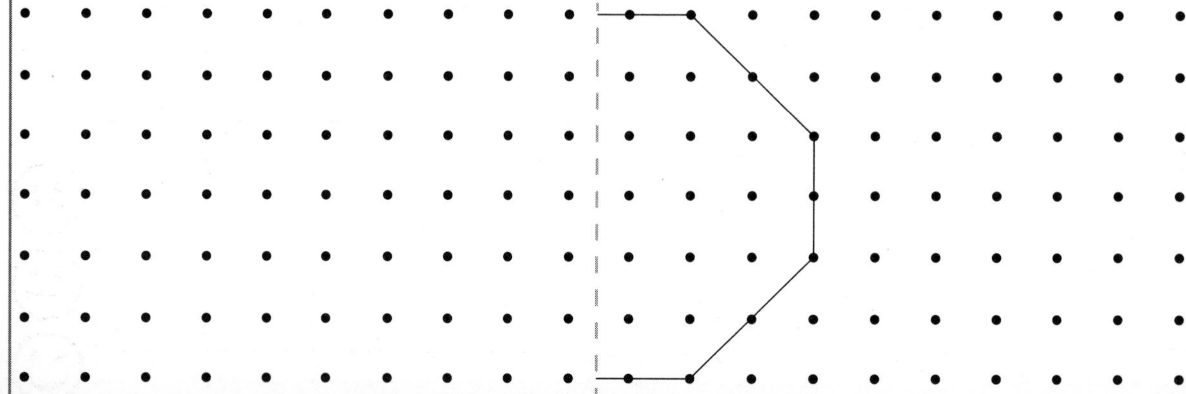

2 These are halves of some shapes. Draw the whole shapes. What shapes have you drawn? Label each one.

a

b

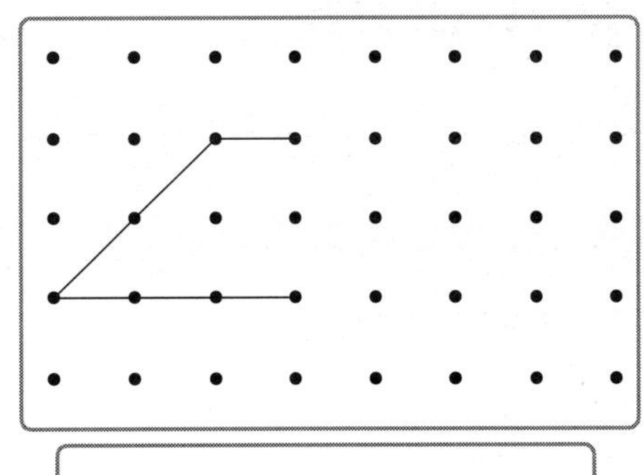

c

d

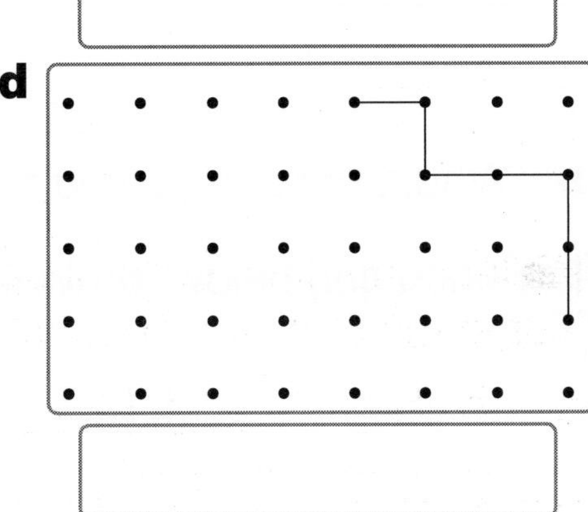

Challenge **3** Design a pattern on one side of the mirror line. Complete it on the other side. Make sure it is symmetrical.

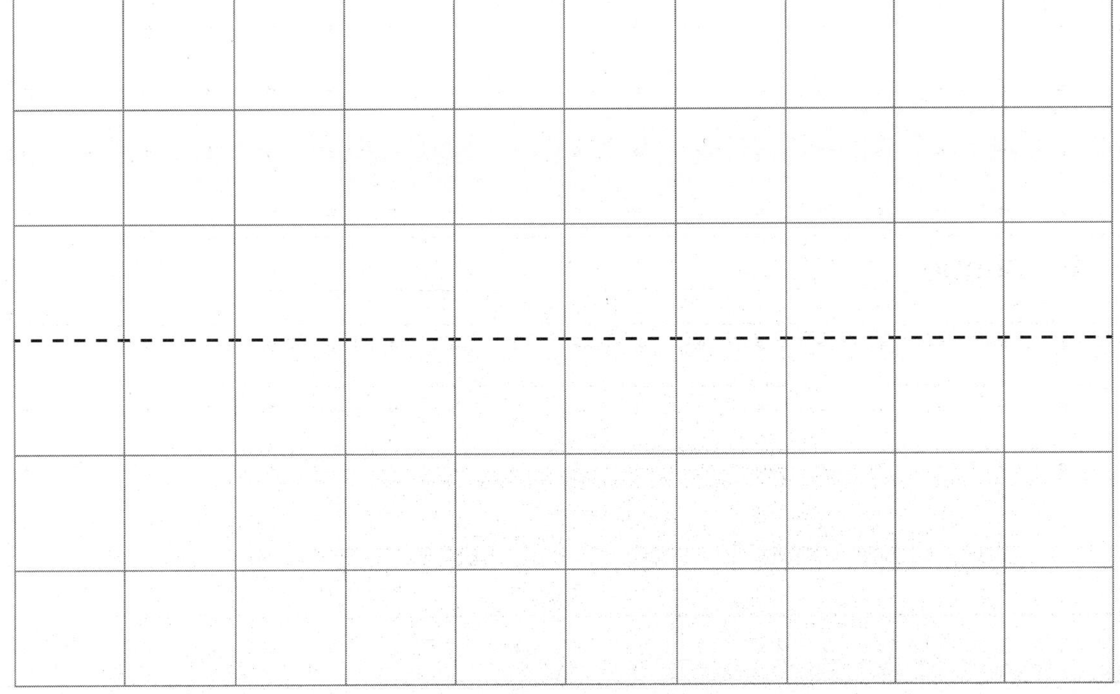

Geometry

Lesson 7: **Reflecting along a line of symmetry**

- Reflect 2D shapes and patterns along a line of symmetry

You will need
- ruler

1 a Complete this pattern so that it is symmetrical.

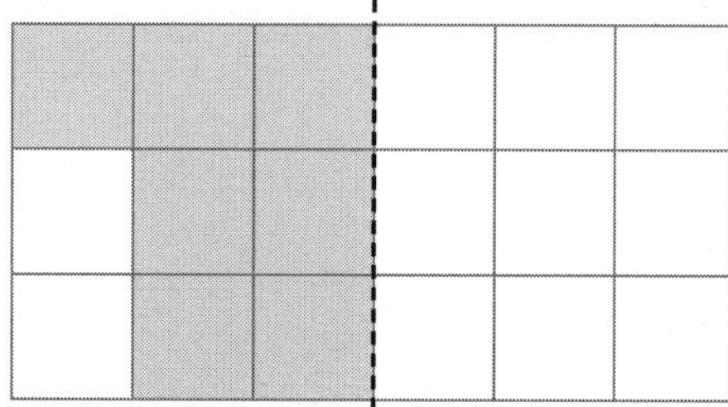

b What shape have you made? ______________________

1 For each grid below, draw the reflected images of the dots.

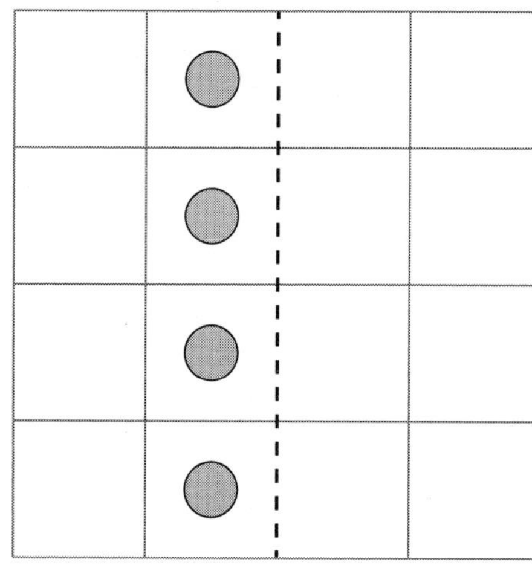

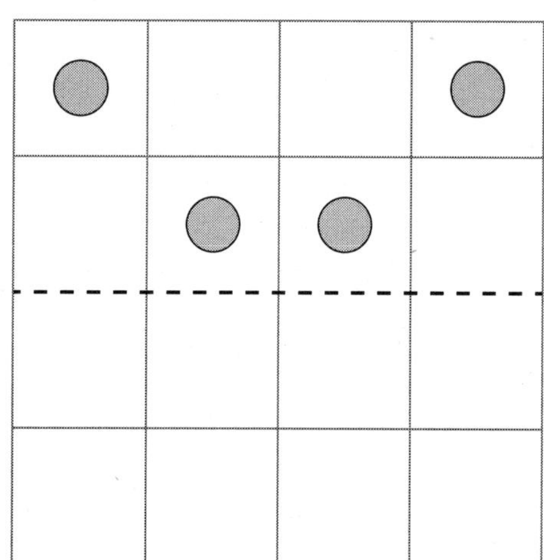

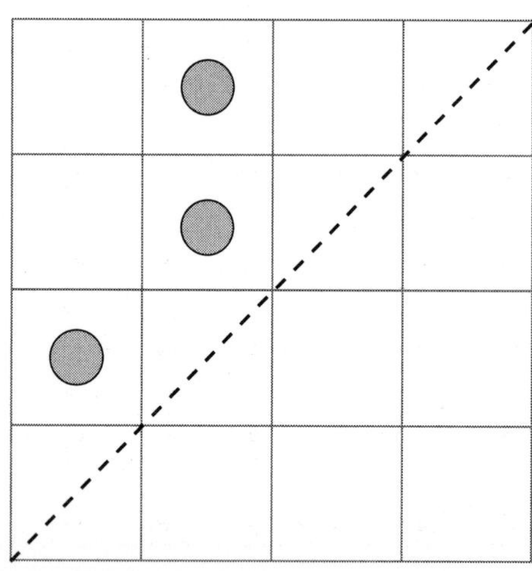

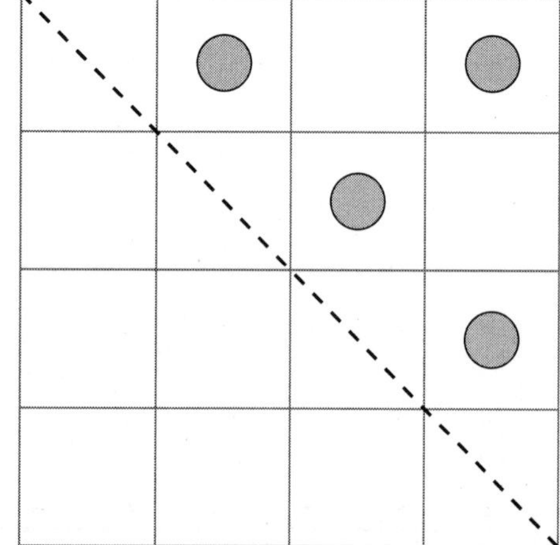

2 Reflect these shapes across the mirror line.

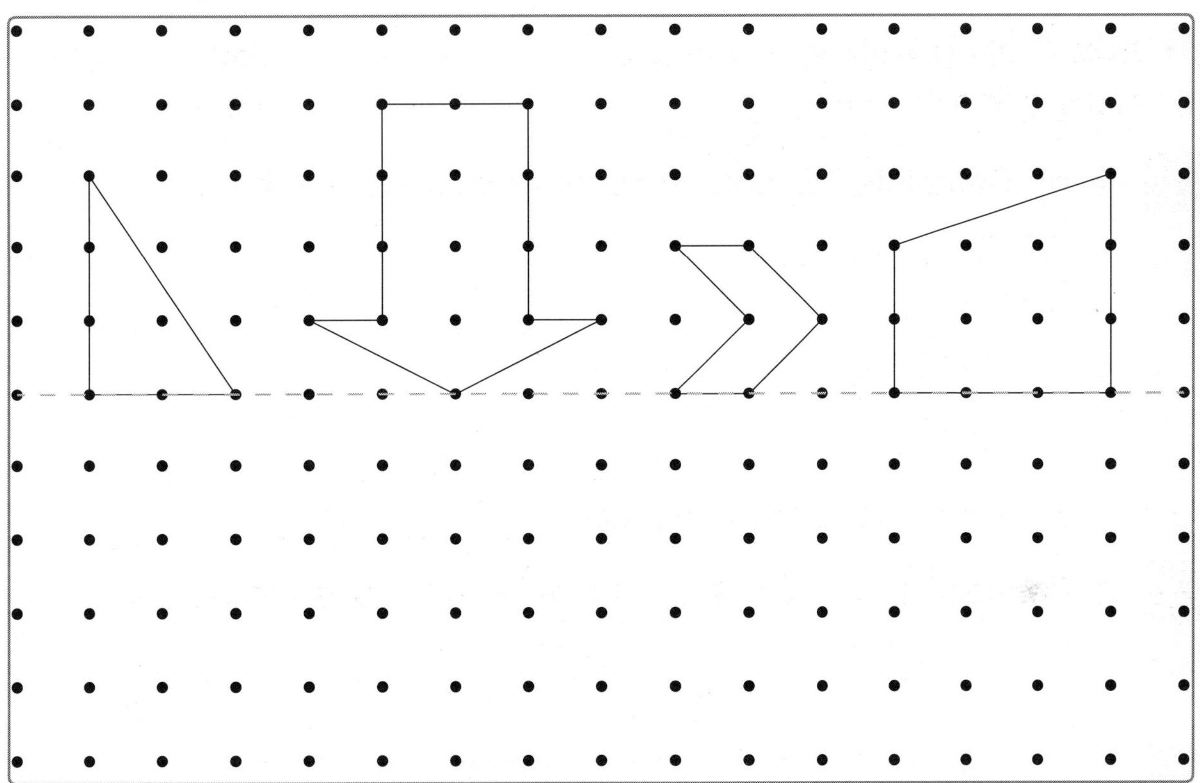

Challenge **3** Reflect this shape across the mirror line.
Use a mirror to check you are correct.

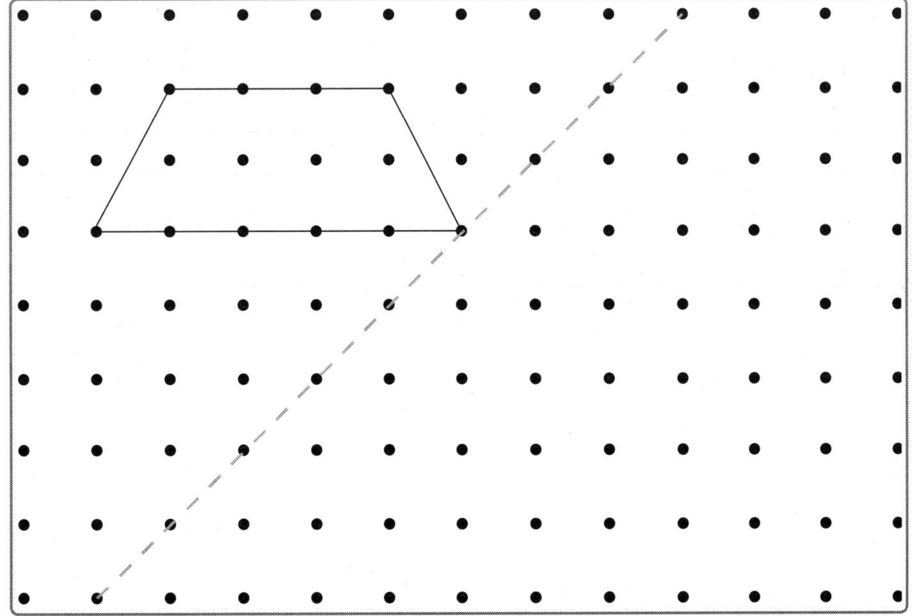

Geometry

Lesson 8: **Repeated reflection to make patterns**

- Repeatedly reflect 2D shapes and patterns along a line of symmetry

You will need
- ruler

Challenge 1

1 Complete this sentence.
A reflection is a shape as it would be seen in a ______________.

2 Reflect this pentagon across the mirror line.

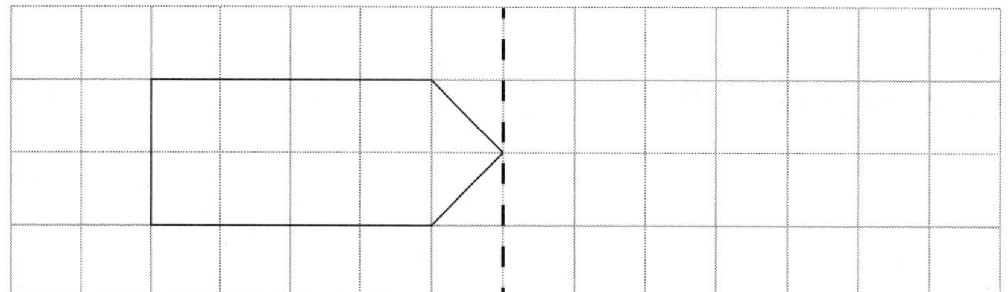

Challenge 2

1 Draw the next two shapes in this reflection sequence.

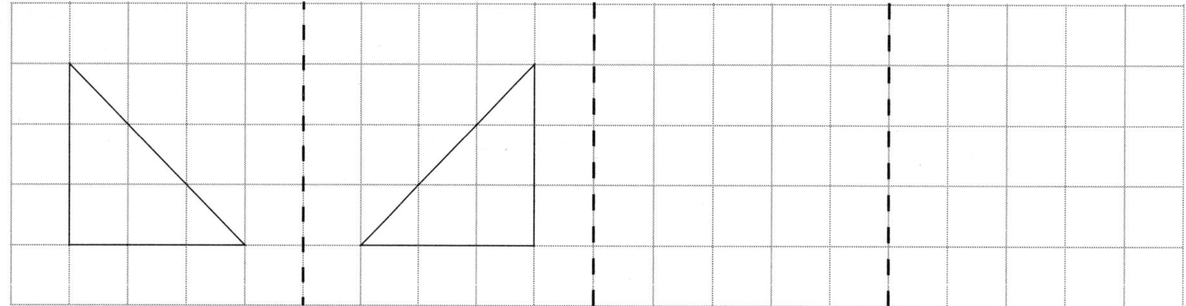

2 What do you think the 10th and 11th shapes will be?
Draw them below.

10th shape  11th shape 

3 Explain why you drew these shapes.

____

____

____

____

____

____

1 Draw a shape and reflect it three times.

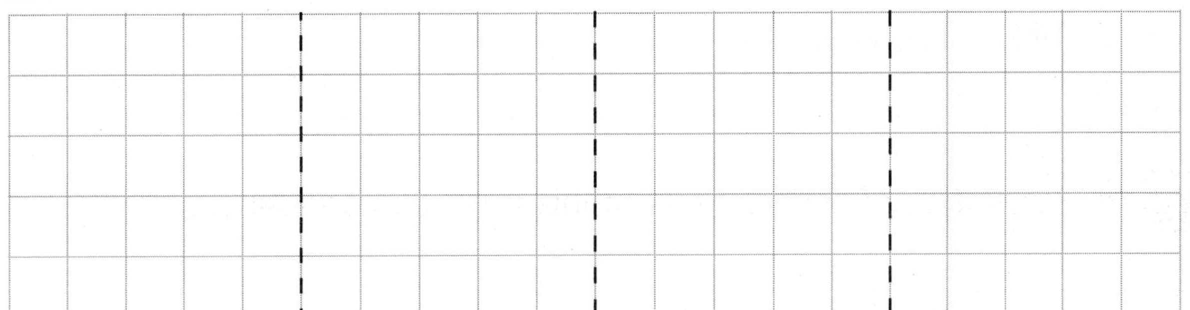

2 Draw another shape and reflect it three times.

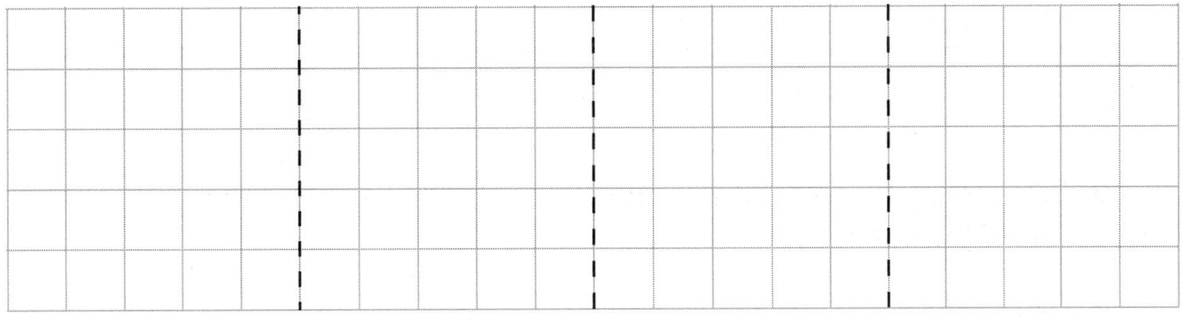

Geometry

Lesson 1: Identifying 3D shapes

- Identify and describe a range of 3D shapes
- Identify similarities and differences between 3D shapes

Challenge 1

1 Name these shapes.

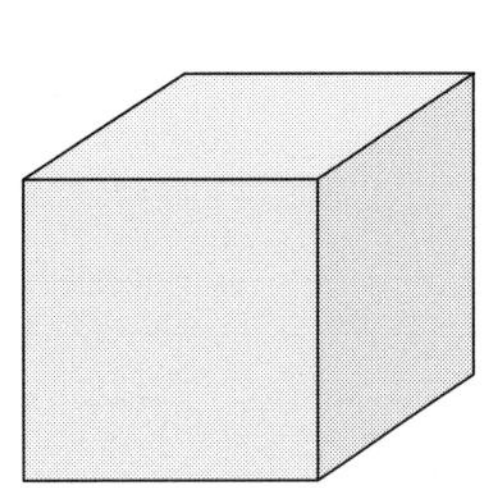 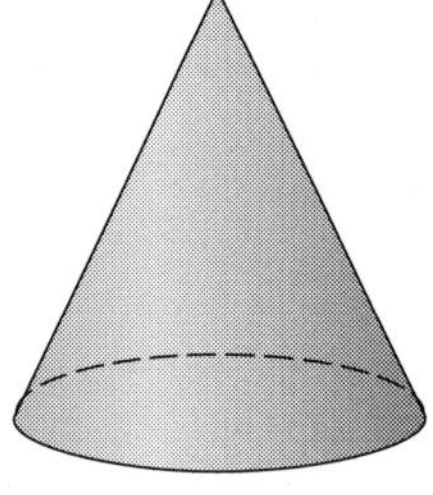 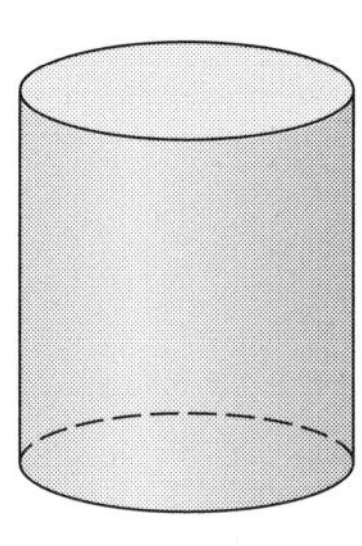 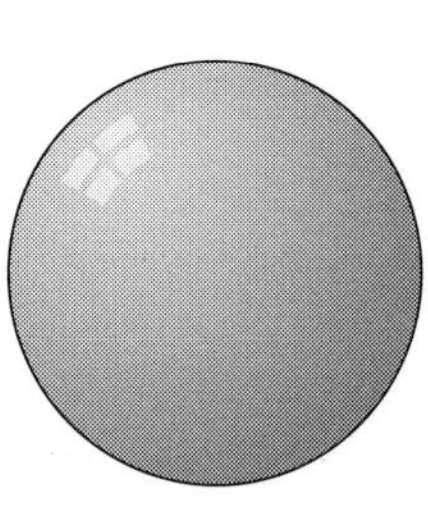

______ ______ ______ ______

2 Tick the polyhedra.

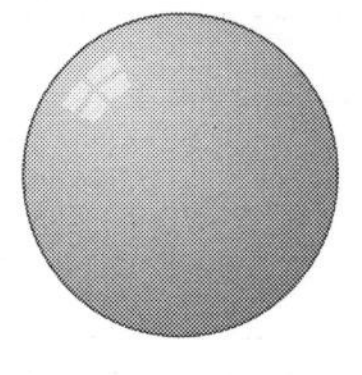 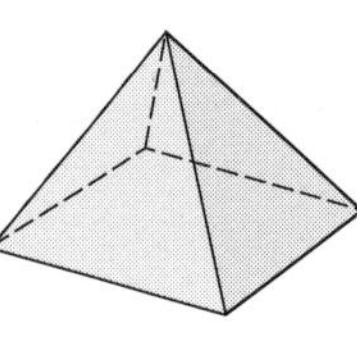 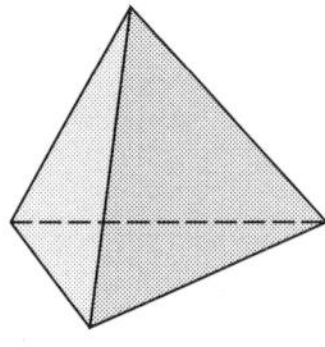 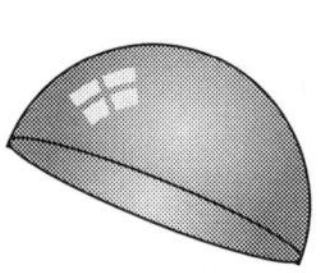 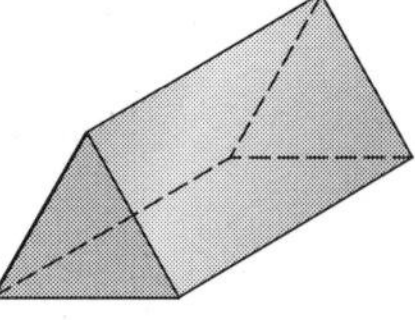

Challenge 2

1 The shape below is a face from a 3D shape.
Which 3D shapes could it be?

______

______

2 Why is a cone not a polyhedron?

______

______

______

3 List the properties of these shapes. Don't forget to include whether or not they are prisms or pyramids.

a Square-based pyramid ______________________________

____

____

____

b Tetrahedron______________________________

____

____

____

c Hexagonal prism______________________________

____

____

____

d Cylinder______________________________

____

____

____

Challenge 3

1 I have 6 faces, 4 are rectangular, 12 edges and 8 vertices. I am a prism. What shape am I?______________________________

2 Make up your own clues like this for a 3D shape of your choice.

____

____

____

____

____

____

____

Lesson 2: Recognising 3D shapes

- Recognise a wider range of 3D shapes in different orientations

Challenge 1

1 Name these shapes.

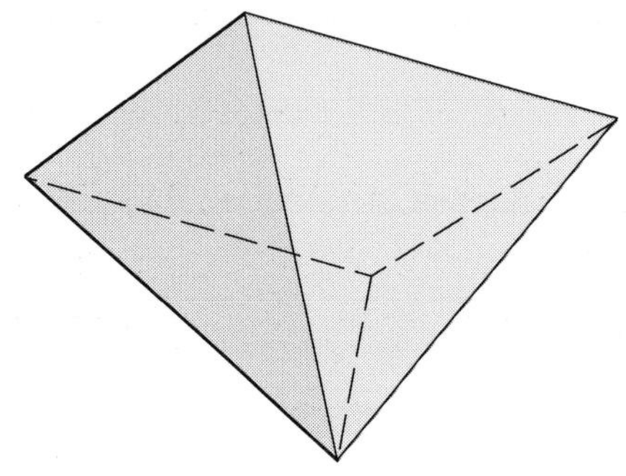

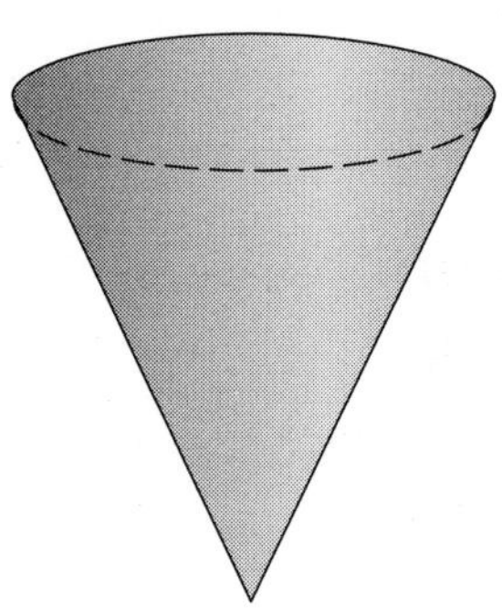

_______________ _______________

2 Look at the two shapes in Question **1**.

a How are they the same?

____

____

____

b How are they different?

____

____

____

Challenge 2

1 How can you identify a prism?

____

____

2 How can you identify a pyramid?

____

____

3 Why is a pentagonal pyramid always a pentagonal pyramid, no matter where it is positioned?

____

____

____

____

4 Look around the classroom, or outside, for examples of 3D shapes. Sketch as many different examples as you can see. Try and look for shapes in unusual orientations or positions.

Challenge 3 3D shapes are used in many aspects of everyday life, for example, in packaging. Think of three more examples where 3D shapes are commonly used. Write about how they are used and why you think that particular 3D shape is used.

____

____

____

____

____

____

Geometry

Lesson 3: **Classifying 3D shapes**

- Classify a range of different 3D shapes

Challenge 1

1 Draw two shapes in this Carroll diagram.

Polyhedron	**Not polyhedron**

2 Label this Carroll diagram.

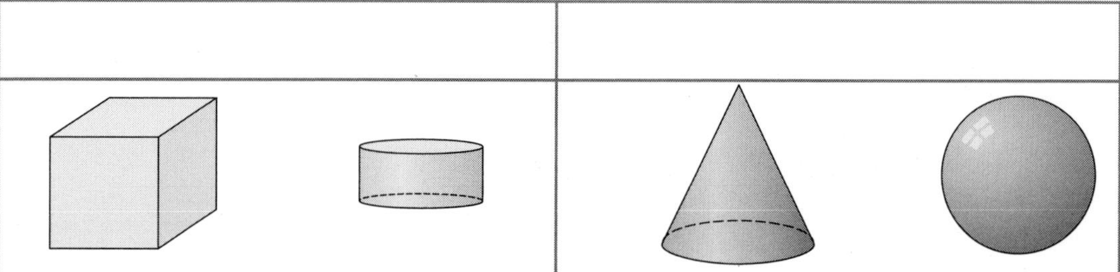

Challenge 2

1 Draw a 3D shape in each section of this Carroll diagram.

	Prism	**Not prism**
Polyhedron		
Not polyhedron		

2 Write the names of two 3D shapes that have at least one regular 2D shape face.

____

____

Challenge 3 For each statement, write whether it is sometimes, always or never true. Explain your answer, using drawings if you wish.

a 'Pyramids have one apex.' ______________

b 'Non-polyhedrons are not prisms.' ______________

c 'Irregular shapes are not symmetrical.' ______________

Lesson 4: **Nets**

- Visualise 3D objects from 2D nets and make nets of 3D shapes

You will need
- ruler

Challenge 1

1 Is this the net of a cube?

Explain your answer.

____

____

2 Add a square to make this into the net of a cube.

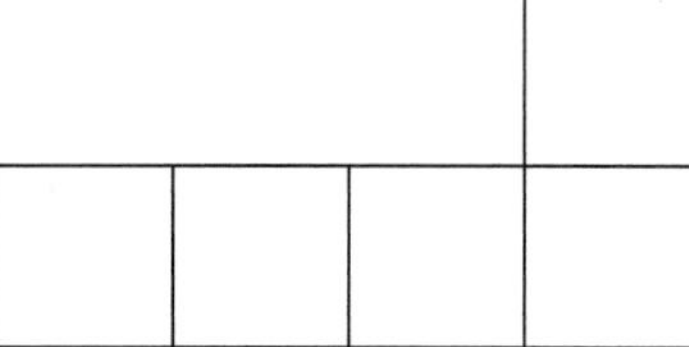

1 How is the net of a cuboid the same as the net of a cube?

____

How is it different?

____

2 Finish this net.

What 3D shape will it make?

____

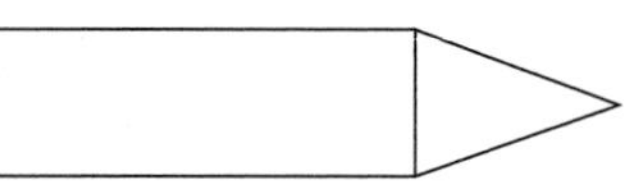

3 This is part of a net.

What 3D shape will it make?

____

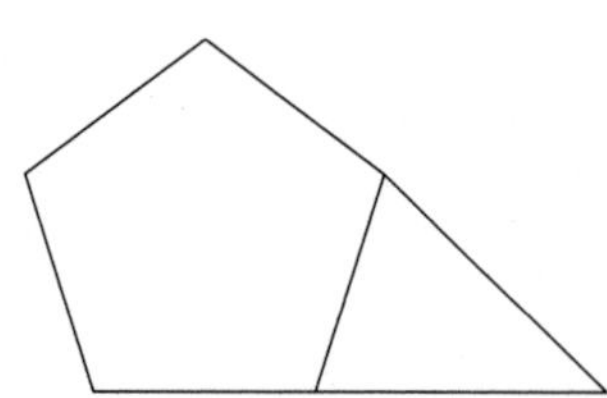

4 What 3D shape can you make with four parallelograms?

____

Challenge 3 What 3D shape has two regular hexagonal faces? Draw the net of the shape and the shape itself.

Geometry

Lesson 1: **Recognising and describing positions**

- Describe and identify positions on a grid

Challenge 1

Look at this grid.

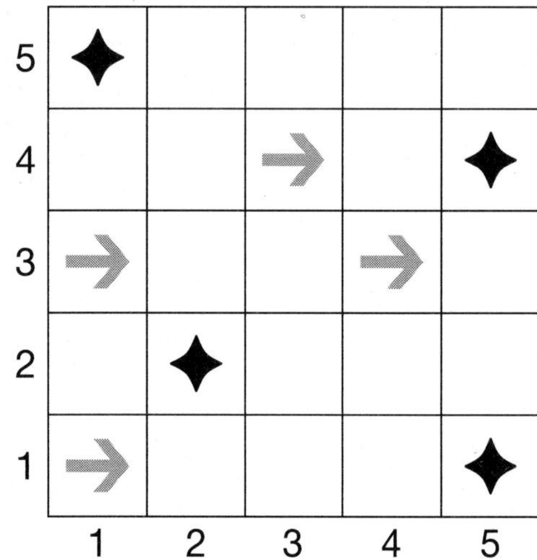

a List the co-ordinates for the stars.

b List the co-ordinates for the arrows.

Challenge 2

1 Look at this grid.

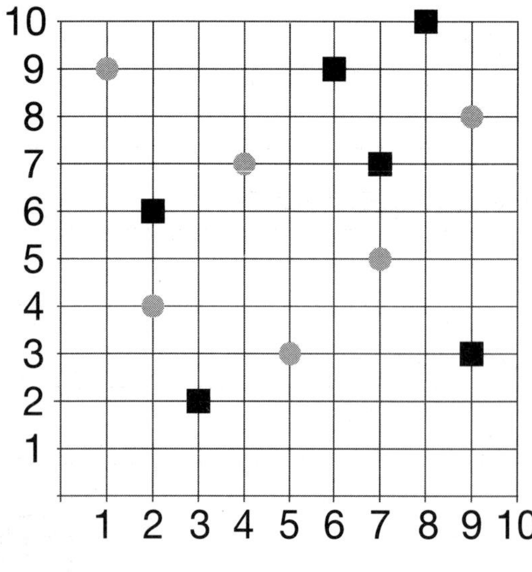

a List the co-ordinates for the circles.

b List the co-ordinates for the squares.

2 a Look at Question **1**. Draw 10 small shapes of your own on the grid below. You decide where to put them.

b List the co-ordinates for your shapes.

Shape	Co-ordinates

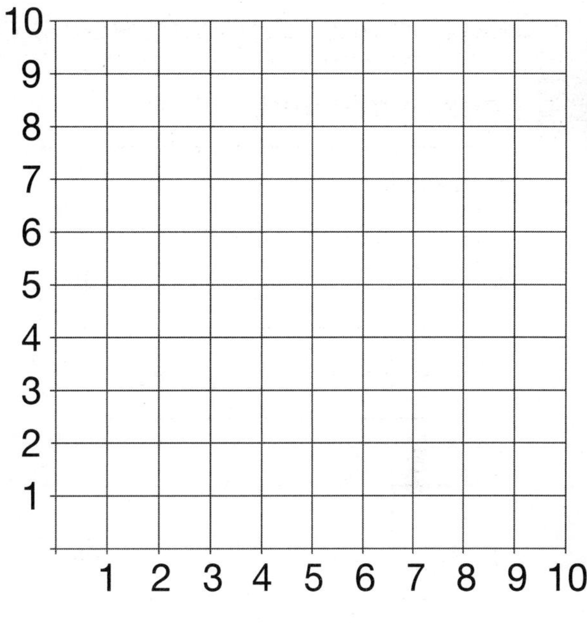

Challenge 3 Draw these three shapes onto the grid and write the co-ordinates of the vertices of each shape.

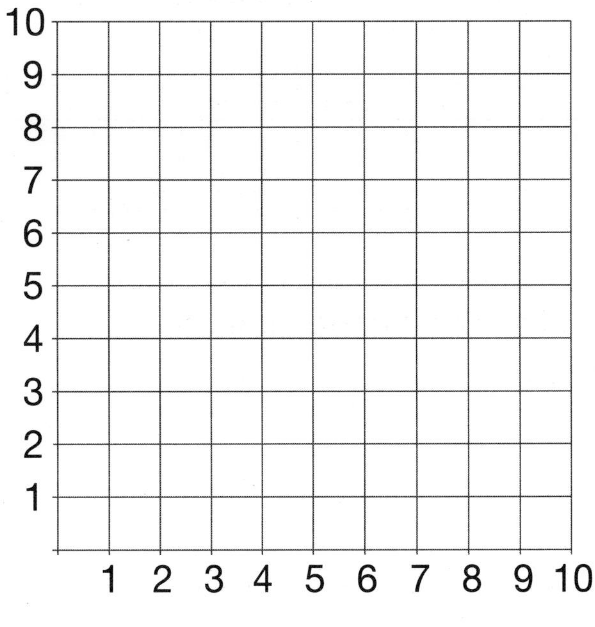

a square

b irregular pentagon

c trapezium

Lesson 2: **Recognising and describing directions**

- Give directions to follow a given path

Challenge 1

Move your finger around the white squares of the grid from A to B. Show three different ways that you can do this.

a

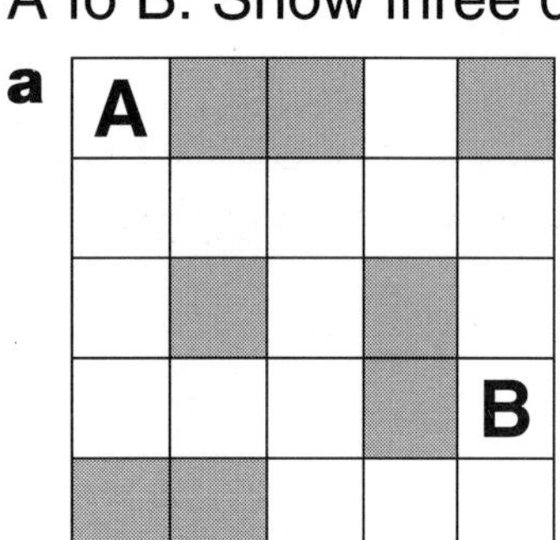

b

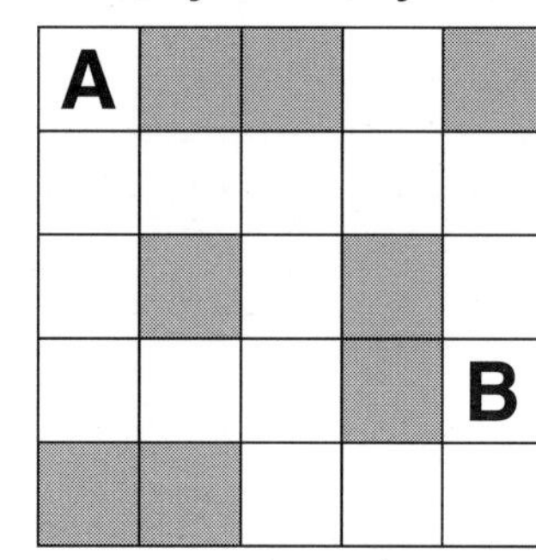

c

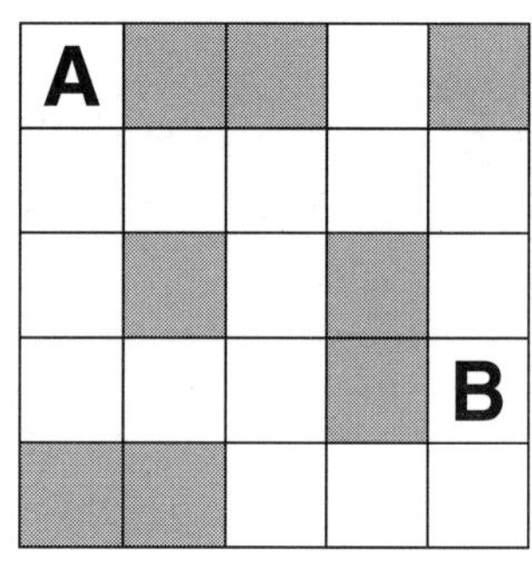

Challenge 2

1 Write eight words that would be helpful when you give directions.

____

____

2 Use some of the words in Question **1** to write the shortest route from A to B in the grid in Challenge **1a**.

____

____

3 Write a set of instructions for a route along the white squares from the star to the moon.

____

____

____

____

____

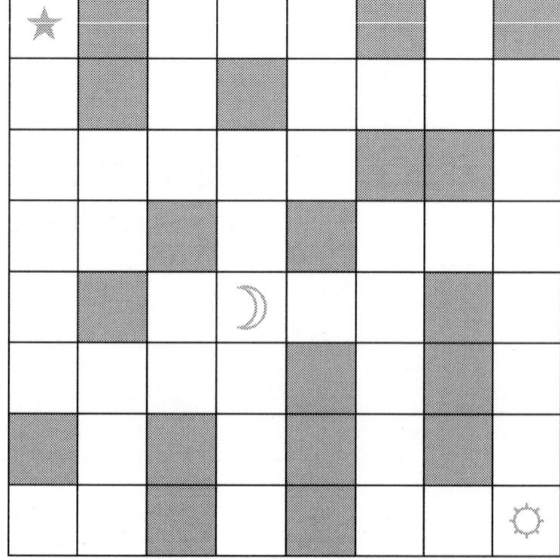

4 Write a set of instructions for the shortest route along the white squares from the star to the sun.

____

____

____

____

Challenge 3

1 Shade five squares on each row of this grid. Create a path of white squares to move you from the triangle to the square.

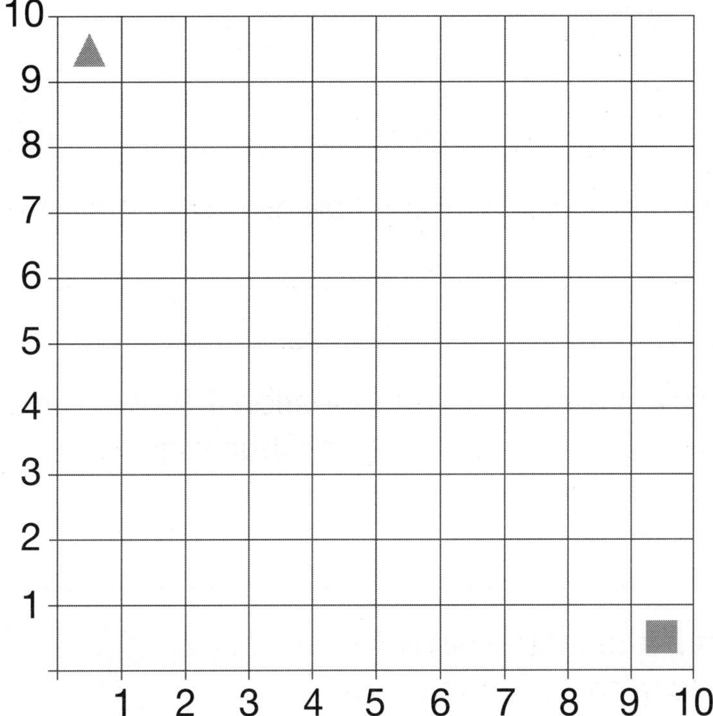

2 a Write instructions to show a route you can take along the white squares from the triangle to the square.

____

____

____

____

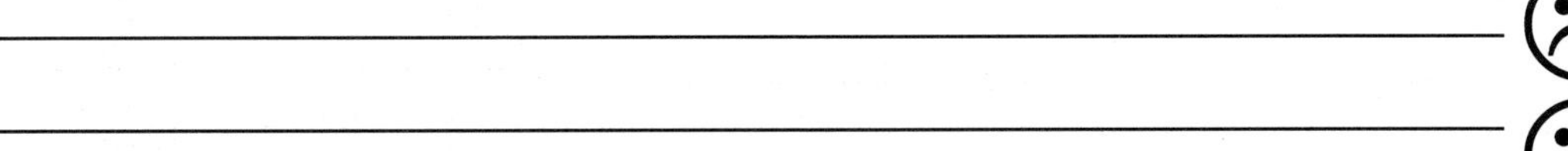

b Write the co-ordinates at a point where you make a turn.

____

Lesson 3: Angles

- Know that angles are measured in degrees
- Know that one whole turn is 360° which is equal to four right angles

You will need
- set square

Challenge 1

1 Tick the right angles.

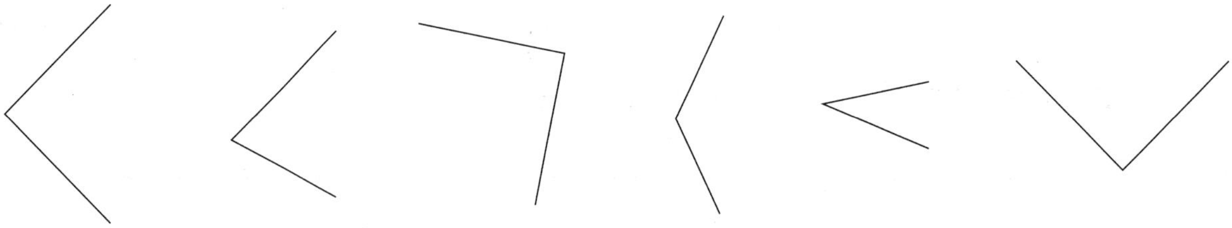

☐ ☐ ☐ ☐ ☐ ☐

2 a How many right angles make a straight line? ☐

b Draw a straight angle.

Challenge 2

1 a How many degrees are there in a whole turn? ☐°

b How many right angles is this equivalent to? ☐

2 a Draw a pentagon that has three right angles.

b What can you say about the other two angles?

____

____

3 a Draw a trapezium with two right angles.

b Describe the other two angles.

____

4 Draw a diagram to show 270° using right angles.

Challenge 3

1 Draw a right angle, an acute angle and an obtuse angle inside this circle. Make sure the sides of your angles touch the outside of the circle.

Label each angle.

2 Write definitions for these angles:

a acute ______________________________

b obtuse ______________________________

c right angle ______________________________

Lesson 4: **Comparing and ordering angles**

- Compare and order angles less than 180°

You will need

- set square

Challenge 1

1 Draw four different angles larger than a right angle.

2 Draw four different angles less than a right angle.

1 Look at these shapes.

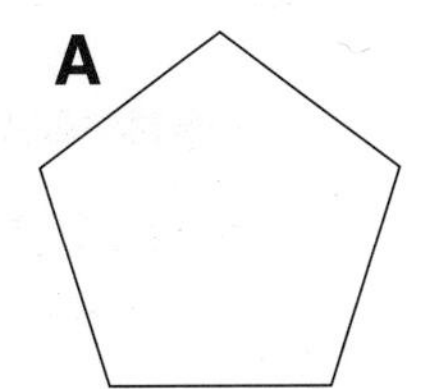

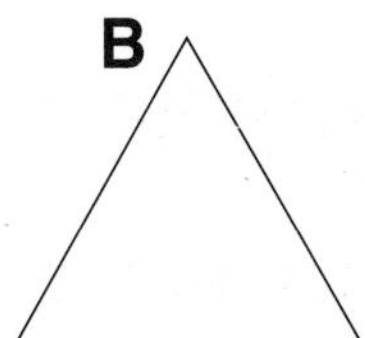

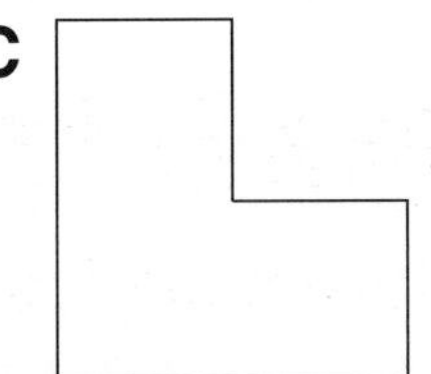

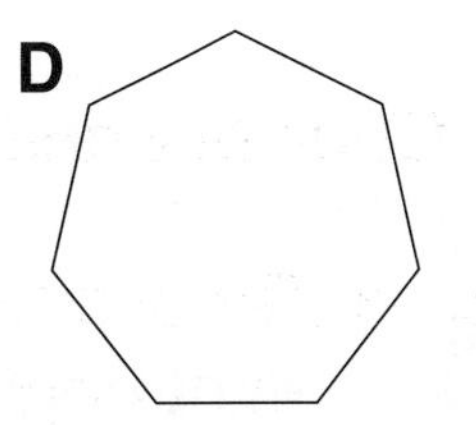

a Which shape has the largest angle? ____________

b Which shape has the smallest angle? ____________

c Which shape only has right angles? ____________

2 Order these angles, from least to greatest.

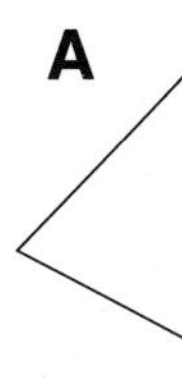

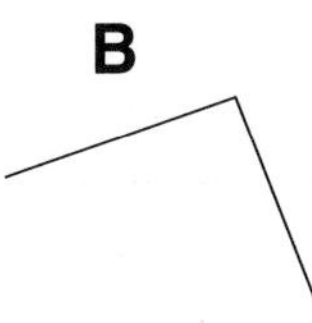

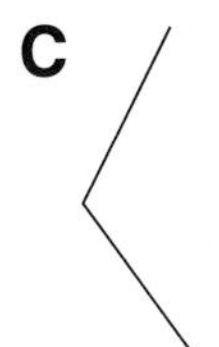

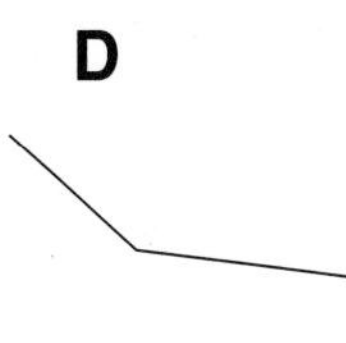

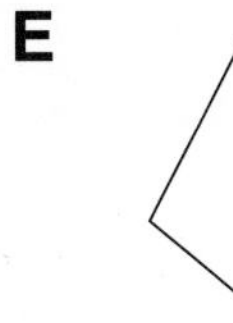

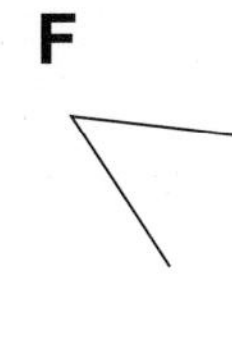

Challenge 3

Draw an irregular hexagon. It must have two right angles, one obtuse angle and one acute angle. What are the other three angles?

____

Measure

Lesson 1: **Units of length**

- Choose and use units to measure length
- Record length in mm, cm, m and km

You will need
- ruler

1 Write mm, cm, m or km next to each picture to show which unit you would use to measure the length.

2 Measure three different pencils and record their lengths in centimetres:

Pencil A: ______ Pencil B: ______ Pencil C: ______

1 Circle the smallest length in each row.

a 10 m 10 mm 10 cm

b 35 km 35 cm 35 m

2 Circle the largest length in each row.

a 50 km 50 cm 50 m

b 72 mm 72 m 72 cm

3 Find four objects to measure in the classroom. Estimate the length of each object then measure it. Don't forget to use the unit of measure: mm, cm or m.

Object	Estimate	Actual length

4 Would you use km or m to measure these distances?

a From your desk to the board. ☐

b From one town to another town. ☐

c From one side of a field to the other. ☐

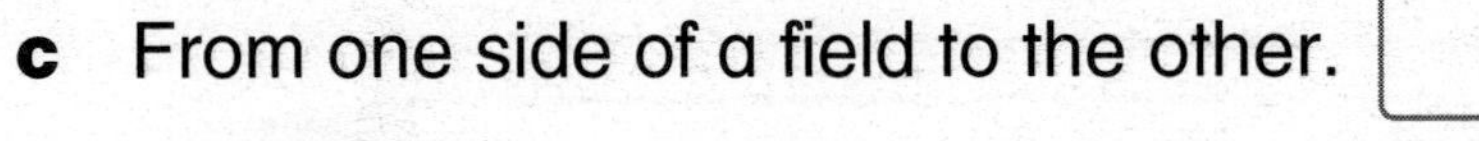

Challenge 3 Answer the questions using whole numbers.

a How many cm in $3\frac{1}{2}$ m? ☐

b How many m in $2\frac{1}{4}$ km? ☐

c How many mm in 3 cm? ☐

Lesson 2: **Reading and interpreting length**

- Read and show length on a ruler or metre rule that is only partially numbered

You will need

- ruler
- metre rule
- red and blue pencils

Challenge 1

1 How long is this rectangle? ☐ cm

0 5 10 15 20

2 How long is this ribbon? ☐ cm

0 5 10 15 20

Challenge 2

1 What is the length of the string? ☐ cm

0 10 20

2 What is the length of the pen? ☐ cm

0 10 20

3 Draw a crayon 12 cm long.

0 10 20

4 a What is the height of the fence? ☐ cm

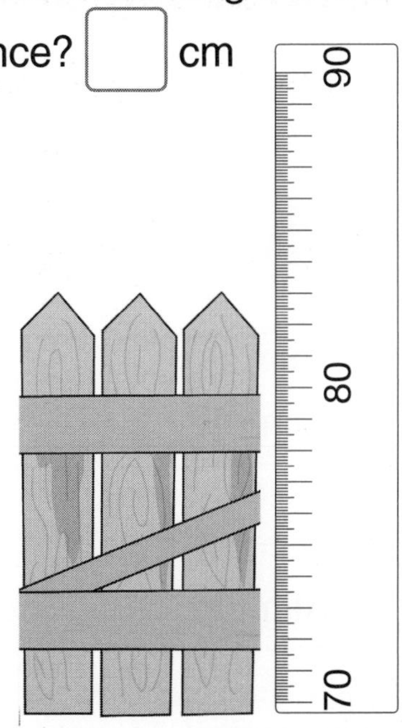

b What is the height of the wall? ☐ cm

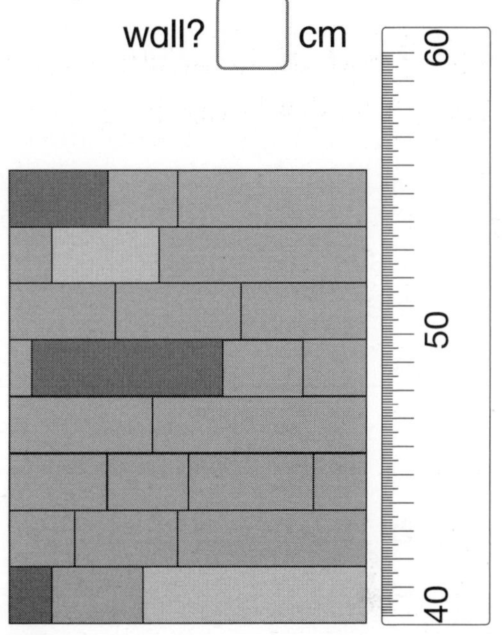

5 Mark where 13 belongs on this ruler.

Explain the strategies you used to work this out.

____

____

1 Mark where the numbers 10, 20, 30, 40, 60, 70, 80 and 90 belong on the ruler.

2 Make a red mark where you think 25 belongs.

3 Make a blue mark where you think 59 belongs.

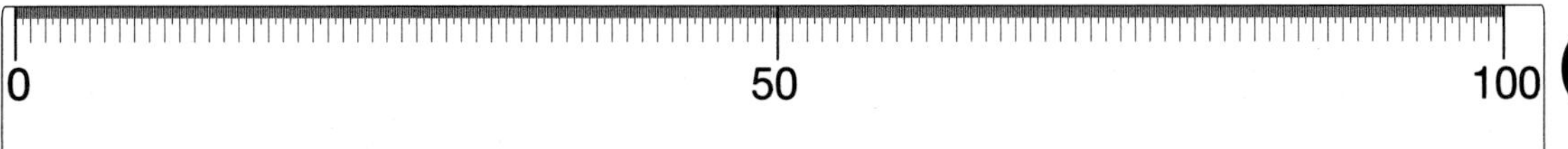

Lesson 3: **Estimating, measuring and recording length**

- Estimate lengths and distances
- Record length in metres and centimetres

You will need
- ruler
- metre rule
- chalk

Challenge 1

1 Estimate the length of each snake.
Record your estimate in centimetres.

a 1 cm — estimate [ ] — actual length [ ]

b 1 cm — estimate [ ] — actual length [ ]

c 1 cm — estimate [ ] — actual length [ ]

2 Now, measure the length of each snake. Record the actual length in centimetres.

Challenge 2

1 Tick the line that you estimate to be 7 cm long.

a ______________________________________ [ ]

b __________________________ [ ]

c ___________________ [ ]

d ____ [ ]

2 Now measure the lines in Question **1** and record their actual lengths in centimetres in the boxes.

3 This line is 10 cm long.

Turn your ruler over so that you cannot see the numbers and use it to draw lines that you estimate to be the following lengths:

a 4 cm

b 12 cm

c 7 cm

4 Now measure your lines and record their actual lengths to the nearest centimetre.

a ☐ cm **b** ☐ cm **c** ☐ cm

Challenge 3

1 Make a mark on the floor with chalk where you estimate 3 m to be from the wall. Measure the actual distance from the wall to your mark and record the distance:

a in metres and centimetres ☐ cm ☐ m

b to the nearest metre ☐ m

2 Think about how close your line was to 3 m in Question **1** and use this information to draw a mark at a point that you estimate to be closer to 3 m.

Measure the distance and record it:

a in metres and centimetres ☐ cm ☐ m

b to the nearest metre ☐ m

Lesson 4: **Problems involving length**

- Solve word problems involving length

For each word problem, show your answer and how you worked it out.

Challenge 1

1 Brad needs to share two baguettes between 5 friends. Each baguette is 20 cm long. How much can each friend have?

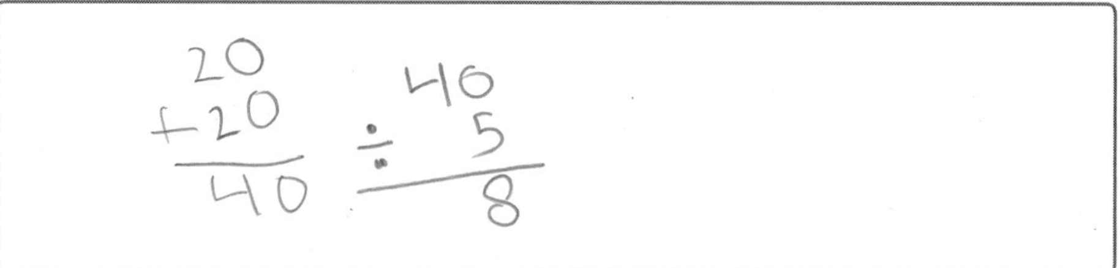

2 Amira has 12 cm of ribbon. Leila has 30 cm of ribbon. Sabeen has 27 cm of ribbon. How much ribbon do they have altogether in centimetres?

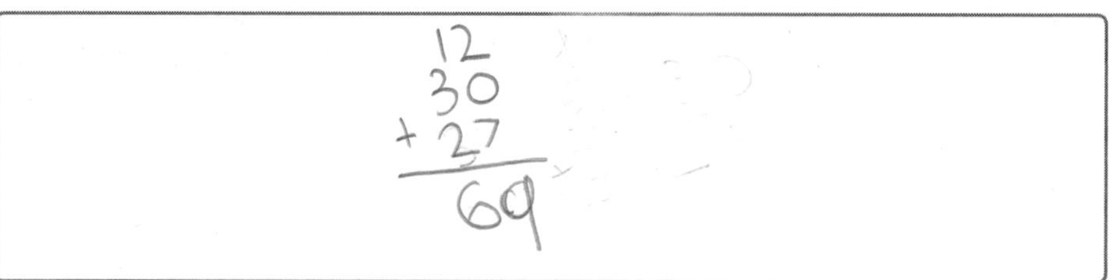

Challenge 2

1 Rahim cuts 6 pieces of string that are each 14 cm in length. How much string has he cut in total?

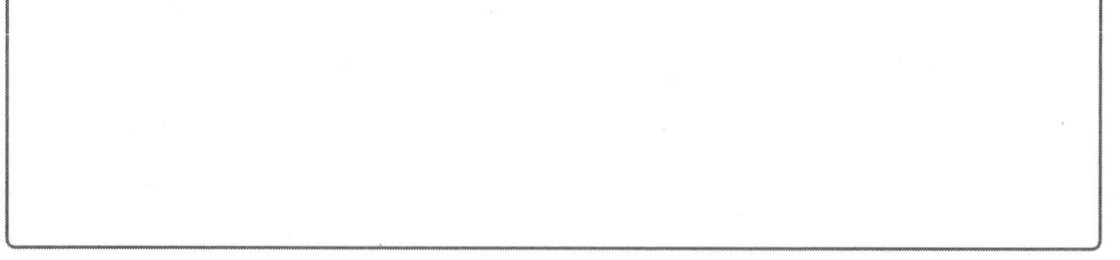

2 Malik has cut a plank of wood into 9 pieces. Each is 20 cm long. What was the total length of the plank before Malik started? How many equal pieces can he cut?

3 It is a 46 km journey into town. Jamal has travelled 18 km so far. How many kilometres must he still travel?

Challenge 3

1 David's trousers are too long. They are 108 cm long. He needs to cut 13 cm off each leg, so they will be the correct length. How long will the trousers be when he has done this?

2 Write a length or distance problem that uses division or multiplication. Make sure you have worked out the answer. Then ask someone to answer your problem.

3 Make up a number story for this calculation. 76 ÷ 4.

Measure

Lesson 1: **Units of mass**

- Choose and use units to measure mass
- Understand the relationship between g and kg

Challenge 1

1 Write g or kg next to each object to show which unit you would use to measure its mass.

2 Name an object you would weigh in grams.

____

3 Name an object you would weigh in kilograms.

____

Challenge 2

1 3000 g = ☐ kg **2** 2 kg = ☐ g

3 Circle the smallest mass in each row.

a 5 g 5 kg 50 g

b 500 kg 50 kg 5000 g

4 Circle the largest mass in each row.

a 250 kg 2500 g 250 g

b 8000 g 5 kg 800 g

5 a How many grams in 4 kg? ☐ g

b How many grams in $2\frac{1}{2}$ kg? ☐ g

c How many kilograms in 6000 g? ☐ kg

d How many kilograms in 2500 g? ☐ kg

e How many kilograms in 1100 g? ☐ kg

f How many grams in $3\frac{1}{4}$ kg? ☐ g

Challenge 3 Answer each question, showing your working.

a How many kilograms is 3750 g?

b How many grams is $5\frac{1}{4}$ kg?

c How many kilograms is 6250 g?

d How many grams is $\frac{1}{4}$ of a kg?

e How many kilograms is 2250 g?

Measure

Lesson 2: **Reading and interpreting mass**

- Read and show a mass on a scale that is only partially numbered

Challenge 1

1 What is the mass shown on the scales? ☐ g

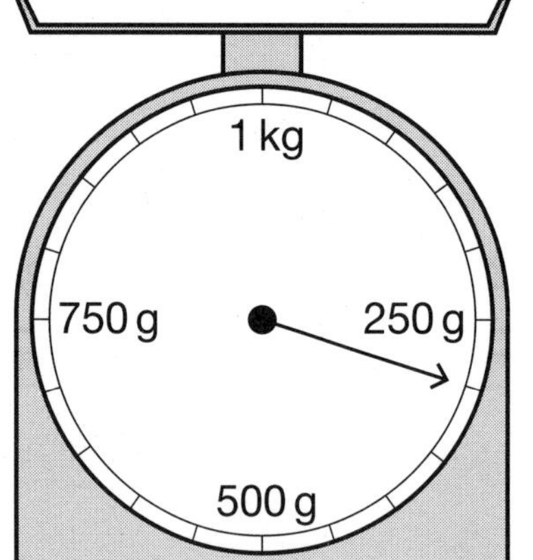

2 What is the mass shown on the scales? ☐ g

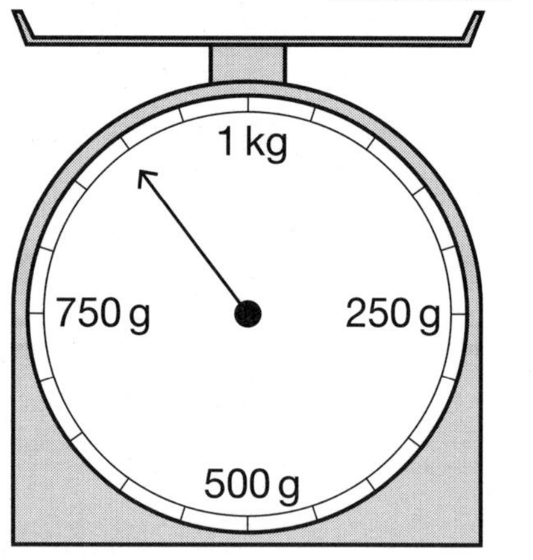

Challenge 2

1 a Show 500 g on the scales.

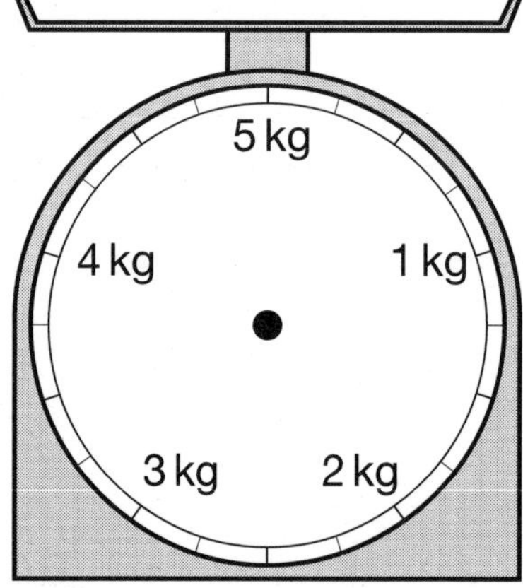

b Show $3\frac{1}{2}$ kg on the scales.

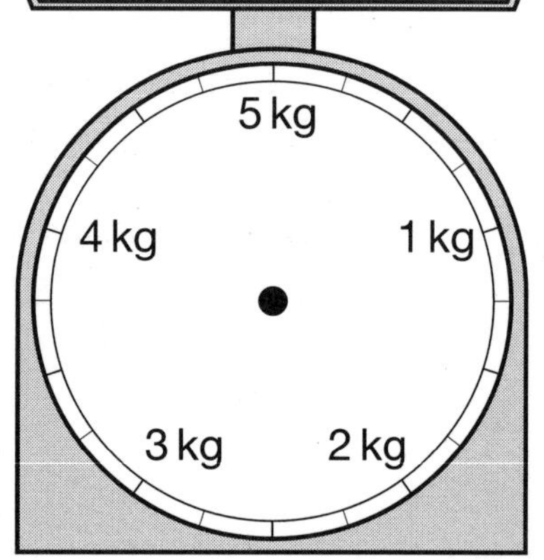

c Show 2250 g on the scales.

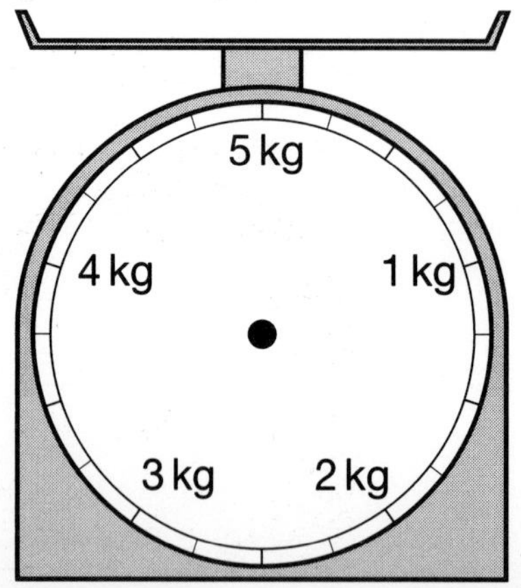

d Show $4\frac{3}{4}$ kg on the scales.

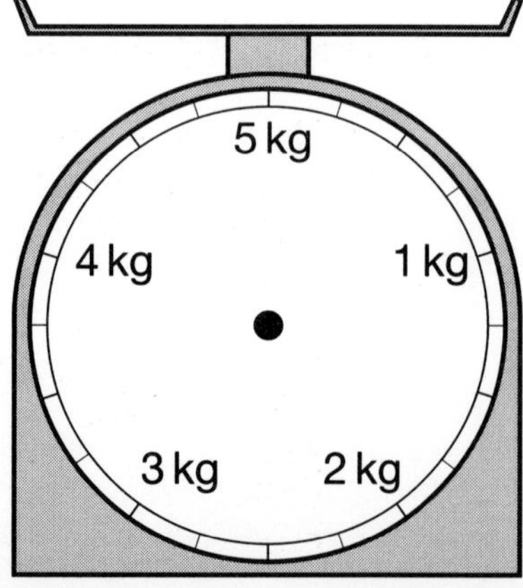

2 a What is the mass of the toy car? ☐ g

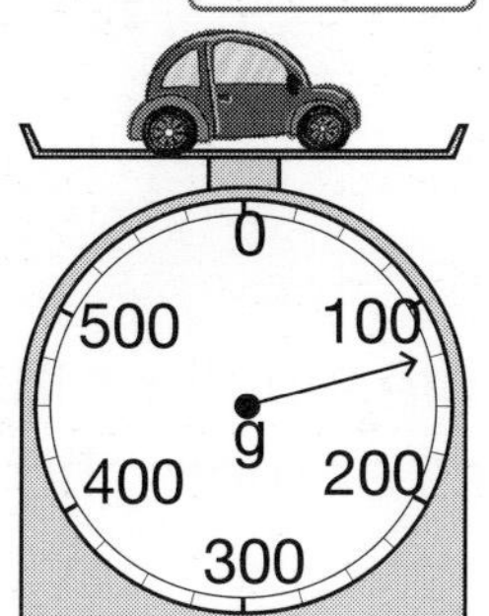

b What is the mass of the teddy bear? ☐ g

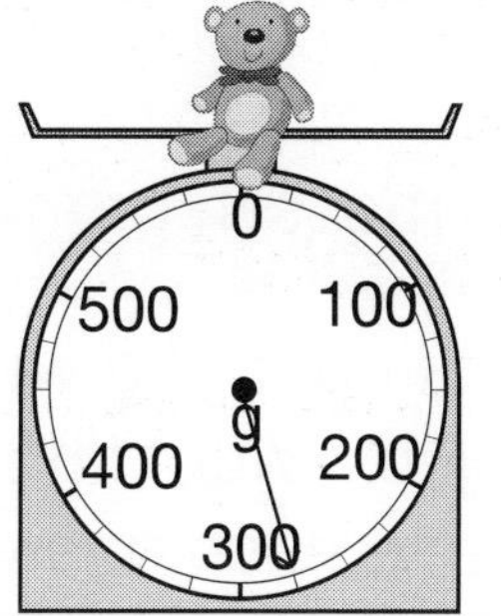

c What is the mass of the apples? ☐ kg

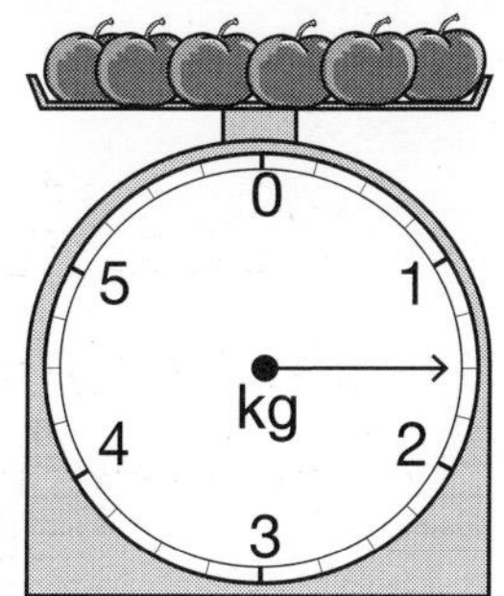

d What is the mass of the books? ☐ kg

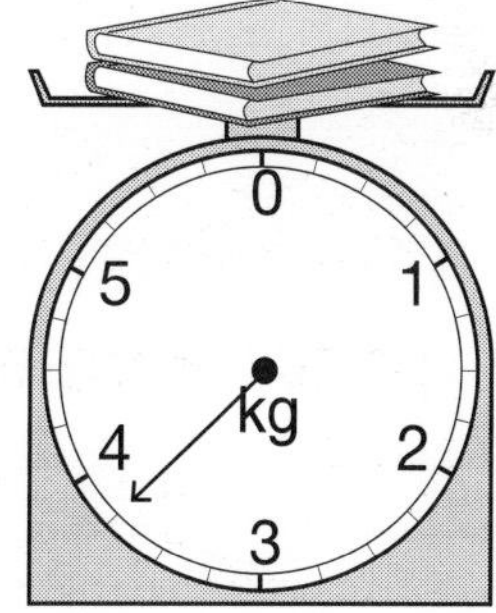

Challenge **3**

1 Show 180 g on the scale.

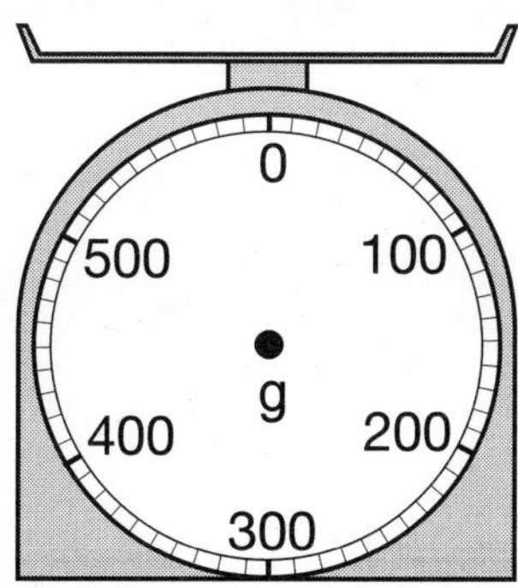

2 Show $\frac{1}{4}$ kg on the scale.

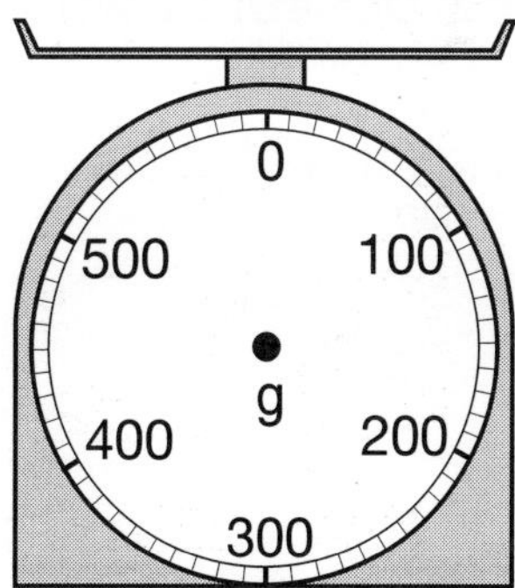

3 Show $3\frac{1}{4}$ kg on the scale.

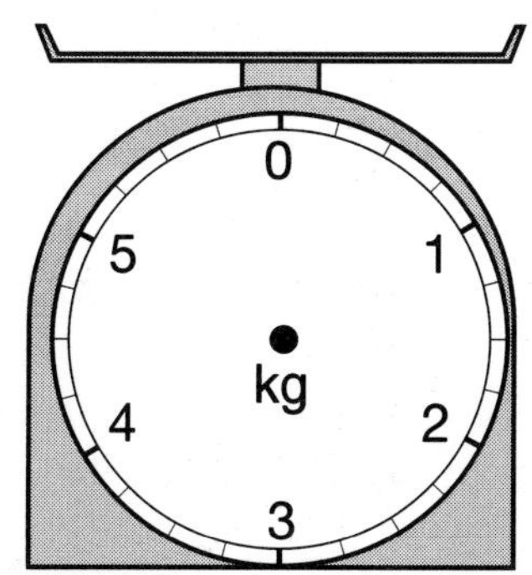

4 Show $4\frac{3}{4}$ kg on the scale.

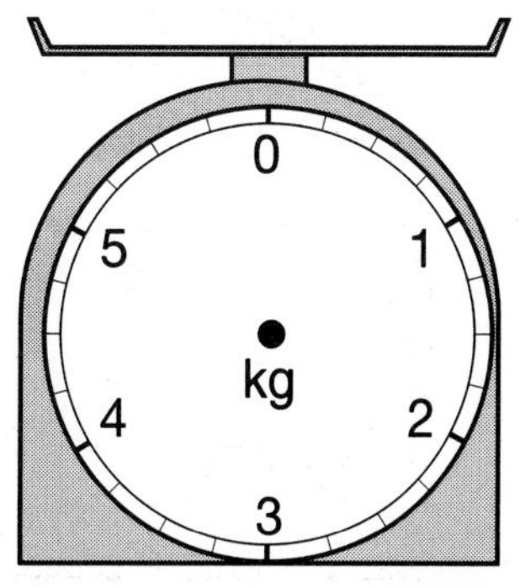

Measure

Lesson 3: **Estimating, measuring and recording mass**

- Estimate mass
- Record mass in grams and kilograms

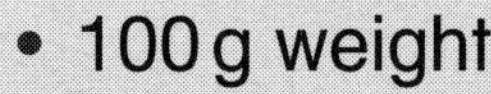

- 1 kg weight
- 100 g weight

1 Pick up a 1 kg weight and then estimate whether these objects would have a mass that is less or more than 1 kg. Circle each answer.

a mouse: less than 1 kg more than 1 kg

b pencil sharpener: less than 1 kg more than 1 kg

c basket of washing: less than 1 kg more than 1 kg

1 Tick the objects that you estimate have a mass of about 1 kilogram.

2 Tick the objects that you estimate have a mass of about 100 grams.

3 Pick up a 1 kg weight and feel how heavy it is. Now find three objects in the classroom that you estimate to have a mass of about 1 kg. Write them here.

____

____

____

4 Pick up a 100 g weight and feel how heavy it is. Now find three objects in the classroom that you estimate to have a mass of about 100 g. Write them here.

____

____

____

Challenge 3

1 Pick up a 1 kg weight and feel how heavy it is. Now find three objects in the classroom that you estimate to have a mass of about half of this weight (500 g). Write them here.

____

____

____

2 Weigh your objects on a set of scales and record their actual mass.

____

____

____

Lesson 4: **Problems involving mass**

- Solve word problems involving mass

For each word problem, show your answer and how you worked it out.

Challenge 1

1 Louise is standing on the scales. She has a mass of 28 kg. She picks up her 3 pet rabbits, which have a mass of 4 kg; 2 kg and 5 kg. What will the reading on the scales show now?

2 I have a bunch of bananas. Each banana has a mass of 80 g and there are 5 in the bunch. What is the total mass of the bunch of bananas?

Challenge 2

1 David has to load 7 bags of corn onto a truck. Each bag of corn has a mass of 20 kg. What is the total mass of corn?

2 I have 65 g of sweets. I give three friends 15 g of sweets each. What mass of sweets do I have left?

3 Sarah is carrying a bag of 4 books. Each book has a mass of 20 g. She picks up another, identical, bag of 4 books. What is the mass of the books she is carrying now?

Challenge 3

1 Jamal carried a 1 kg bag of flour home. It leaked and he lost 350 g of the flour. How much flour is left?

2 Write a mass problem that uses division or multiplication. Make sure you have worked out the answer. Then ask someone to answer your problem.

3 Make up a number story for this calculation. 23 g × 8 = 184 g.

Measure

Lesson 1: **Units of capacity**

- Choose and use units to measure capacity
- Understand the relationship between ml and *l*

You will need

- red, blue and yellow coloured pencils

Challenge 1

1 Write *l* or ml next to each picture to show which unit you think would have been used to measure the liquid.

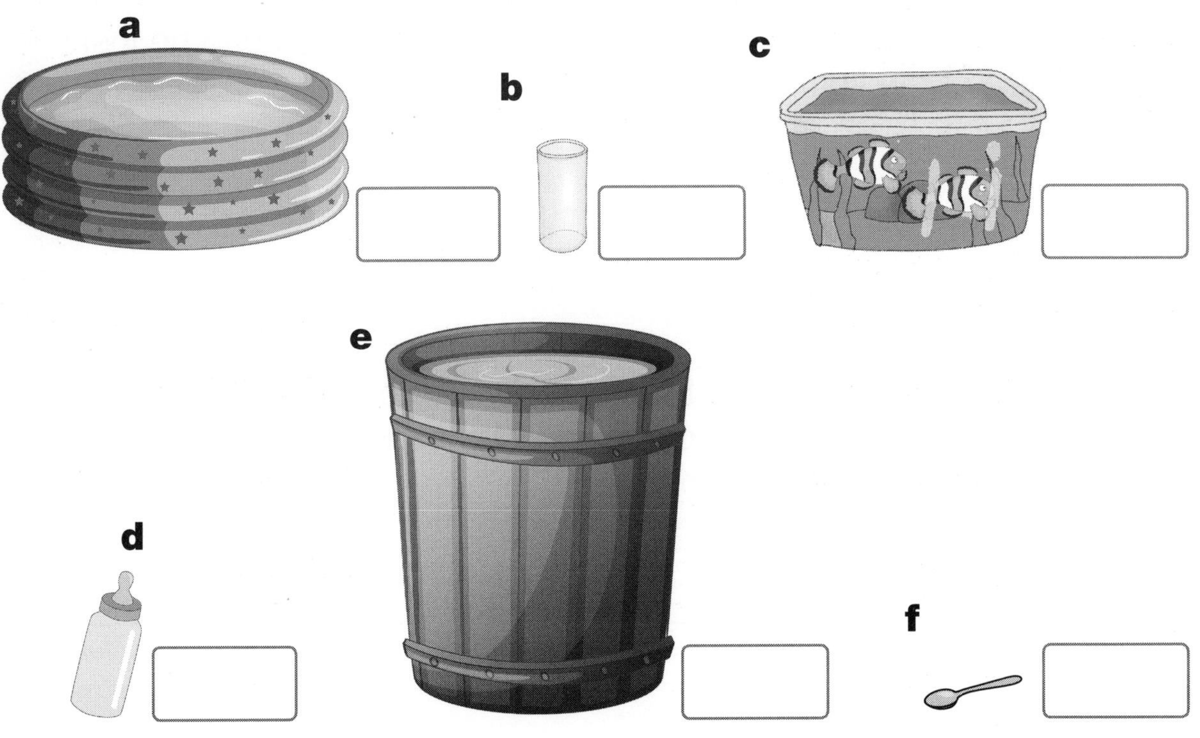

2 Write an example of when you would measure liquid in litres.

____

3 Write an example of when you would measure liquid in millilitres.

____

1 7000 ml = ☐ l

2 3 l = ☐ ml

3 $9\frac{1}{2}$ l = ☐ ml

4 a Colour the container red to show 200 ml.

b Colour another half a litre yellow.

c Colour another 100 ml blue.

d How many more millilitres would you have to colour to reach 1 litre? ☐

5 Draw lines to match the amounts that are equal.

500 ml •	• $\frac{3}{4}$ of a litre
1 litre •	• 250 ml
100 ml •	• 1000 ml
750 ml •	• 3 litres
3000 ml •	• $\frac{1}{10}$ of a litre
$\frac{1}{4}$ of a litre •	• $\frac{1}{2}$ a litre

1 $\frac{4}{10}$ l = ☐ ml

2 $3\frac{1}{4}$ l = ☐ ml

3 $\frac{7}{10}$ l = ☐ ml

4 1250 ml = ☐ l

5 2750 ml = ☐ l

6 810 ml = ☐ l

Lesson 2: **Reading and interpreting capacity**

• Read and show capacity on a scale that is only partially numbered

1 Write the amount of liquid shown in each container.

a [ ]

50 ml
40 ml
30 ml
20 ml
10 ml

b [ ]

500 ml
400 ml
300 ml
200 ml
100 ml

1 Show 125 ml of liquid in the container

500 ml
400 ml
300 ml
200 ml
100 ml

2 Show 475 ml of liquid in the container.

500 ml
400 ml
300 ml
200 ml
100 ml

3 Show 350 ml of liquid in the container.

500 ml
400 ml
300 ml
200 ml
100 ml

4 Show 225 ml of liquid in the container.

500 ml
400 ml
300 ml
200 ml
100 ml

5 How much water is in this measuring jug?

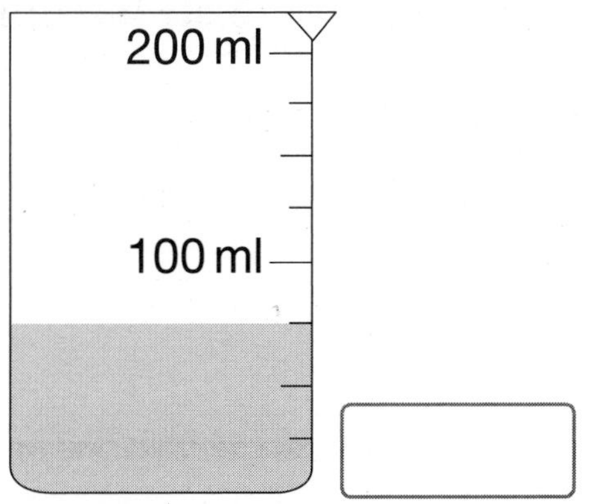

6 How much water is in this measuring jug?

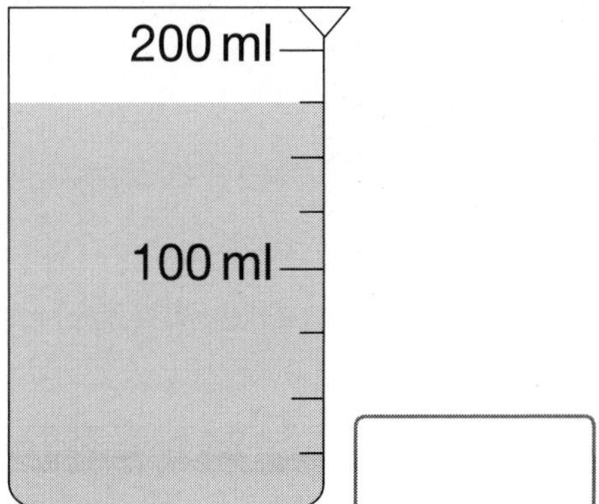

1 **a** Mark where you think 2 *l* 175 ml would be on this scale.

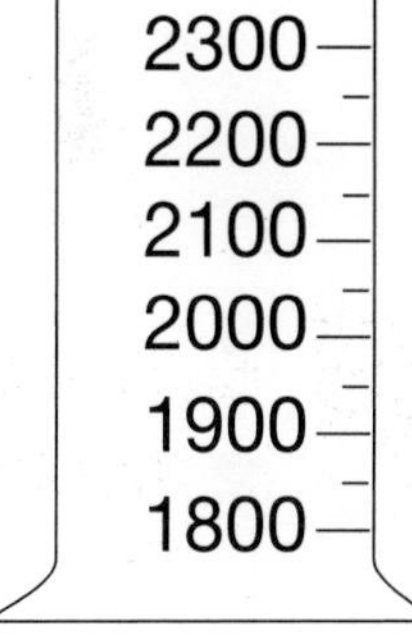

b How much is 2 *l* 175 ml in millilitres?

2 **a** Show 110 ml of liquid in the container.

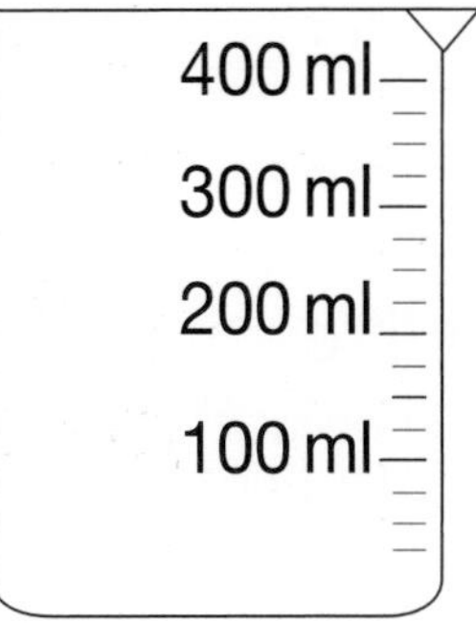

b Show 260 ml of liquid in the container.

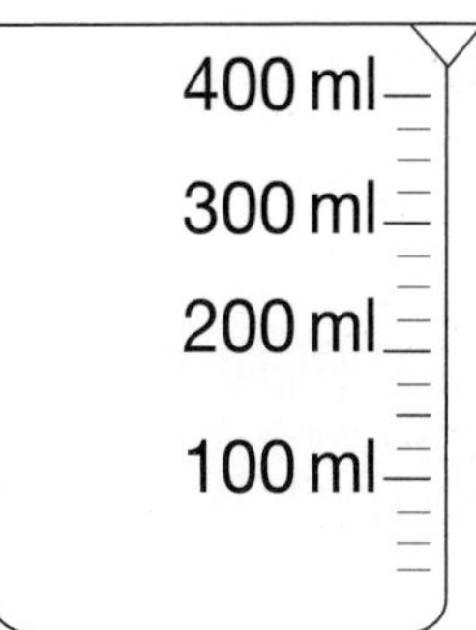

c Show 370 ml of liquid in the container.

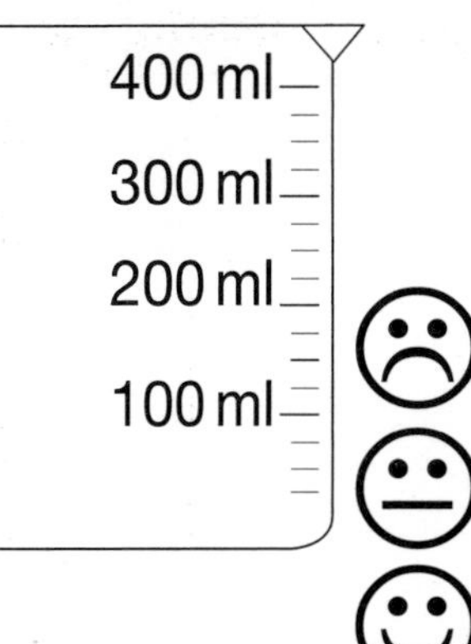

d Explain the strategies that you used to place the numbers.

____

____

____

____

____

Measure

Lesson 3: **Estimating, measuring and recording capacity**

- Estimate capacity and record it in litres and millilitres

You will need
- selection of plastic containers

Challenge 1

1 Estimate whether these containers hold less, or more, than 100 ml. Circle your estimate.

a

less more

b

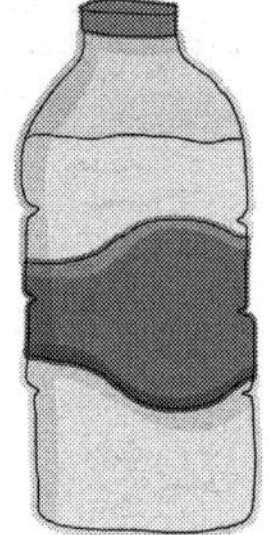

less more

c

less more

d

less more

2 Estimate whether these containers hold less, or more, than 1 litre. Circle your estimate.

a a basin: less than 1 litre more than 1 litre

b a drinking glass: less than 1 litre more than 1 litre

c a washing machine: less than 1 litre more than 1 litre

Challenge 2

1 Draw a line to match each container to the capacity that you estimate it to have.

 •  • 5 ml

•  • 200 ml

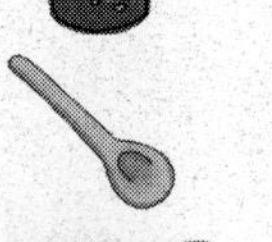 •  • 8 litres

 • • 330 ml

 • • $1\frac{1}{2}$ litres

2 a Look at a container that has a capacity of 250 ml. Now, find a different container that you think has the same capacity. Pour water from the second container into the first to check. Were you correct?

Yes / No

b What was the difference between the capacities in ml? ☐

3 a Look at a container that has a capacity of 500 ml. Now, find a different container that you think has the same capacity. Pour water from the second container into the first to check. Were you correct?

Yes / No

b What was the difference between the capacities in ml? ☐

1 If container A holds 200 ml of liquid, how much liquid do you estimate container B holds? ☐ ml

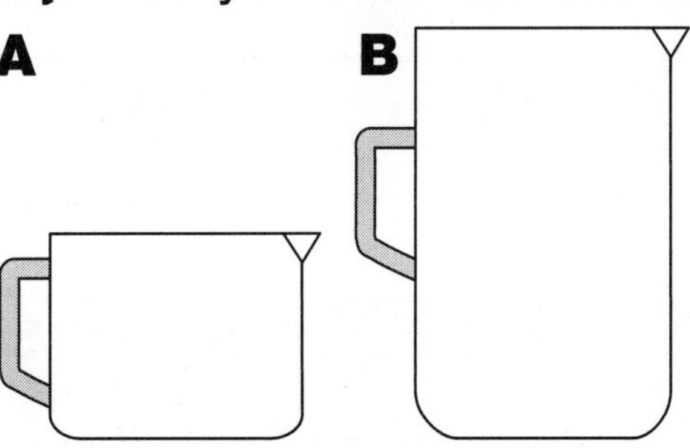

2 If container A holds 100 ml of liquid, can you tell how much liquid container B holds?

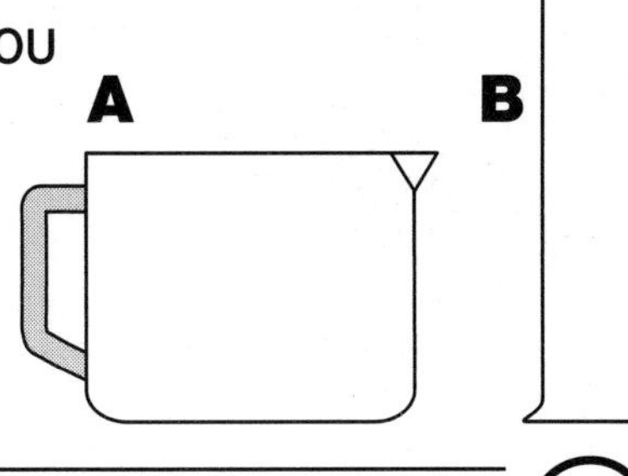

Yes / No

Explain your reasoning.

___

___

___

___

___

Lesson 4: **Problems involving capacity**

- Solve word problems involving capacity

For each word problem, show your answer and how you worked it out.

Challenge 1

1 Ben has filled a paddling pool with 13 litres of water. He makes another three trips and puts in 7 litres, 4 litres and 6 litres, which fills the pool. What is the capacity of the pool?

2 Jamal opens a 1 litre carton of apple juice. He drinks 300 ml. How much apple juice is left in the carton?

Challenge 2

1 Six children are painting. There is 450 ml of paint in the pot. How much paint will be left over if each child has 60 ml of paint?

2 Seven people each pour 20 ml of water into a container. The container is now completely full. What is the capacity of the container?

3 Aida has a bottle with a capacity of 1500 ml. She fills it with water, spills 230 ml, then adds another 50 ml to it. How much water is in the bottle now?

Challenge 3

1 Surinder's dad bought 40 litres of fuel for his car. The next day, only 13 litres of fuel were left. How many litres of fuel did the car use?

2 Write a two-part capacity problem that uses addition, subtraction, division or multiplication. Make sure you have worked out the answer. Then ask someone to answer your problem.

3 Make up a number story to go with this calculation.
$22\,l + 41\,l = 63\,l$. $63\,l \div 7\,l = 9\,l$.

Lesson 1: **Revising length**

- Estimate and measure length in metres and centimetres
- Record length using decimal notation

You will need
- ruler
- coloured pencils

1 Write each length using decimal notation.

a 50 cm = 0·☐ m **b** 70 cm = 0·☐ m

c 1 m 30 cm = ☐·3 m **d** 4 m 60 cm = ☐·☐ m

2 Write each length in metres and centimetres.

a 0·40 m = ☐ cm **b** 0·80 m = ☐ cm

c 2·20 m = ☐ m ☐ cm **d** 3·10 m = ☐ m ☐ cm

1 Find the matching lengths and colour them with the same colour. Choose a different colour for each pair of matching lengths.

25 cm 0·81 m 6 m 70 cm

10 cm 81 cm

4·32 m 0·25 m 4 m 32 cm

6·7 m 0·1 m

2 Write each length using decimal notation.

a ☐ m

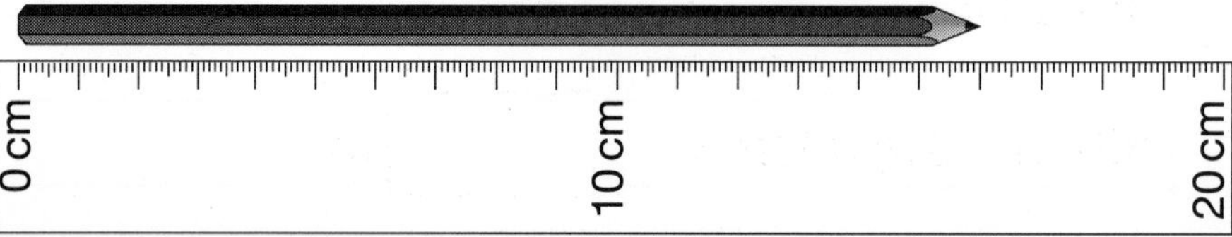

b [ ] m

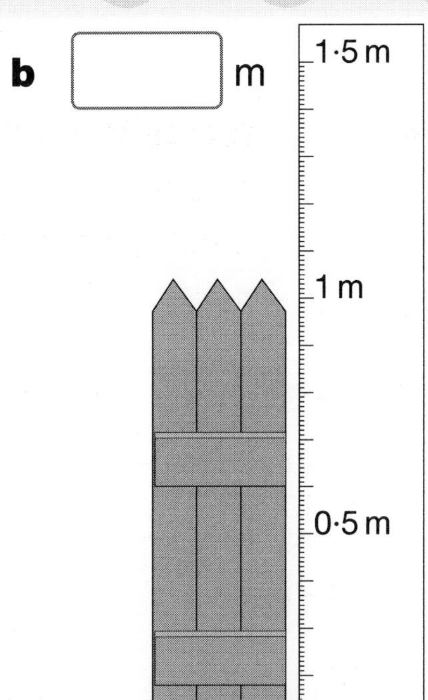

c [ ] m

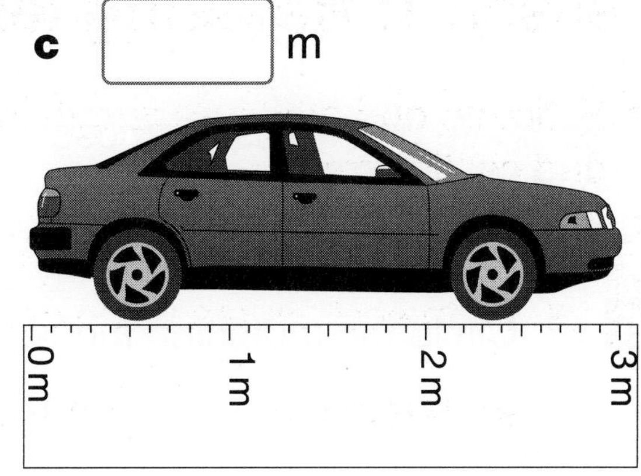

3 Measure your hand span with a ruler. Record the measurement:

a in centimetres [ ] cm

b using decimal notation [ ] m

1 Circle the length that is **not** equal to the others.

a $\frac{3}{4}$ of a metre   0·75 m   1 m 75 cm

b 6 m 10 cm   6·01 m $6\frac{1}{10}$ of a metre

c 2·60 m $2\frac{6}{10}$ of a metre   260 cm

2 Complete each calculation and write the answer using decimal notation.

a 67 cm + 21 cm = [ ] m

b 1 m 53 cm + 3 m 39 cm = [ ] m

c 8 m 88 cm + 32 cm = [ ] m

Measure

Lesson 2: **Revising mass**

- Estimate and measure mass in grams and kilograms
- Record mass using decimal notation

You will need

- weighing scales

Challenge 1

1 Circle the matching mass.

a	600 g =	0·5 kg	0·6 kg	4·6 kg
b	800 g =	0·8 kg	1·8 kg	8·8 kg
c	1 kg 50 g =	0·15 kg	1·5 kg	1·05 kg
d	4 kg 100 g =	4·1 kg	0·41 kg	4·6 kg

2 Write each mass using decimal notation.

a 300 g

. kg

b 900 g

. kg

c 500 g

. kg

Challenge 2

1 Draw lines to match the masses that are equal.

750 g •	• 5·89 kg
2 kg 600 g •	• 0·1 kg
5 kg 890 g •	• 2·3 kg
50 g •	• 0·05 kg
2 kg 300 g •	• 2·6 kg
100 g •	• 0·75 kg

Measure

2 Write each mass in kilograms and grams.

a

b

c

3 Weigh your shoe on the scales. Record the mass:

a in grams  g

b using decimal decimal notation ☐ kg

4 Write the equivalent mass using decimal notation.

a $3\frac{3}{4}$kg = ☐ kg

b $1\frac{7}{10}$kg = ☐ kg

c $\frac{5}{10}$kg = ☐ kg

Challenge 3

1 Circle the mass that is **not** equal to the others in each row.

a	$\frac{1}{2}$ of a kilogram	0·5 kg	50 g
b	0·3 kg	$\frac{1}{4}$ of a kilogram	250 g
c	$\frac{1}{10}$ of a kilogram	200 g	0·2 kg

2 a Which is larger 0·6 kg or 0·06 kg? ☐

b Explain how you know.

____

____

____

3 Complete each calculation and write the answer using decimal notation.

a 43 g + 11 g = ☐ g

b 1 kg 34 g + 5 kg 19 g = ☐ kg

c 7 kg 77 g + 33 g = ☐ kg

Measure

Lesson 3: **Revising capacity**

- Estimate and measure capacity in litres and millilitres
- Record capacity using decimal notation

You will need
- selection of plastic containers
- measuring jug

Challenge 1

1 Circle the matching capacity.

a	600 ml =	0·2 *l*	6·0 *l*	0·6 *l*
b	1 *l* 200 ml =	1·2 *l*	2·1 *l*	1·0 *l*
c	0·3 *l* =	3 ml	30 ml	300 ml
d	4·1 *l* =	4 *l* 1 ml	4 *l* 0 ml	4 *l* 100 ml

2 What volume of liquid is in each jug?
Write your answer in millilitres.

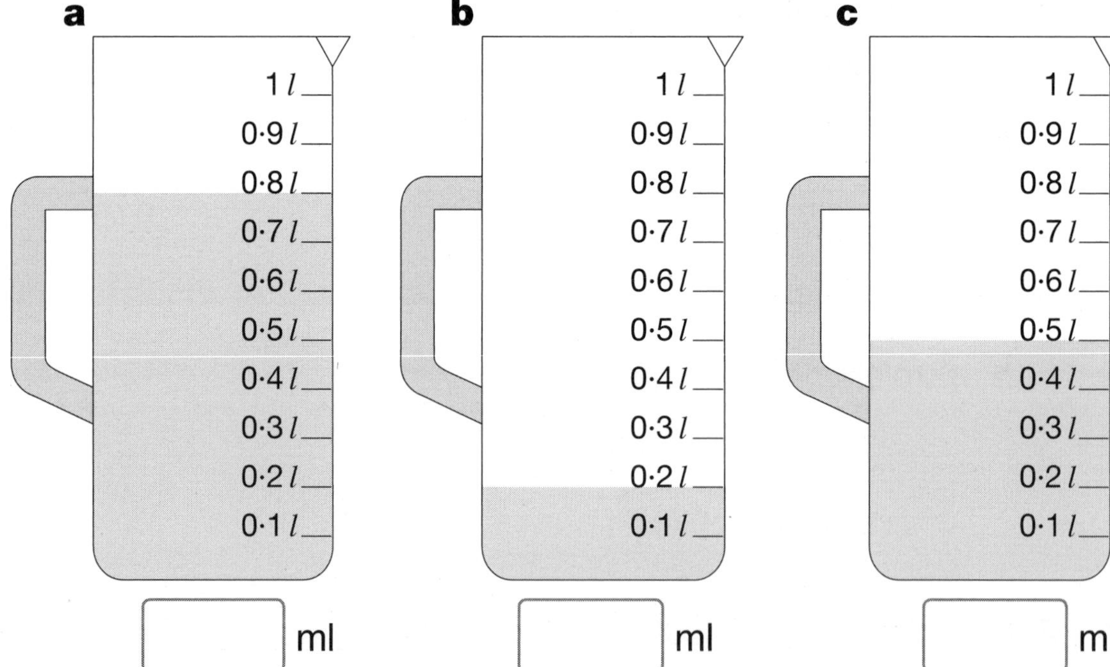

Challenge 2

1 Write each capacity using decimal notation:

a $\frac{1}{2}$ of a litre ☐ *l*   **b** $\frac{1}{4}$ of a litre ☐ *l*

c $\frac{1}{10}$ of a litre  *l*   **d** $\frac{3}{4}$ of a litre ☐ *l*

2 Write each capacity in litres and millilitres.

a

b

c

3 Pick a container. Estimate its capacity:

a in millilitres ☐ ml

b using decimal notation ☐ *l*

4 Now work out the container's capacity using a measuring jug. Write the capacity below:

a in millilitres ☐ ml

b using decimal notation ☐ *l*

Challenge 3

1 Complete each calculation and write the answer using decimal notation.

a 450 ml + 420 ml = ☐

b 3 *l* 500 ml + 2 *l* 120 ml = ☐

c 6 *l* 240 ml + 1 *l* 310 ml = ☐

2 a Which is smaller 3·40 *l* or 3·04 ml? ☐

b Explain how you know.

____

____

____

Lesson 4: **Problems involving measures**

- Solve word problems involving measures
- Record measures using decimal notation

Work out the answer to each word problem in the space provided. Write all answers using decimal notation.

Challenge 1

1 There were 0·7 kg of mixed nuts in the jar. Adiba sold 200 g of them yesterday. What is the mass of the nuts that are left now?

kg

2 Leila ran 2300 m today, 1100 m yesterday and 1500 m the day before that. How far has she run altogether?

m

Challenge 2

1 Some children are filling a bucket with water. Prahalad pours in 1·3 *l*. Fatima pours in 400 ml. Manir pours in 1·1 *l*. How much water is there in the bucket now?

l

2 Jamal and his family are walking at a speed of 7600 m per hour. They have been walking for half an hour. How many kilometres have they travelled?

km

3 Hakan is packing books into a box. Each book weighs 250 g. The parcel weighs 3·75 kg. How many books are in the parcel?

4 Make up a number story for this calculation. 27 + 82 = 109

Challenge 3

1 Lily had a bath. The bathtub had a capacity of 25 *l*. She let $\frac{3}{5}$ of the water out. How much water was left in the bath?

l

2 Write a measurement problem that uses two of the following: addition, subtraction, division or multiplication. You can decide whether it is about length, mass or capacity. Make sure you have worked out the answer. Then ask someone to answer your problem.

3 Write a measures number story for this calculation.
476 – 380 = 96. 96 ÷ 8 = 12.

Lesson 1: **Telling the time on an analogue clock**

- Read and tell time to the nearest minute on an analogue clock
- Use a.m. and p.m.

1 Circle the words we use when telling the time.

hands	co-ordinates	o'clock	angles	minutes
hours	metres	degrees	seconds	half past

2 Write these times.

a 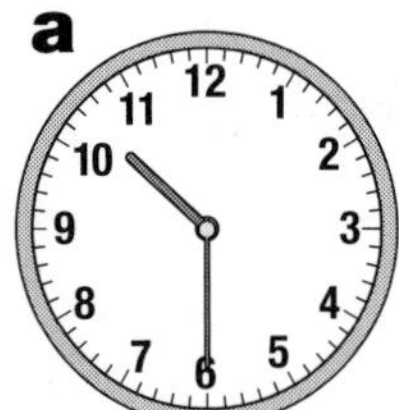

b 

c 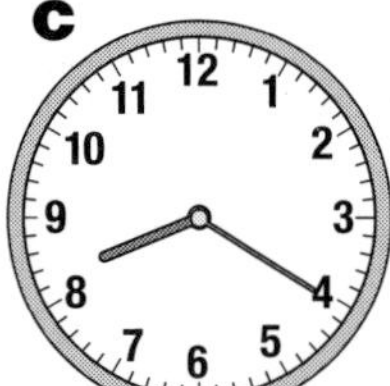

d 

e 

1 Draw these times.

a 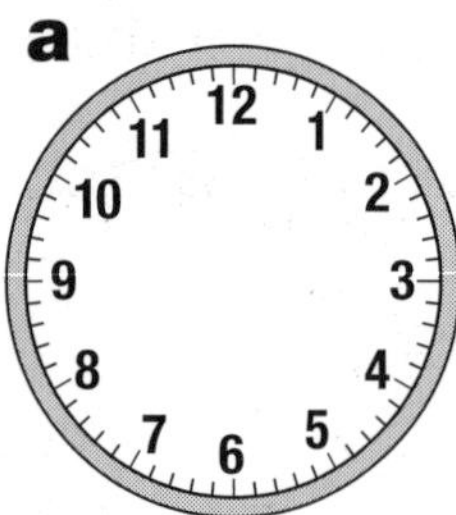

23 minutes past 9

b

47 minutes past 2

c 

22 minutes to 7

d 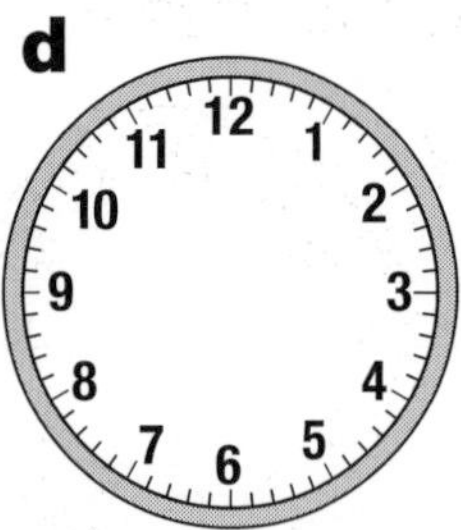

11 minutes past 5

e 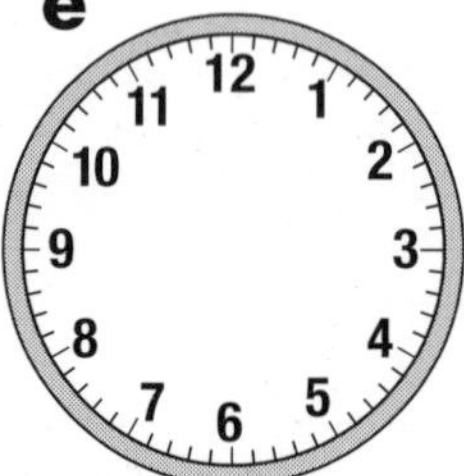

9 minutes to 4

f 

28 minutes past 1

2 Write these times in an equivalent analogue clock time.

a 40 minutes past 3 ____________________

b 10 minutes past 10 ____________________

c 33 minutes past 7 ____________________

d 10 minutes to 1 ____________________

e 27 minutes to 4 ____________________

f 11 minutes past 9 ____________________

3 Write these times. Include a.m. or p.m.

a  afternoon

b  morning

c  evening

Challenge 3 On the clocks, draw the times that are 30 minutes after these times.

a 6 minutes past 8

b 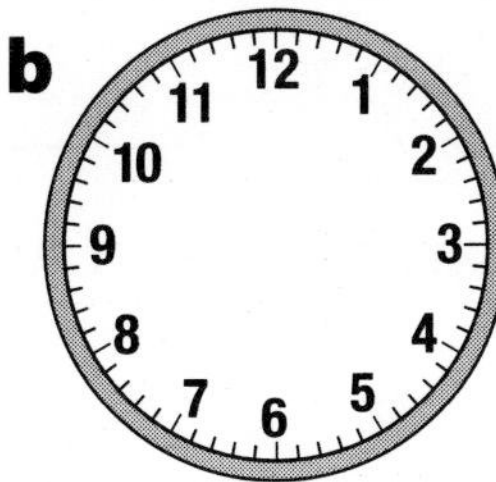 24 minutes to 11

c  13 minutes to 5

d  18 minutes past 3

e  23 minutes to 1

f  11 minutes past 7

Lesson 2: **Telling the time on a digital clock**

- Tell the time correctly to one minute on analogue and digital clocks

Challenge 1

1 Write these analogue times as digital times.

a 25 past 3 [:] **b** 10 past 4 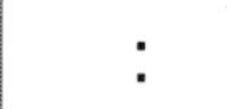

c 35 past 6 [:] **d** 45 past 8 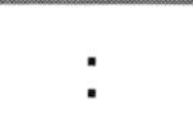

e 55 past 10 [:] **f** 15 past 7 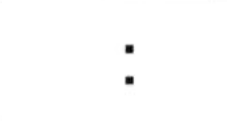

2 Order these times, from earliest to latest.

4:30	4:45	4:05	4:50	4:20	4:55

____

Challenge 2

1 Write the equivalent analogue times beside these digital times.

Example: 12:26 26 minutes past 12 o'clock

a 10:46 ______________________

b 4:53 ______________________

c 6:11 ______________________

d 8:55 ______________________

2 Write the times on these clocks in two different ways.

a

[ ]

[:]

b

[ ]

[:]

c

[ ]

[:]

Measure

3 Show or write the missing times in each question.

a

10:22 a.m.○ p.m.●

b

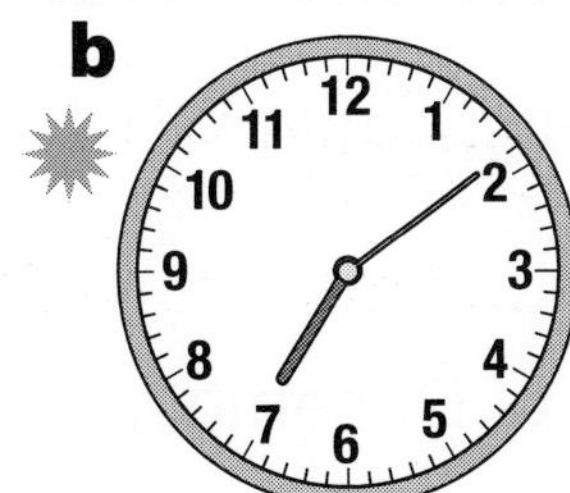

: a.m.○ p.m.○

c

12 minutes to 8 in the evening

: a.m.○ p.m.○

d

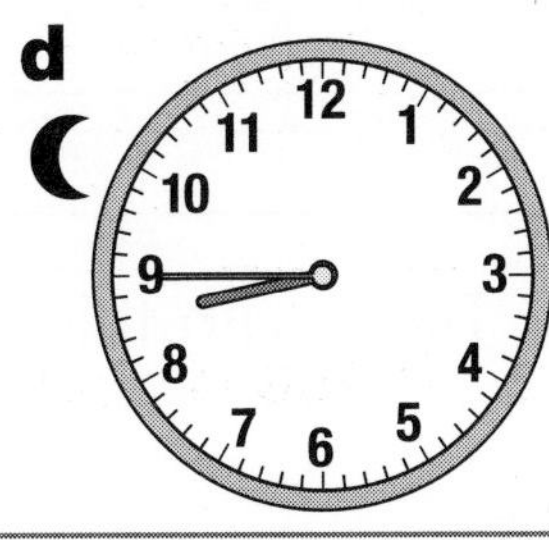

: a.m.○ p.m.○

e

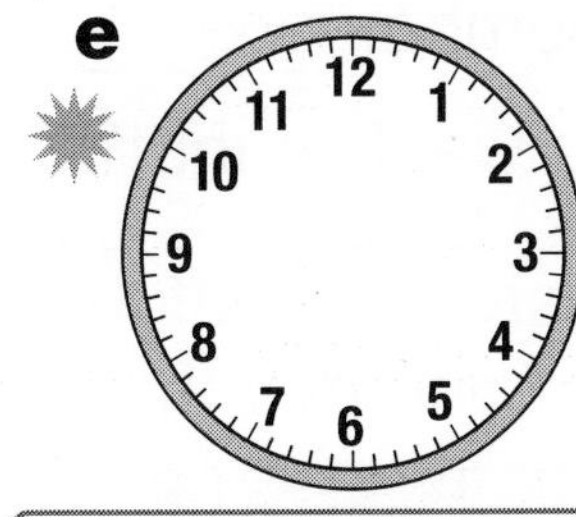

26 minutes past 11 in the morning

: a.m.○ p.m.○

f

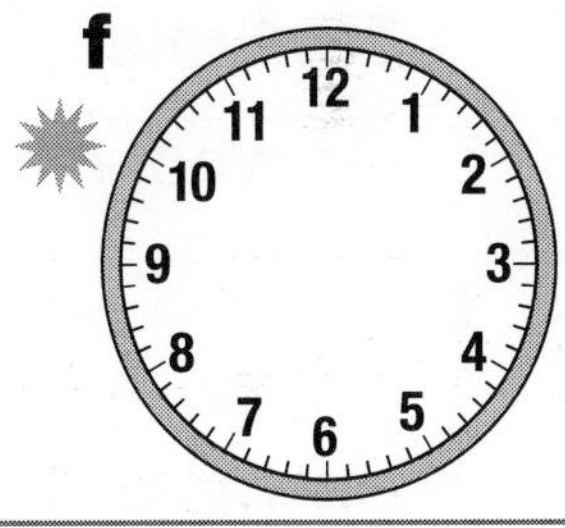

06:37 a.m.● p.m.○

Challenge 3 These clock faces have lost their numbers! Estimate the times that they are showing. Write them in three different ways.

a

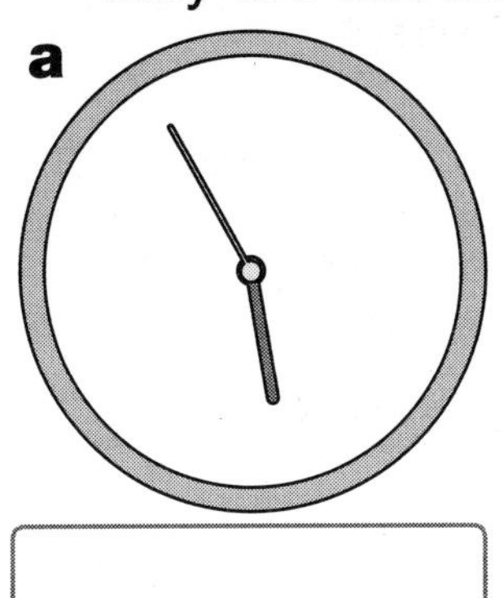

:

b

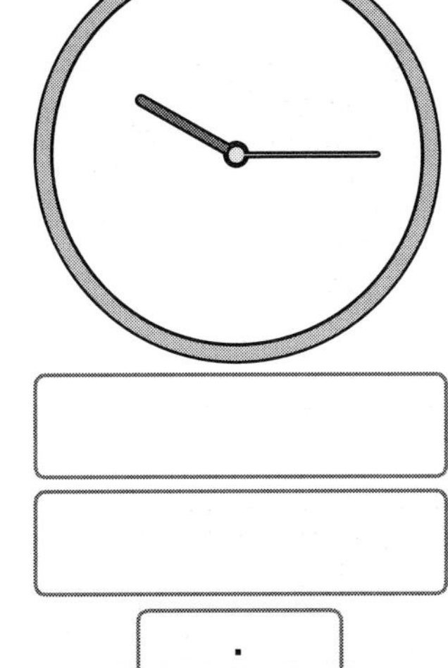

:

c

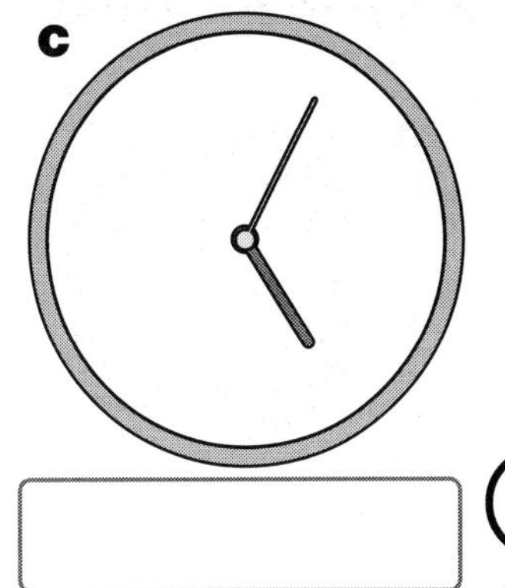

:

Measure

Lesson 3: **Timetables and calendars**

- Read a calendar and timetable and work out time intervals

You will need

- page from a calendar showing 12 months

Challenge 1

1 Look at the month of December on your calendar.

a Which is the first day in December? ______________________

b Which is the last day in December? ______________________

c How many days are there in December? ________________

2 Use the calendar to find out which date is two weeks and three days after 8th December. ______________________

On what day of the week is that? ______________________

Challenge 2

1 Use the blank classroom timetable below. Fill it with things that you do in school on one day this week.

Lesson	Start time	Finish time

2 Which is the longest lesson you have?

____

3 Use the bus timetable to answer the questions.

	Arrival time				
Bus	**A**	**B**	**C**	**D**	**E**
Town Centre	7:00 a.m.	9:00 a.m.	11:00 a.m.	1:00 p.m.	3:00 p.m.
Library	7:09 a.m.	9:11 a.m.	11:09 a.m.	1:09 p.m.	3:11 p.m.
Luton Street	7:14 a.m.	9:16 a.m.	11:14 a.m.	1:14 p.m.	3:16 p.m.
Superstore	7:22 a.m.	9:24 a.m.	11:22 a.m.	1:22 p.m.	3:24 p.m.
Mill Road	7:31 a.m.	9:33 a.m.	11:31 a.m.	1:31 p.m.	3:33 p.m.
Brook's Hill	7:38 a.m.	9:40 a.m.	11:38 a.m.	1:38 p.m.	3:40 p.m.
Railway station	7:43 a.m.	9:45 a.m.	11:43 a.m.	1:43 p.m.	3:45 p.m.

a Where is Bus D at 1:22 p.m.? ____________

b Which bus is at Brook's Hill at 9:40 a.m.? ____________

c Which stop is before Luton Street? ____________

d How long does it take Bus E to travel from the Town Centre to the Superstore? ____________

e Write one statement about the information in the timetable.

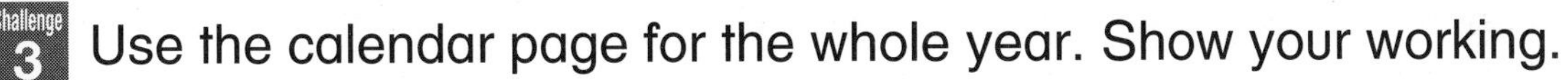

Challenge 3 Use the calendar page for the whole year. Show your working.

a How many weeks and days are there between 23rd June and 12th August?

b How many months, weeks and days are there from 14th April to 24th November?

c How many weeks is that? How many days?

Lesson 4: **Measuring time intervals**

Measure

- Choose units of time to measure time intervals

Challenge 1

1 Calculate these time differences. Draw a number line to help you.

a 7:30 to 8:30 [ ]

b 10:00 to 11:30 [ ]

c 12:15 to 2:00 [ ]

d 3:10 to 5:30 [ ]

2 Approximately how long do you spend in school each day? [ ]

Challenge 2

1 Use the words below to describe the time intervals.

minutes hours days weeks

a The length of time you watch TV each week.

____

b The length of time it takes you to get to school in the morning.

____

c How long it is until the end of term. ______________

d How long it is until home time. ______________

e How long it takes you to sharpen a pencil. ______________

2 Calculate these time differences and choose the best unit of time for your answer. Draw a number line to help you.

a 8:25 a.m. to 9:50 a.m.

b 11:45 a.m. to 12:20 p.m.

c 11:55 a.m. to 3:15 p.m.

d 2:05 p.m. to 5:55 p.m.

e 3:35 p.m. to 8:05 p.m.

Challenge **3**

1 Which of these is the greatest time difference? Underline your answer.

7:15 a.m. to 4:35 p.m. or 12:25 p.m. to 7:55 p.m.

Explain how you worked out the answer

2 Farrah left home at 8:35 a.m. It took her 20 minutes to walk to her friend's house. She stayed there for 2 hours and 55 minutes, then she walked back home.
What time does she arrive home?

Show how you worked this out on a number line.

Lesson 1: **Perimeter (1)**

- Draw rectangles to specific measurements
- Measure and calculate their perimeters

Challenge 1 Write the perimeters of these rectangles.

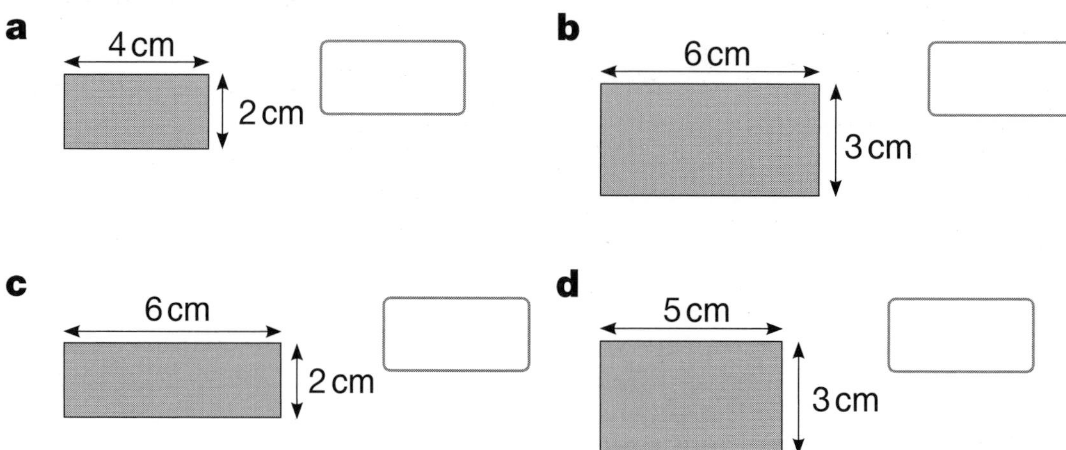

Challenge 2

1 Draw a rectangle that has a length of 10 cm and a width of 2 cm

What is the perimeter of your shape?

2 Write the perimeters of rectangles that measure:

a 10 cm by 3 cm

b 12 cm by 5 cm

c 6 cm by 6 cm

d 7 cm by 10 cm

e 15 cm by 12 cm

f 11 cm by 13 cm

Challenge 3

1 A square has a perimeter of 32 cm. How long is each side? Draw the square and label each side.

2 A rectangle has a perimeter of 32 cm. How long could each side be? Draw your rectangle and label each side.

Lesson 2: **Perimeter (2)**

- Draw rectangles to specific measurements
- Measure and calculate their perimeters

Challenge 1

Write the perimeters of these rectangles.

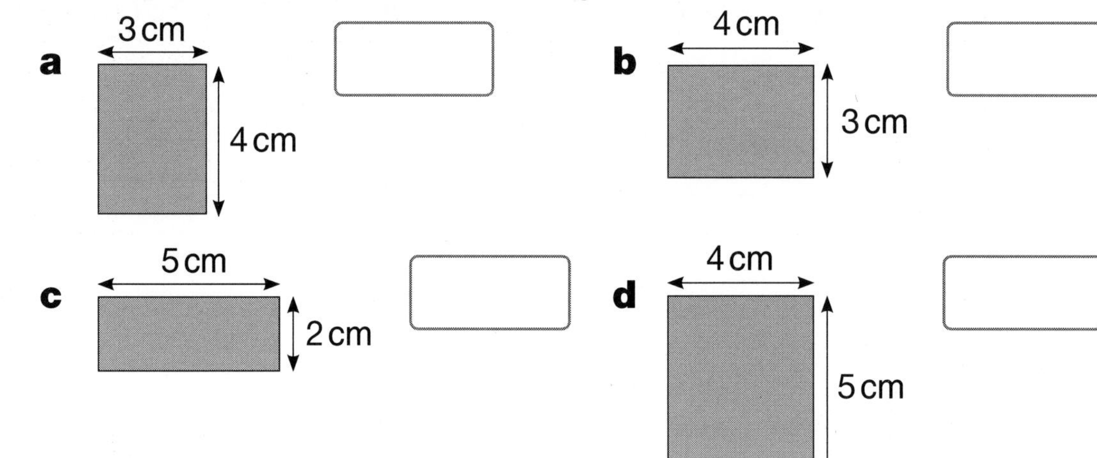

Challenge 2

1 Dana drew a rectangle that was 15 cm by 12 cm. What was its perimeter? Show how you worked out your answer.

2 Hamzah drew a square. He said that it had a perimeter of 48 cm. What were the lengths of the sides of his square? Show how you worked out your answer.

3 Abi drew a rectangle. Two sides were each 14 cm in length. The perimeter was 40 cm. What were the lengths of each of the other sides? Show how you worked out your answer.

Measure, label and work out the perimeter of each shape.

a

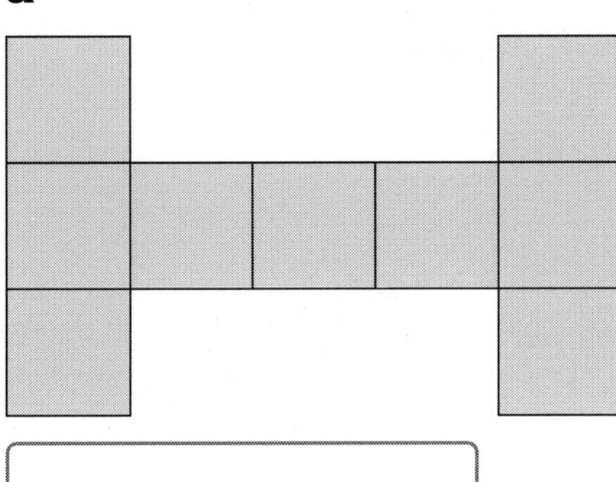

b

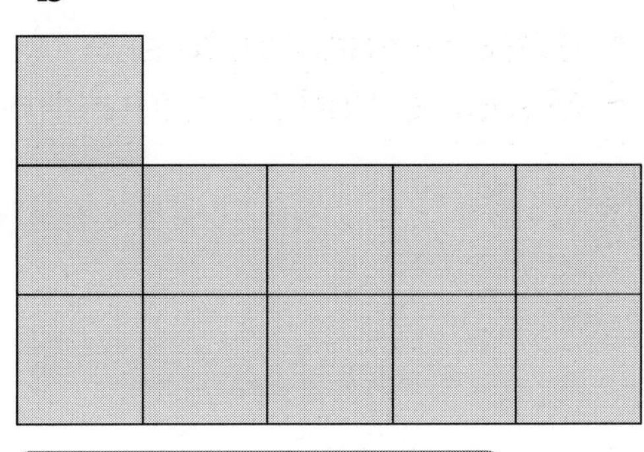

c

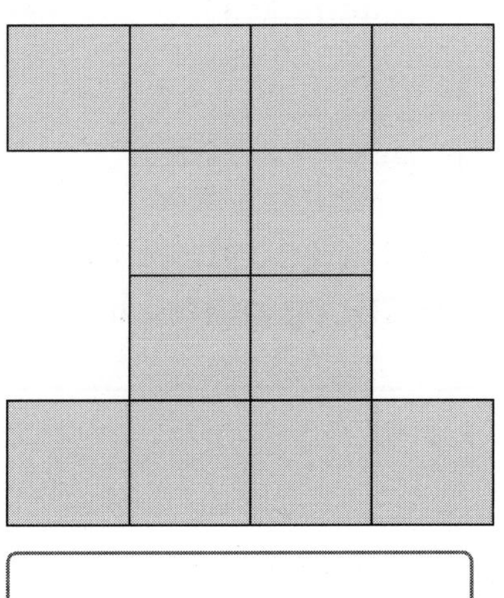

d

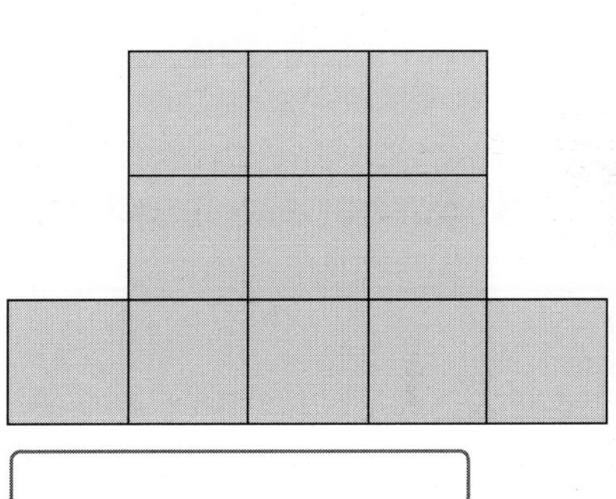

e

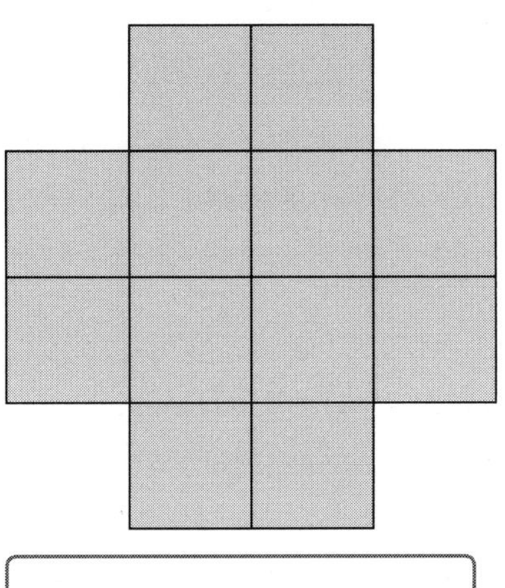

f

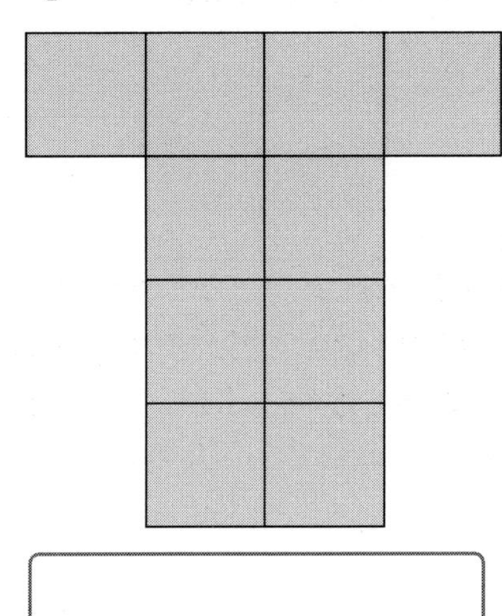

Measure

Lesson 3: **Area (1)**

- Understand that area is measured in square units and find the area of rectangles

Challenge 1 Write the area of these squares.

a 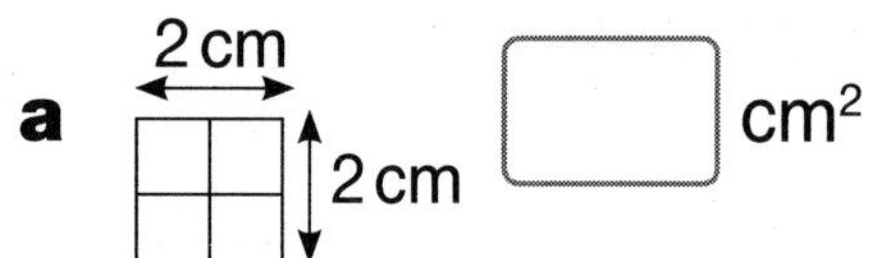

☐ cm^2

b 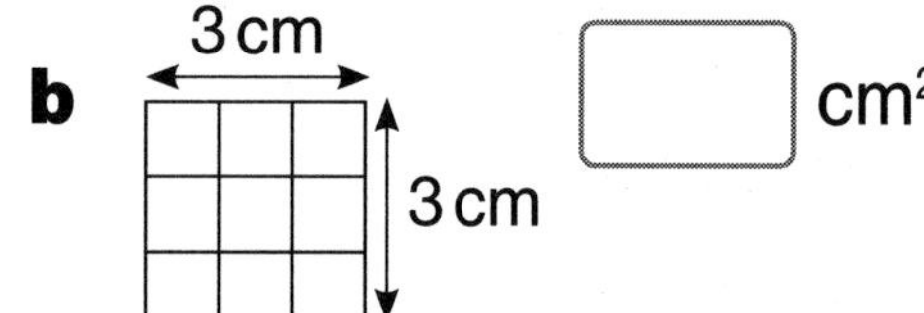

☐ cm^2

c 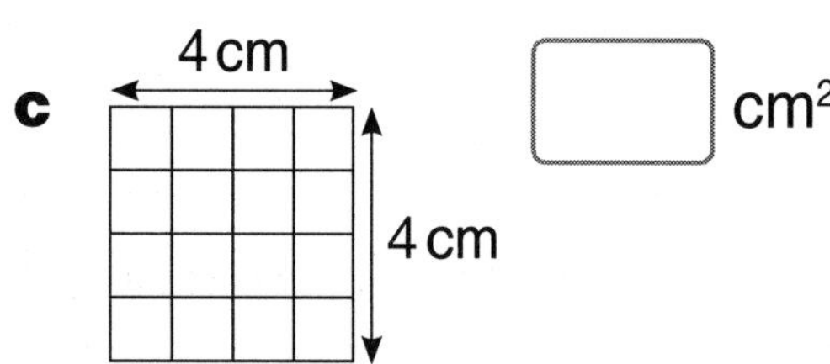

☐ cm^2

d 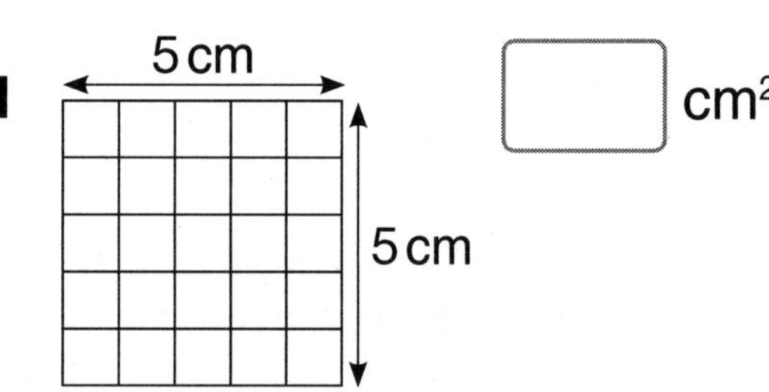

☐ cm^2

Challenge 2 **1** Sasha drew a rectangle. It measured 12 cm by 3 cm. Draw it below.

a What is the area of Sasha's rectangle? ☐

b What is the perimeter of Sasha's rectangle? ☐

2 Find the area and perimeter of rectangles with these dimensions:

a 8 cm by 4 cm

Area = Perimeter =

b 9 cm by 7 cm

Area = Perimeter =

c 5 cm by 6 cm

Area = Perimeter =

d 12 cm by 3 cm

Area = Perimeter =

Challenge 3

1 A square has an area of 144 cm^2. How long is each side? Show how you worked out your answer.

2 A rectangle has an area of 48 cm^2. How long could each side be? Show how you worked out your answer.

3 Thalia made three squares all of the same size. They looked like this:

Thalia thought she could put these together to make other shapes of different areas. Is she correct? Explain your answer.

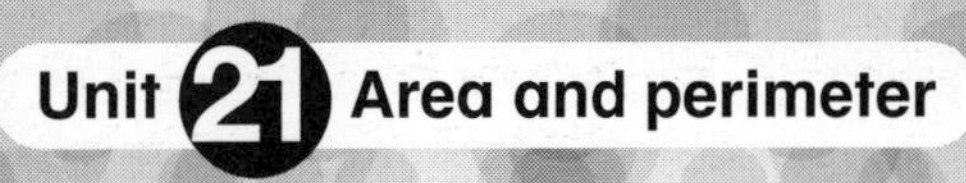

Measure

Lesson 4: **Area (2)**

- Understand that area is measured in square units and find the area of rectilinear shapes

Challenge 1 Find the areas of these rectangles.

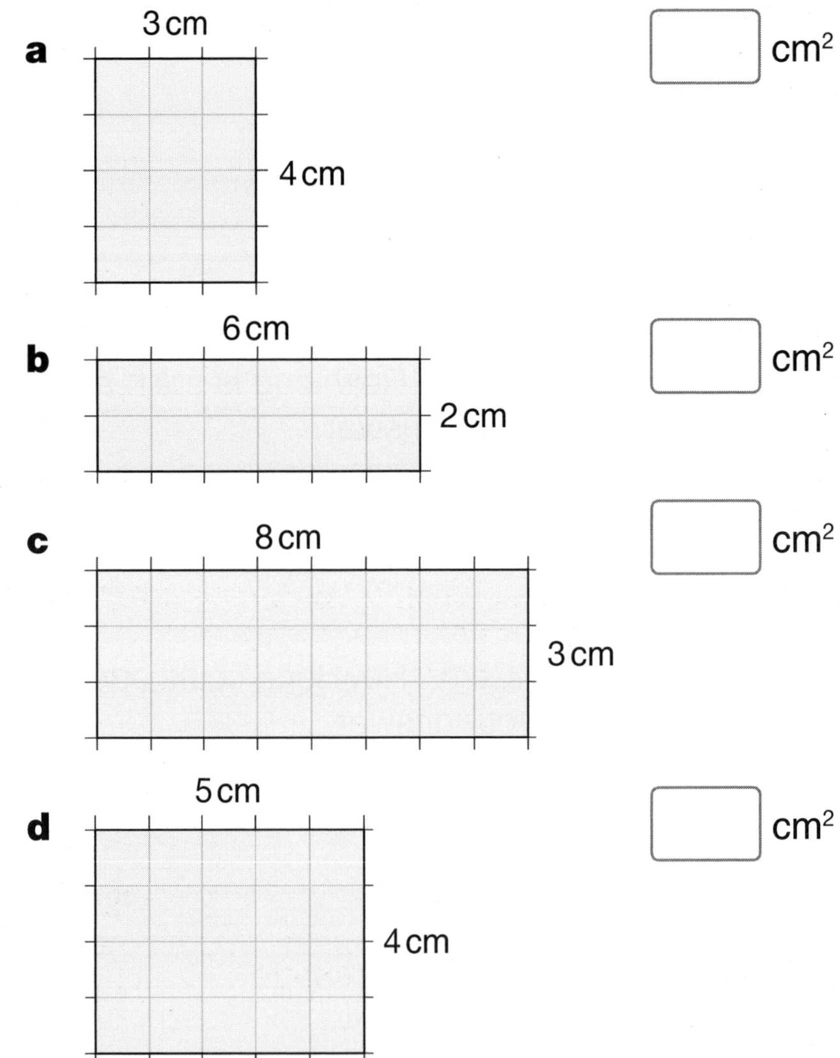

a ☐ cm^2

b ☐ cm^2

c ☐ cm^2

d ☐ cm^2

Challenge 2 **1** Tick the rectilinear shapes.

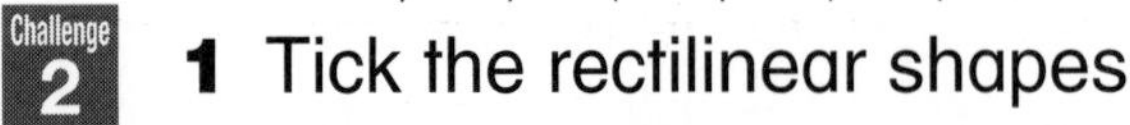

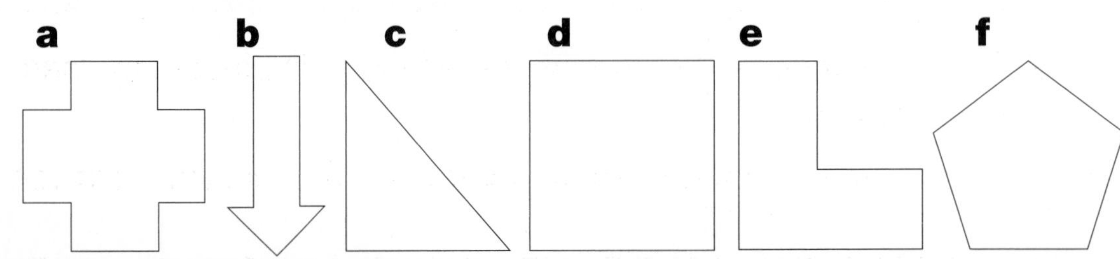

2 Write the areas of these rectilinear shapes.

☐ = 1 square centimetre (cm^2)

a

b

c

d

e

f

3 a Draw a rectilinear shape below. It cannot be a rectangle!

b What is its area?

c What is its perimeter?

Challenge 3

1 Describe what is meant by rectilinear shape.

____

____

2 Sameer thinks, 'If the area of something gets bigger, so does the perimeter.'

Is this always, sometimes or never true? Explain your answer.

____

____

Lesson 1: **Tables, diagrams, tally charts and frequency tables**

- Collect and sort information using tally charts and frequency tables

Challenge 1

Complete the table by totalling the frequency from the tally.
Favourite snacks in Class 4A

Snack	Tally	Frequency
crackers	||	
popcorn	𝍸 𝍸 ||||	
fruit	𝍸 ||||	
vegetables	𝍸	5

Challenge 2

1 Hassan asked some people, 'Where do you go to buy your bread?' He made a tally chart for their answers.

Location	Tally	Frequency
supermarket	𝍸 𝍸 𝍸 𝍸 |||	
corner shop	𝍸 𝍸 |	
market stall	𝍸 𝍸 𝍸	
bakery	𝍸 𝍸 ||	

a Count the tally marks. Write the totals in the Frequency column.

b Where do most people buy their bread? ____________

c Which is the least popular location? ____________

d How many more people shopped at the supermarket than at the market stall? [ ]

e How many people did Hassan ask altogether? [ ]

1 Complete the tally and frequency table to show the sale of bakery items, using data from the pictures.

Bakery item	Tally	Frequency
chocolate cake		
cupcakes		
bread		
doughnuts		

2 What is the most popular bakery item?

____

3 How many more people prefer cupcakes to bread? [ ]

4 Write a statement about the information in the table.

____

____

____

____

Lesson 2: **Venn and Carroll diagrams**

- Use Venn and Carroll diagrams with two and three categories to organise information or objects

Challenge 1

Complete the simple Carroll diagram.

345 417 124 208 736 453 319

602 863 780 204 576

Less than 500	500 or more

Challenge 2

1 Class 4 wanted to know what types of books learners prefer to read. The categories were: fantasy fiction, realistic fiction and non-fiction. Below are the results of their survey.

Name	Fantasy fiction	Realistic fiction	Non-fiction
Aida	✓		✓
Amira		✓	✓
Ben	✓	✓	
David	✓		
Jamal			✓
Louise	✓	✓	✓
Malik		✓	
Omar		✓	✓
Pita	✓	✓	
Rahim		✓	✓
Sarah	✓		
Surinda			✓
Ravinda	✓		✓
Zubin	✓	✓	✓

Show the results of the survey in the Venn diagram.

Books Class 4 like to read

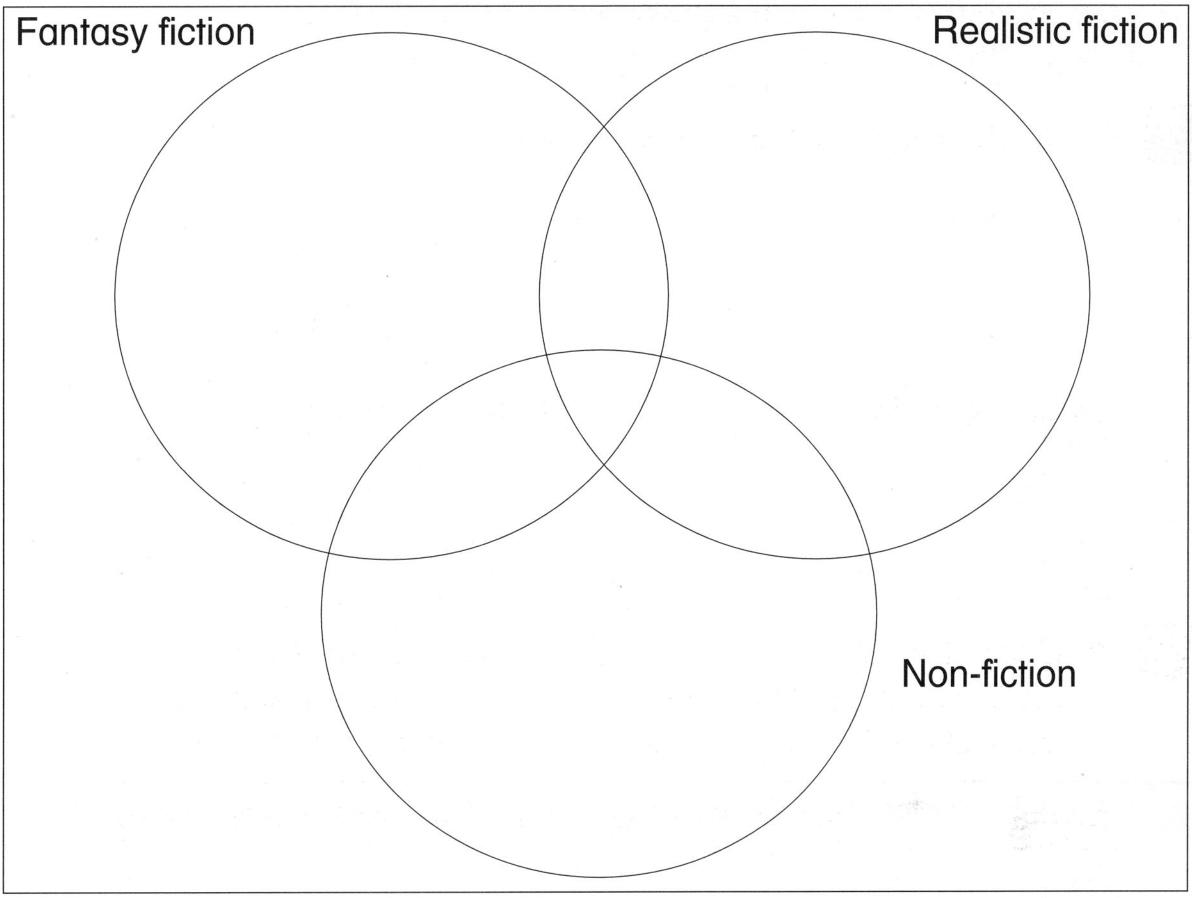

2 Use the data in the Venn diagram to answer these questions.

a What types of books does Pita like to read?

____

b Who likes to read realistic fiction and non-fiction?

____

c How many children only prefer to read one type of book?

☐ Who are they? ______________________________

Find the errors in the Carroll diagram and circle them.

	Less than 20	20 or more
Odd	25, 11, 13, 15, 17, 19, 21, 23	10, 12, 14, 16 18
Even		20

Lesson 3: Pictograms (1)

- Construct and read pictograms with quantities of 2, 5, 10 or 20 represented by one picture

Challenge 1

Read the frequency chart and key, then complete the pictogram.

Balloons sold

Colour	Frequency
red	4
blue	6
purple	8
pink	6
green	2

Balloons sold **Key** (balloon) = 2

red	blue	purple	pink	green

Challenge 2

1 This pictogram shows the favourite flowers of the mothers who have children in Class 4.

Mothers' favourite flowers

violet	✿ ✿ ✿ ✿
lily	✿ ✿ ✿
orchid	✿ ✿ ✿ ✿ ✿ ✿ ✿
rose	

Key ✿ = 5 mothers

a How many mothers like orchids best? ☐

b Which is more popular violets or lilies? ☐

c 4 mothers said they prefer roses. Add this to the pictogram.

d How many more mothers prefer orchids to lilies? ☐

2 A Nature Club recorded how many butterflies they spotted in a day. Use the data in the frequency table to complete the pictogram.

Key = 10

Number of butterflies spotted in one day

Name	Frequency
Hiba	30
Youssef	50
Miriam	20
Joseph	10

Number of butterflies spotted in one day

Hiba	
Youssef	
Miriam	
Joseph	

Challenge **3**

1 The total number of pies sold in January was 60.

How many pies does one symbol on the pictogram represent? Complete the key.

Key = ☐

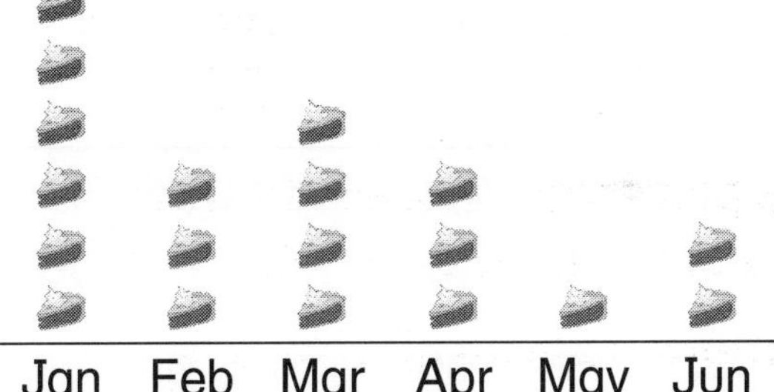

2 Use the data in the pictogram to answer these questions.

a 60 pies were sold in January. In which month were half this number sold? ____________________

b How many pies were sold in March? ☐

c In which two months were the same number of pies sold?

____________________ and ____________________

How many pies was this? ☐

d Altogether how many pies were sold in April, May and June? ☐

Handling data

Lesson 4: **Bar charts (1)**

- Construct and read bar charts with intervals of 2, 5, 10 or 20 on the vertical scale

You will need
- 5 different-coloured pencils
- ruler

Challenge 1

Use the data in the bar chart to answer the questions.

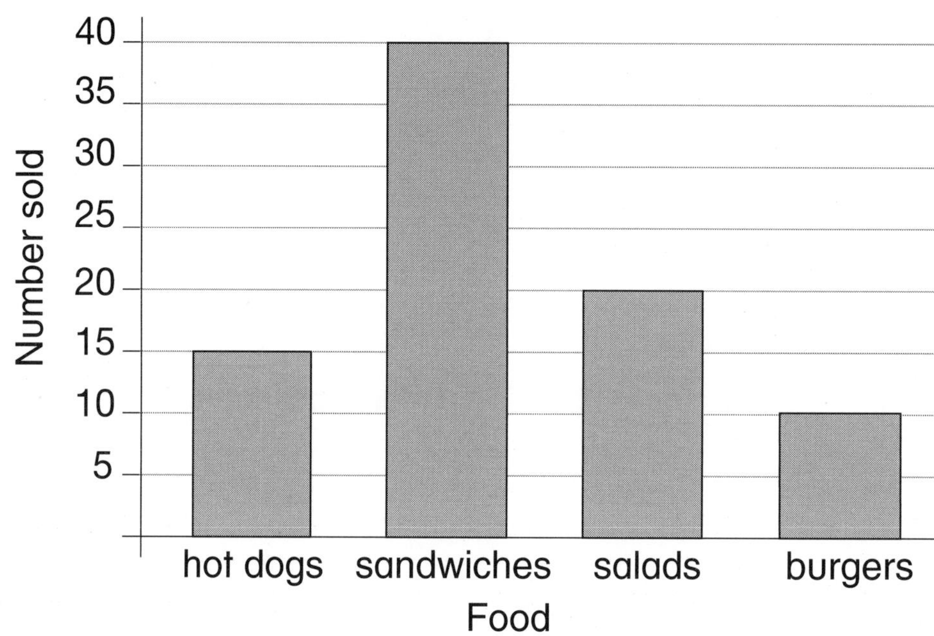

a How many sandwiches did the shop sell?

b How many more salads were bought than burgers?

c The owner bought 20 hot dogs and buns to sell. How many did he have left?

Challenge 2

The owner of the shop has decided to find out the most popular sandwich filling. The frequency table shows the results.

Sandwich filling	Quantity sold in a day
egg	5
hummus with salad	10
chicken and mayo with salad	15
tuna and peppers	10

Use the data to draw a bar chart with a scale that goes up in intervals of 5. Then use the first word of each filling as labels.

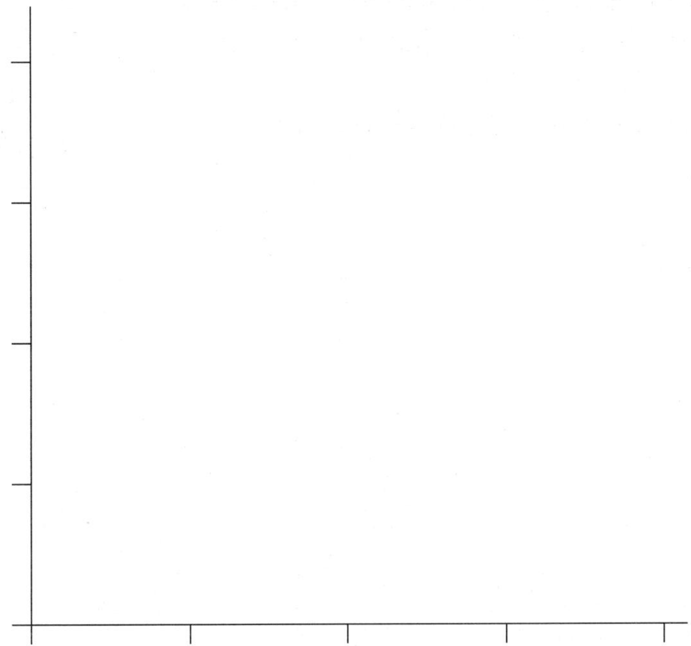

Challenge 3 Use the data in the bar chart below to answer these questions.

a What is the most popular type of film? ____________________

b What is the least popular type of film? ____________________

c How many people like comedy films? [ ]

d How many learners took part in the survey? [ ]

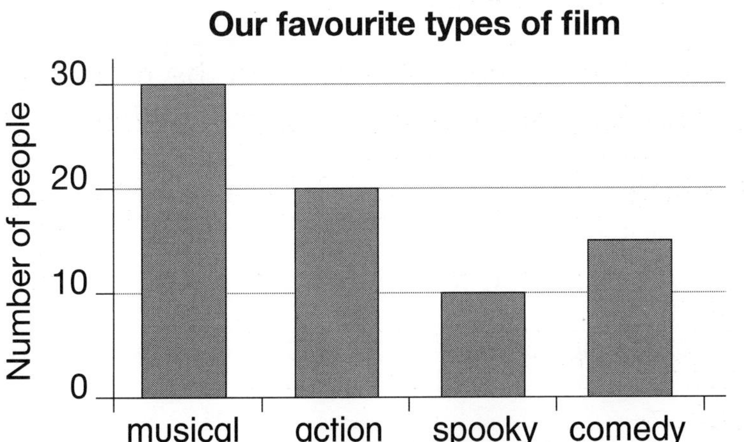

Lesson 1: **Pictograms (2)**

- Read pictograms with whole and half symbols

Challenge 1

A school checks how many sports shirts it has. How many shirts of each colour does the school have?

Numbers of shirts

red = ☐

blue = ☐

green = ☐

yellow = ☐

Sports shirts stock take

red	☺☺☺☺☺☺
blue	☺☺☺☺☺◐
green	☺☺☺◐
yellow	☺☺◐

Key: ☺ = 2 shirts

Challenge 2

1 A local council have planted sunflowers around the town. They used a pictogram to record how many sunflowers they planted each day.

Sunflowers

Monday	✿✿✿
Tuesday	✿✿✿✿✿✿✿
Wednesday	✿✿✿✿✿✿◐
Thursday	✿✿✿✿✿
Friday	✿✿✿✿✿◐

Key: ✿ = 10 sunflowers

a How many sunflowers did they plant on Friday? ☐

b On what day did they plant the most sunflowers?

____

c How many more sunflowers did they plant on Wednesday, compared to Thursday? ☐

d Write one statement about the data in the pictogram.

____

____

Student's Book page 117

Handling data

2 Complete a pictogram based on the data in the frequency table.

Chocolates produced by a chocolate factory in a day

Type of chocolate	Frequency
caramel chocolate	80
dark chocolate	90
milk chocolate	110
white chocolate	60

Key: ◇ = 20 chocolates.

Challenge 3 Use the data in the pictogram below to answer these questions.

Shoes we wore to school today

buckles	● ● ●
sandals	● ● ● ◖
boots	● ● ◖
trainers	● ● ● ● ● ● ●
laces	● ● ● ●

Key:
● = 2 shoes

a How many children are wearing boots? ☐

b How many more children are wearing sandals than boots? ☐

c Write one statement about the data in the pictogram.

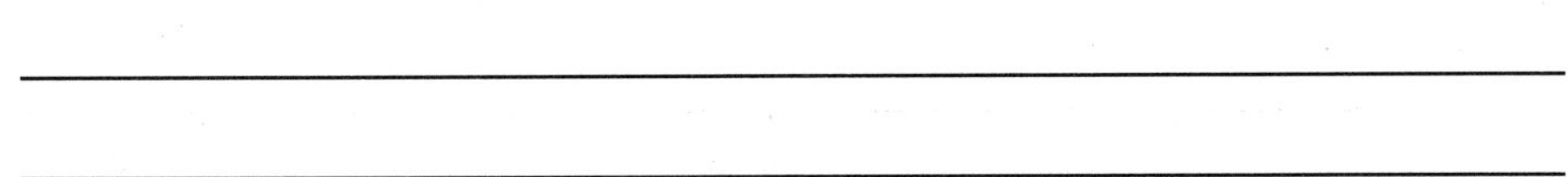

Lesson 2: **Pictograms (3)**

- Read and construct pictograms where the symbol represents different units

You will need
- coloured pencils

Add the data from the frequency chart to the pictogram.

Sports played by Year 4 Learners

baseball	⚽ ⚽ ⚽ ⚽ ⚽
soccer	
cricket	
basketball	⚽ ⚽ ⚽ ⚽

Sport	Number of learners
cricket	5
soccer	15

Key: ⚽ = 10 learners

1 Read the data in the frequency table then represent it in a pictogram. Start by completing the key. Choose a suitable symbol and quantity.

Group points this term

Group	Points
squares	5
circles	9
pentagons	6
hexagons	11

Key ☐ = ☐

Group points this term

squares	
circles	
pentagons	
hexagons	

2 Draw another pictogram to represent the data in the frequency table on page 236. Use the same symbol but where it represents a different quantity.

Key ☐ = ☐

Group points this term

squares	
circles	
pentagons	
hexagons	

A Swimming Club records the number of swimmers over a week.

Represent the data on the two pictograms. Choose a suitable symbol and decide on a different quantity for the symbol in each pictogram.

Day	Number of swimmers
Monday	12
Wednesday	30
Friday	18

Key: ☐ = ☐

Mon			
Weds			
Fri			

Key: ☐ = ☐

Mon			
Weds			
Fri			

Handling data

Lesson 3: **Bar charts (2)**

- Read and construct bar charts

You will need
- coloured pencils
- ruler

Challenge 1

Prepare the bar chart for data by following these instructions.

a Write these labels in the spaces on the horizontal line: woods, hills, beach, city.

b Label the horizontal line: Place.

c The marked intervals on the vertical line go up in 10s from zero.

d Label the vertical line: Number.

e Give the bar chart the title: Our favourite places

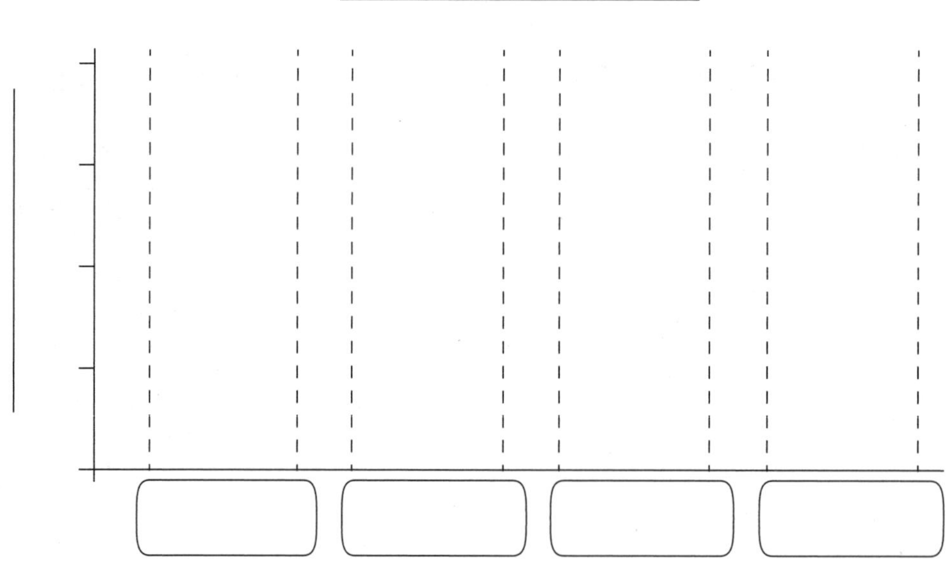

Challenge 2

Use the data in the pictogram to draw a bar chart on the next page. Use the key to help you decide on the intervals for the scale.

Month	Number of houses built
January	🏠🏠🏠🏠🏠
April	🏠🏠🏠🏠
July	🏠🏠🏠🏠🏠🏠🏠
October	🏠🏠🏠🏠🏠🏠🏠🏠

Key: 🏠 = 20 houses

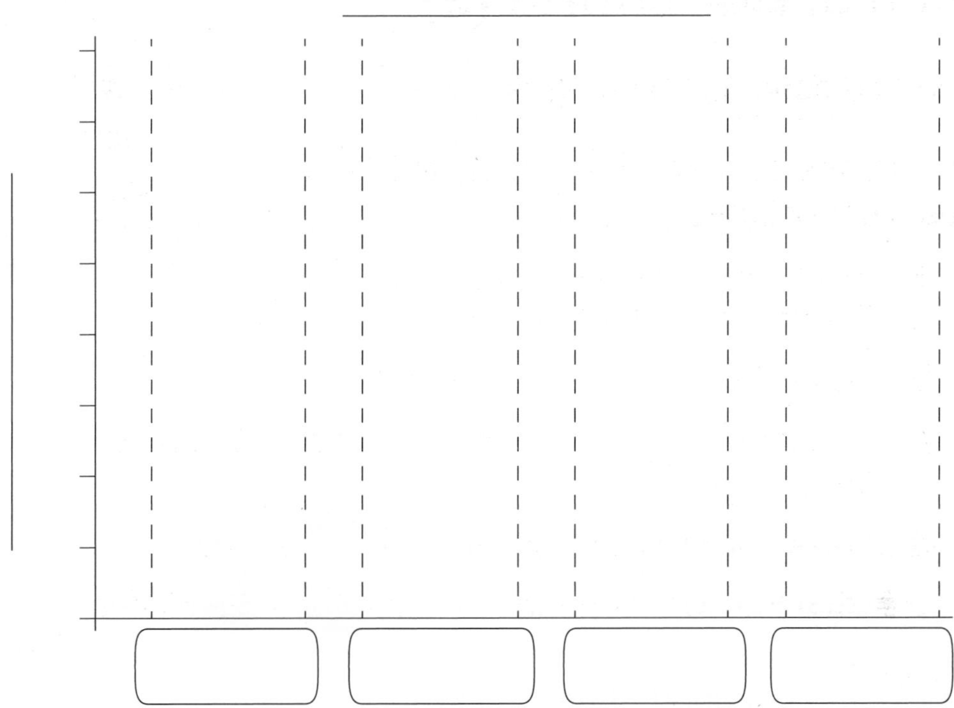

Challenge 3 Use the data from the frequency table to draw a bar chart.

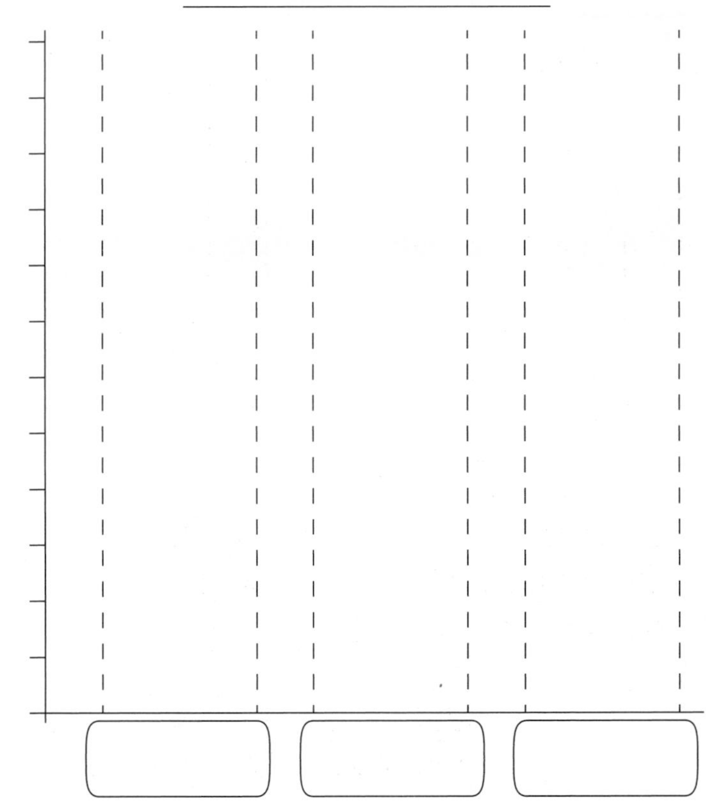

Most popular drums

Name of drum	Frequency
tabla	12
conga	24
bongo	18

Lesson 4: **Bar charts (3)**

Handling data

- Read bar charts, interpreting frequencies between two labelled divisions

Challenge 1 Look at the bar chart, then answer the questions.

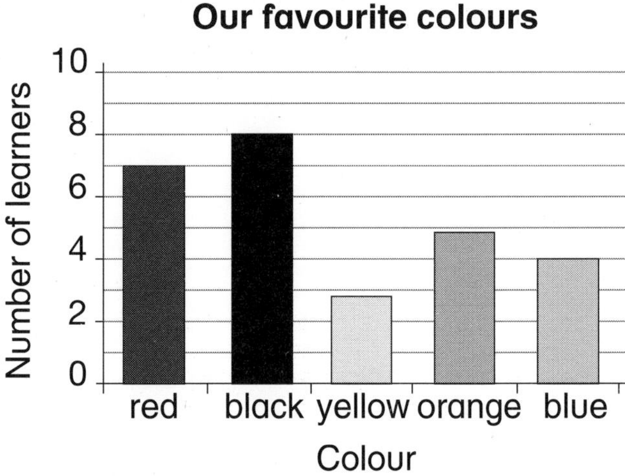

a How many learners voted for blue?

b How many voted for red?

c What colour has the least votes?

Challenge 2 Look at the bar chart, then answer the questions.

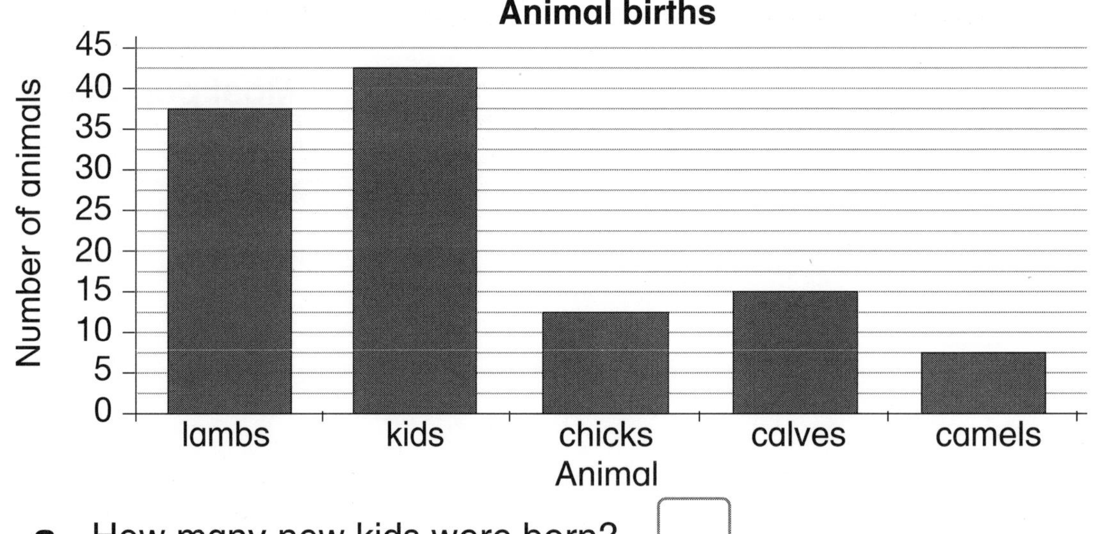

a How many new kids were born?

b How many baby camels were born?

c How many more lambs were born than baby chicks?

d How many more kids were born than calves?

e Write one statement about the data in the bar chart.

Use the data in the frequency table to draw two bar charts, each with a different scale. Label one chart in intervals of 5 and the other in intervals of 10.

Favourite ice cream flavours of Stage 4 learners

Ice cream flavour	Frequency
chocolate	35
vanilla	40
banana	25

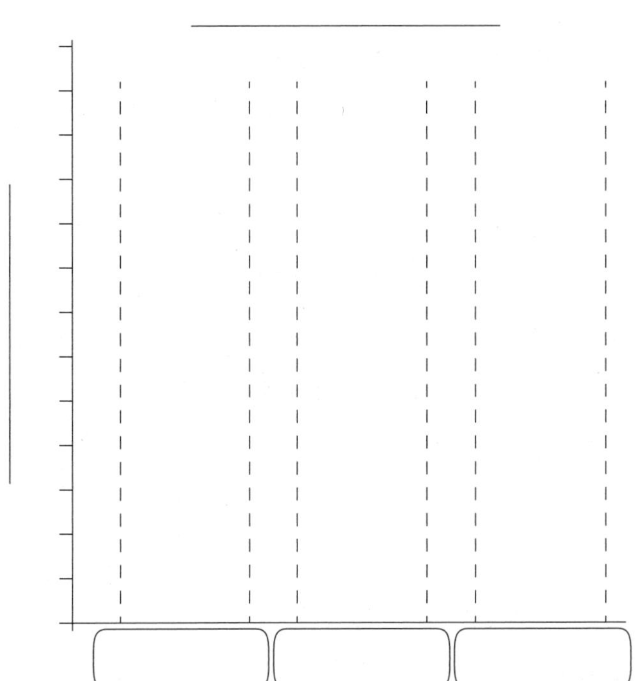

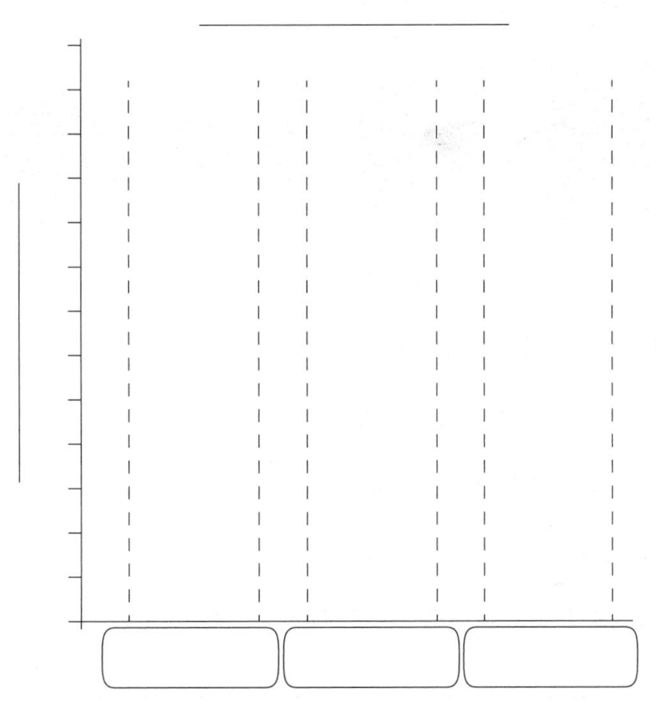

Notes

Notes

Notes

Notes

Notes

Notes

Notes

Notes

Notes

Notes

Notes

32
32
32
+ 32

1,28

Notes

Notes